Student Activism

Student Activism

Town and Gown in Historical Perspective

Alexander DeConde, Editor

Charles Scribner's Sons · New York

Printed in the United States of America
Library of Congress Catalog Card Number 74–162754
SBN 684–12546–3 (Trade cloth)
SBN 684–12545–5 (Trade paper)

Preface

This book is built on the simple premise that the worldwide youth rebellion of the 1960s has roots in the past and should therefore be viewed in historical perspective. The selections, taken mainly from the writings of scholars concerned with student activism or of participants, represent a wide spectrum of opinion and offer explanations of student turmoil all over the world, from medieval times to the present. Most of the essays are analytical, but a few, where literature on the subject is limited, are descriptive. All should contribute to an understanding of activism as a historic part of student culture, as a phenomenon that has frequently occurred when students formed a community of their own. The volume, as a whole, also tells something of how the struggle of generations became institutionalized.

Ralph Brax, my graduate research assistant, did so much of the footwork in tracking down sources that he was virtually a co-editor. He is doing extensive original research on American student activism, and hence his own evaluations of the readings were invaluable. Another graduate research assistant, Alberta Sanders, helped considerably in the project's early stages.

Alexander DeConde

Santa Barbara, California

Contents

Introductory Essay

In Perspective   *Alexander DeConde*   3

I   Medieval Student Life

1 The Earliest Universities   *Charles H. Haskins*   19

2 Town and Gown   *Robert S. Rait*   33

3 Scottish Student Life in the
   Fifteenth Century   *Annie I. Dunlop*   39

II   Student Movements in Western Europe

4 Students on the Barricades:
   Germany and Austria, 1848   *Priscilla Robertson*   59

5 The French Student Movement   *Jean-Pierre Worms*   72

6 Italy: From Reform to Adventure *Federico Mancini*   87

7 Students' Opposition in Spain   *Enrique Tierno
                                     Galván*   102

III   The Activist Tradition in Eastern Europe

8 Students and Politics in Russia *Nicholas Hans*   127

9   Social Cleavage: Warsaw   George Z. F.
                                     Bereday   135

10 Students and Politics in Turkey Leslie L. Roos, Jr.,
                                     Noralou P. Roos,
                                     and Gary R. Field   143

        IV   Student Communities in Asia and Africa

11 Reflections on the Modern Chinese
    Student Movement   John Israel   165

12 Comparison Between Pre- and
    Post-War Student Movements
    in Japan   Michiya Shimbori   190

13 The Transformation of the
    Indian Student Movement   Philip G. Altbach   204

14 Korean Students and Politics   William A. Douglas   221

15 African Student Organizations: Donald K.
    The Politics of Discontent   Emmerson   235

        V   Latin America's Student Power

16 Students in Latin-American
    Politics   Francis Donahue   253

        VI   Student Rebellion in the United States

17 The Oxford-Cap War at Harvard   Kenneth Wiggins
                                     Porter   273

18 Revolt on the Campus:
    April 13, 1934–April 12, 1935   James Wechsler   280

19 "Student Power" in Berkeley   Nathan Glazer   295

20 Confrontation at Cornell   William H.
                                     Friedland and
                                     Harry Edwards   318

    Selected Bibliography   337

Introductory Essay

In Perspective

Alexander DeConde

Accustomed to a tradition that places the university within society's ruling establishment and unaware of the history of academic turmoil and political activism in other lands, Americans of the sixties were surprised, shocked, and angered by the eruption of protest among their own student population. This reaction is understandable: Vehement concern with the large external problems of society was not expected in a country where the student community has historically been considered passive or apolitical. When campuses exploded over social, political, and educational issues, student behavior appeared unpredictable, inconsistent, and mystifying to established authority—and difficult to accept.

Baffled Americans were at least aware that contemporary student activism was not a uniquely American phenomenon. The mass media, particularly television, had made them realize that student dissent in Berkeley and New York had much in common with violent demonstrations in Paris, Rome, and Tokyo. Instant communication between youth cultures, as well as increased student travel, had made the younger generation's protests a matter of international concern. Through the media, which brought youthful rage and violence into the living room, and through organized militant protest, students everywhere were assaulting traditional values. In the United States they jolted the underpinnings of the university and shattered the complacency of older generations toward them.

Scholars, most of whom knew little about the history of student activism because they had neglected or virtually ignored it as a field of serious study, were also surprised by the new militance on American campuses. Social scientists have long been interested in various aspects of education, school systems, curricula, teachers, and relations between schools and government, but seldom have they looked at student culture as a social phenomenon. The outbursts of the sixties finally thrust upon them a concern for campus activity as a force in social change. The effectiveness of this force is difficult to analyze over any extended period because student movements are extremely fluid—constantly shifting in power, ever changing in constituency, and generally unstable. They often lose popular support as swiftly as they gain it, and their leadership, usually comprising a small dedicated group, rises and falls just as rapidly. Moreover, such movements cannot be understood unless they, and the university, are related to the total environment and the contemporaneous problems of society.

Despite these obstacles to thorough investigation, out of the turbulence of the sixties came an extensive literature on student activism, most of it concerned with sociological and psychological analyses of contemporary protest. While much of this writing is of excellent quality, especially in explaining student motivation, it generally lacks historical dimension, or even a sense of history. This missing ingredient is a vital one because student agitation has a long history. It is as old as the universities. Students, in one way or another, have always been active in the affairs of their universities, their communities, and their nations. They have frequently functioned as barometers of deep-seated unrest and social change.

Student rebellions against established authority have occurred in practically every country with significant university communities. Civil disturbances involving town and gown erupted in the Middle Ages virtually as soon as students began living together in university towns as members of a recognized group set off from the larger society. Since that time hostility between the academic community and townspeople has been traditional. Although each generation thinks of its problems as unique, students have often merely refought yesterday's battles.

The records of medieval universities are filled with accounts of clashes between students and professors on one side and townsfolk on the other, with both sides suffering injuries. Town-and-gown animosity often had deep underlying causes, such as differences over how much freedom students and faculty should have from local law, or whether town or university authorities should have jurisdiction over student activities outside the classroom. Students generally had a privileged status that gave them freedoms and prerogatives ordinary people were denied. Similarities in background, outlook, and environment often built up a sense of community among students that placed a screen between them and the older nonstudent generation. Even their sense of alienation from their families and society set them off as a unique culture group. Townsfolk resented their privileged, elite status; trivial incidents could frequently bring this feeling to a boiling point, and violence would follow.

In modern Europe university students, coming mainly from well-born and wealthy parents, retained their elite status until recently. Since they were or would become part of the ruling establishment, they did not usually act as agents stimulating social change. Generally they organized themselves into syndicates, or student unions, devoted to the advancement of their own welfare as apprentice elitists. When they did turn to politics, established authority could safely ignore their demands because even though students acted with urgency, heat, and emotion, they seldom had enough sustaining power to compel meaningful change.

There were times, however, when student groups in nineteenth-century Europe showed staying power, mainly by providing support and recruits for revolutionary movements. Until 1848 student societies in Germany, the *Burschenschaften,* functioned as centers of radical, democratic, and anti-establishment activities. Russian students of the late nineteenth and early twentieth centuries were known as active foes of the Tsarist government. They were so deeply involved in the agitation that led to the revolution of 1917 that some writers consider the initial revolutionary activism in Russia virtually a student movement.

In the twentieth century, as Europeans and others entered the era of mass education and universities opened their doors to the sons of shopkeepers and workers, students saw their elitist status eroded. They also lost importance as individuals. To regain their identity many turned to a deeper, more broadly organized activism than in the past, challenging established policies and traditions. They formed true student movements, or associations inspired by ideological doctrines and often devoted to political action. When these groups took to the streets, their clashes with authority had far greater social significance than the traditional town-and-gown violence.

This radiating social impact was especially evident in France where national issues aroused students. In 1958 student groups mounted massive protests against a colonial war in Algeria; they became the nation's conscience, comprising one of the few well-organized forces to speak out against the government's war policy. A decade later the French youth movement shook the foundations of the republic itself. Students pressured labor into calling a general strike, compelled the dissolution of the National Assembly, and forced the holding of national elections. The events of May 1968 captured headlines all over the world and had long-lasting effects in France. Students claimed considerable credit for the fall of Charles de Gaulle in the following year. Their uprising brought no lasting social change, however; the old ills, such as overcrowded classrooms and miserable living conditions in the universities, persisted.

Italy, too, experienced large-scale student rebellion in these years, the biggest in her history. In 1967–68, as in France, militants struck against an archaic system of higher education and demanded reform and a voice in university administration. Student activism in Italy was as belligerent as anywhere else in the world, and it had lasting repercussions in the large society. Almost everywhere students won their battles for free speech, but as in France, they failed to force basic improvement in the universities.

Even dictatorships, with their unchecked power for suppression of dissent, have been unable to avoid the protest movements of student activists. In 1926 Spanish students organized to oppose the military dictatorship of Primo de Rivera. In the sixties they awakened to demand freedoms from Francisco Franco. They did not gain true liberty, but through strikes and demonstrations they wrenched some concessions from the government. In authoritarian Portugal students in the sixties also struck against government restrictions. As in France, a colonial war in Africa aroused Portuguese students. One twenty-two year old spoke for many. "Nobody," he said, "asked us students what we thought about shipping thousands of our colleagues to Angola and Mozambique."

Ruthless regimes can easily crush student movements and have sometimes exterminated them. In the early twenties most activists at Moscow University supported Leon Trotsky. Josef Stalin's police destroyed the movement. Yet some dissent has persisted even within "official" youth movements in totalitarian societies. Much of the political ferment in Poland during the late fifties came from government-sanctioned student groups and their publications. In the Hungarian uprising of October 1956 against a communist dictatorship controlled by Russia, students from Budapest University started the movement and students made up much of the resisting force. Student protests against maltreatment in Czechoslovakia in 1967 brought brutal suppression by police and also widespread criticism of the government. As a result, the government investigated grievances and made concessions.

Although student activism has not succeeded in undermining governments in the totalitarian societies of Eastern Europe, it has done so in Turkey, South Korea, South Vietnam, Indonesia, Bolivia, Venezuela, and Cuba. Students have been particularly successful in forcing changes in government policy in the developing nations of Asia, Africa, and Latin America. They formed key elements in the political and economic development in many of these states, serving as the primary source of technologically trained manpower and as instruments for modernization. Student populations in these countries were small, relatively homogeneous, and self-consciously elitist. The governing elites were usually recruited from their ranks.

Where there had been colonial rule students often provided leadership, or inspired it, in independence movements. Even before completing their educations they assumed political responsibilities and stimulated social action. Government leaders were unusually sensitive to the uses of student political power. At one time, for example, the president of the Ivory Coast believed it necessary to hold a long-distance discussion with student leaders to guarantee their loyalty to his regime. In Burma in 1953 the prime minister was forced to appeal to the nation by radio to cope with a student strike at the University of Rangoon, and finally he had to use military police to break it. China's communist rulers considered it necessary to crush a student movement because it voiced opposition to government policies. In Turkey in 1960 student violence reached such proportions and gained such support that it brought down the regime. Student movements have been so important in the developing nations that one cannot understand the political structures of these countries without analyzing the role of students in them.

Like his counterpart in the West, the activist in traditional societies, whether in Asia, Africa, or the Middle East, found himself an alienated man, but for reasons different from those applicable to Western students. The Afro-Asian was alienated by Western education from his own culture and history. Yet his heritage and color also alienated him from the Western world with its humiliating racism that had stigmatized him and his people as inferiors.

The Chinese student movement was influenced both by Western educational models and by China's own history. Before Western influence became strong in the middle of the nineteenth century, Chinese university students belonged to an elite of privilege and responsibility. After that time the traditional image of the scholar began to suffer because mastery of classical learning had failed to prepare China for the modern age, leaving her a weak nation exploited by foreigners. Rebelling against these conditions, students became agents of intellectual and social ferment. Rejecting their traditional elitist cultural heritage, they supplied cadres for the revolutionary movement that overthrew the Manchu dynasty and established a republic.

When the new government in the thirties promised reforms, students remained relatively quiet, but when it appeared weak and corrupt, as after the Second World War, activism again erupted. Convinced that the main obstacle to national unity was the Kuomintang government, students became Chiang Kai-shek's harshest critics and contributed to the destruction of his regime. Under Mao Tse-tung they were no longer alienated elitists; they had been transformed into working, studying members of the revolutionary establishment. Yet they had no power; some grumbled against tyranny but were unable to stimulate change. At one point, in the "Hundred Flowers Movement" of 1956, some protested, but no revolt followed. With its complete control of the university and society, the communist regime would not tolerate unchanneled student dissent, even from a minority.

In postwar Japan, too, student activism contributed to social upheaval and turmoil in the universities. There students openly intimidated their professors and university presidents. In 1960 a militant leftwing student organization, *Zengakuren,* captured world headlines when it spearheaded demonstrations against an unpopular treaty with the United States, compelled the government to rescind an invitation to President Dwight D. Eisenhower, and overthrew Prime Minister Nobosuki Kishi's government. The radicals succeeded in this instance because they gained support from the labor movement and several political parties, but the radicals could not mount the revolution they desired. They were a minority alienated not only from the rest of society but also from the older leadership of the revolutionary political parties.

Since 1963 student protests have also contributed to political crises in South Vietnam. At various Indian universities students have taken to politics to achieve social and educational goals. The All India Students' Federation, a leftwing group, has been especially active in politics, but student dissent has not been massive or well organized. Sporadic activism has disrupted universities but has not eliminated basic educational evils.

Nowhere has the tradition of student activism in politics been more deeply rooted than in Latin America. There, since Argentine students succeeded in gaining university reforms in the 1920's, students throughout the continent have had a constitutional voice in academic affairs, and they have often been instruments of reform. In much of Latin America student movements have attacked the traditional oligarchic elements in society for resisting economic and social modernization. University students have also frequently been the only ones to combat dictatorships. This role of critic has given them an unusual importance in the social structure. Using the universities as privileged sanctuaries, they are among the few in authoritarian societies who can debate politics, criticize the ruling establishment, and still survive. But student power in Latin America has not always been praiseworthy. In reasonably democratic countries it has threatened academic freedom and kept educational standards low. Student involvement in professional and administrative decision-making within the universities has brought with it corruption, factionalism, and erosion of intellectual life.

In the late fifties Fidel Castro transformed radical student activism in Latin America. His revolution in Cuba became a model for young leftwing reformers thirsting for power, a symbol of the student movement in arms fighting for, not merely talking about, social reform. Since his climb to power radical students in much of Latin America have been better organized than in the past and have replaced intermittent violence with guerrilla warfare within and outside universities.

Historically, youthful activism and student power within the social and educational structure in the United States has never been comparable to that in Latin America, though in the early colleges student participation in decision-making was an established part of academic practice. In the late nineteenth century the faculty gained ascendancy, a development that coincided with the rise of the great universities and of professionalism in academic disciplines. The professional academicians, that is, men trained in the universities to teach and do research in their fields of competence, greatly improved the quality of higher education. Students generally approved this professionalization because they benefited from it, but it did strip them of the power they had previously exercised in matters of curricula and teaching.

Student unrest in the nineteenth century did not stem from a desire for academic power. Not being politically oriented, students seldom attacked established authority. There were no real political or ideological differences among students, faculty, and trustees of the university. When students rebelled they did so for immediate practical reasons. They complained about food in the commons, protested increased requirements in studies, and demonstrated against rigorous examiners. Boisterous and mischievous, they frequently rioted in the old tradition of town *versus* gown, but they organized no real student movement. Such organization did not come until the twentieth century.

In the 1930's students plunged into the labor movement, striving to improve the conditions of workers throughout the country. They were also drawn to other large issues: unemployment, pacifism, and the abolition of compulsory R.O.T.C. on campuses. Many turned to Marxism and different types of socialism as instruments for transforming society. In 1934 two radical organizations, the National Student League and the Student League for Industrial Democracy, carried out a surprisingly successful "Student Strike Against War." In two demonstrations of solidarity in April 1934 and April 1935 students in various colleges walked out of classes and endorsed the Oxford Pledge, as revised for American students, to refuse "to support the United States Government in any war it may conduct." In 1936 a third walkout attracted 350,000 students out of a total college population of 1,000,000.

With the coming of the Second World War this activism faded; American university students fought without protest; and the wartime generation returned to the campuses determined to earn a place within the establishment. They were practical-minded and reputedly politically apathetic. Their successors, the students of the fifties, were termed "the silent generation"; polls indicated that most of them were unconcerned with the deeper issues of society. They gave the impression of being faddists interested more in panty raids than in reform.

The reputation of American students changed drastically in the sixties; they became politicized and known all over the world as committed activists. The young began questioning almost everything, protesting what they disliked, and involving themselves in the university's and society's fundamental problems. College campuses became forums of political controversy and staging areas for attacks on the *status quo*. Universities welcomed participatory democracy, student evaluations of professors, student membership on faculty and administrative committees, special Black and Chicano courses; they witnessed widespread use of drugs and opposition to war, to the draft, and to the establishment.

This new massive student activism began in February 1960 with a wave of sit-ins by black students in the South. University students from the North, white and black, joined the civil-rights crusade, taking summer treks to Mississippi to expose racism and violence. This struggle for social justice for blacks infused life into the previously dormant student movement. For several years the civil-rights battle gave young people an issue unclouded by ambiguity, one that merited a full-hearted response. Those who joined the crusade became the founders of radical politics in American universities.

Nowhere did the radicals flourish more than on the Berkeley campus of the University of California. There in the fall of 1964 militants applied the experience of the civil-rights crusade to a student uprising known as the free-speech movement. For the first time on a large scale, students protested the computerized unresponsive authority of the "multiversity." The most invoked metaphor was that of the IBM card. "I am a UC student," one protestor said, "Please don't bend, fold, or mutilate me." No other student rebellion had ever gripped the public imagination as did that at Berkeley. It acted as a catalyst setting off student explosions in favor of educational, political, and social reform on campuses across the country and in other parts of the world.

Student activists next turned their attention to the Vietnam War. Moved by feelings of moral revulsion against what they deemed a barbarous and unnecessary bloodbath, students and some of their professors became among the first to oppose it. Opposition spread until the conduct of the war became a dominant political issue, one that permeated the entire American student movement. In fighting for civil rights for blacks, students had challenged an outmoded social system; their civil disobedience was based on a widely recognized humanitarianism. Their opposition to the Vietnam War, however, was much more radical; it threatened not only the ruling establishment but also values held by the nonstudent majority.

The war produced a marked deterioration in American political life. The protest it evoked was not just restricted to the nation's leading campuses. However, to the campuses the war brought a special and very harsh message that only force counts, a practical realization that increased youth's alienation and cynicism. Student radicals adopted the principle of force and turned it against the establishment with numerous acts of civil disobedience—the seizure of buildings, random destruction of university property, bomb scares, fires in libraries, and confrontations with police and the National Guard. Within this atmosphere of violence breeding violence occurred the

second most significant student uprising of the era, the protest at
Columbia University over the building of a gymnasium in Harlem's
Morningside Park adjacent to the campus. In April 1968 radical
students abandoned peaceful protest; they used force to wrench
concessions from the university. The Columbia revolt showed that
radical activism could spring up almost anywhere, in Ivy League
schools as well as in sprawling state universities. Violence now became something of a norm in radical insurgency. In the fall of 1968
black students presented a list of "nonnegotiable demands" to the
administration at San Francisco State College, and in April 1969
at Cornell blacks backed their demands for change with rifles and
shotguns. At the University of Wisconsin and the University of
California at Santa Barbara students met violent deaths as a result
of disorder.

The protests, the agitation, the demands, the violence, all stirred
a deep uneasiness in legislators, the courts, parents, alumni, academic
administrators, and the public. In March 1969 a Gallup Poll claimed
that campus disorders had replaced the Vietnam War as the primary
concern of most Americans. On a single day in April student demonstrators were occupying buildings on seventeen campuses. The
stunned American public realized that the youth rebellion, headquartered in the universities, had to be taken seriously. Polls indicated that the public was alarmed, intolerant, and favored hard
responses to the agitation. At Kent State University in Ohio in May
1970 National Guardsmen fired pointblank on students protesting
the American invasion of Cambodia; they killed four unarmed
youths. Students and faculty everywhere were outraged, but most
Americans sided with repressive "law and order." During the legislative sessions of 1969–70 the anti-student backlash struck with full
force; thirty-two states enacted laws designed to prevent or cope with
campus disorders. Other countries, too, experienced a backlash. In
Germany, Italy, and elsewhere legislators prepared bills to curb student outbursts.

Critics pointed out that the youth rebellion was not truly widespread, that activists comprised only a minority of the student
population. This was an accurate observation. The small, private
denominational colleges, teachers' colleges, technological schools,

and most state universities experienced no demonstrations or political activism. Radicals found the environment for dissent most con-
genial at large schools with quality student bodies and faculties, and
often at institutions within urban environments. Despite the small
number of militants, one reason for the public fear of them was the
exaggeration of the scope of the activism by politicians and the mass
media. Newspaper and television reporters seized on dramatic and
violent confrontations, playing them up as though the attitude of
the dissidents represented that of the entire student community.

Yet the student movement was not a phenomenon made up of
refugees from the lunatic fringe. The dissenters came from all levels
of society, but mostly from the middle and upper classes. They were,
on the whole, the intelligent children of America's elite. While the
activists themselves were few, their goals appealed to a broad cross
section of students, hence the massiveness of various protests.

The appeal was strong because the institutions under attack had
much wrong with them and needed reform. Dissidents and others
had no faith in science, government, the political system, and the
university. All seemed immovable and unresponsive to individual
needs. The activists were concerned about the state of higher education and its relationship to a society that seemed to condone war
against small impoverished nations, that perpetuated poverty, and
that fouled the environment. The university, they argued, was an
instrument of the repressive political system; it had become totally
bureaucratic and had lost contact with students, treating them not
as individuals but as "IBM cards, numbers, cogs in a sort of educational factory." To those who viewed the world as dominated by
large, unfeeling authoritarian organizations, the university had become just another impersonal institution.

What the young dissidents did not seem to understand is that
technology, civil law, the military, and politics are all human institutions that can only be reformed by men of good will. The students
exposed real social and institutional flaws, but though they spoke of
creating alternatives, they offered no program of constructive reform.
One of the younger generation's most admired spokesmen of discontent, Paul Goodman, has pointed out that except in isolated
instances, as in Poland and Czechoslovakia where dissatisfied youth

confronted unusually oppressive and outmoded regimes, students usually protested over immediate issues. As one Czech student told his Western European counterparts, "We have a clearly defined objective—we want liberty. We do not know what you want. . . . " The tactics of most student groups have been mainly disruptive, and they have acted without coherent purpose for a better society. Their goals have been fuzzy. But in France, Portugal, and the United States the opposition to colonial or semicolonial wars had in it a concern for the general good as well as for student welfare.

Regardless of its shortcomings, student activism, wherever it has taken place, has seldom been a purely campus phenomenon. Activists have at least attempted to grapple with broad issues in society and in higher education, with war, poverty, discrimination, and the perpetuation of an elitist establishment in the university. Militants have demanded a radical transformation that would make society and the campus more responsive to needs of the masses. Even though activism has differed from country to country and from period to period, it has characteristics that can be found all over the world. University students everywhere have constituted an elite that has long had a political and social significance out of proportion to the numbers involved. Their life at universities has created a student culture made up of marginal men who stand somewhere between childhood and adulthood, a culture that sets students apart from others in society. Their separate identity, their alienation, has long fostered opposition to adult society.

In recent years, as youth's image of the future clashed with the reality of daily experience, students rebelled against adult politics, against an establishment they did not trust. They believed no one was listening to their grievances, so they felt compelled to shout, unleash rage, and show themselves clutched in a crisis against authority. In their revolt against impersonal institutions they expressed an annoyance with authority that was shared by adults. The activists' desire for influence in institutions they would someday control, while not always practical, was legitimate and understandable. "We want so badly," a Stanford student said, "to have an impact on the society in which we live."

Concerned societies recognize this desire, accept the legitimate aspects of student activism, and differentiate between disruption and organized dissent. Such societies would not deny universities the support and resources essential for legitimate self-reform that students know is needed; such societies would use the zeal and energy of youth to effect meaningful change wherever required. Those of the older generation in the seats of authority should not attempt merely to crush student militance but to understand and, where possible, to work with it for constructive ends. The conflict of generations, which has always been with us, does not have to be bloody.

I
Medieval
Student Life

This selection from a larger work describes the origins of the modern university from the medieval institutions at Paris and Bologna. Note how a student class came into existence and quickly gained special privileges from Emperor Frederick Barbarossa. Note also why students organized themselves against townspeople, and how and for what purpose they used their collective power. It is clear that in Paris town-and-gown violence led to special status before the law for students.

1

The Earliest Universities

Charles H. Haskins

Universities, like cathedrals and parliaments, are a product of the Middle Ages. The Greeks and the Romans, strange as it may seem, had no universities in the sense in which the word has been used for the past seven or eight centuries. They had higher education, but the terms are not synonymous. Much of their instruction in law, rhetoric, and philosophy it would be hard to surpass, but it was not organized into the form of permanent institutions of learning. A great teacher like Socrates gave no diplomas; if a modern student sat at his feet for three months, he would demand a certificate, something tangible and external to show for it—an excellent theme, by the way, for a Socratic dialogue. Only in the twelfth and thirteenth centuries do there emerge in the world those features of organized education with which we are most familiar, all that machinery of instruction represented by faculties and colleges and courses of study, examinations and commencements and academic degrees. In all these matters we are the heirs and successors, not of Athens and Alexandria, but of Paris and Bologna.

The contrast between these earliest universities and those of today is of course broad and striking. Throughout the period of its origins the mediaeval university had no libraries, laboratories, or museums, no endowment or buildings of its own. . . . As an historical textbook from one of the youngest of American universities tells us,

From Charles H. Haskins, *The Rise of the Universities* (New York, 1923), pp. 3–36.

with an unconscious touch of local color, it had "none of the attributes of the material existence which with us are so self-evident."
The mediaeval university was, in the fine old phrase of Pasquier,
"built of men"—*bâtie en hommes*. Such a university had no board
of trustees and published no catalogue; it had no student societies—
except so far as the university itself was fundamentally a society of
students—no college journalism, no dramatics, no athletics, none of
those "outside activities" which are the chief excuse for inside inactivity in the American college.

And yet, great as these differences are, the fact remains that the
university of the twentieth century is the lineal descendant of
mediaeval Paris and Bologna. They are the rock whence we were
hewn, the hole of the pit whence we were digged. The fundamental
organization is the same, the historic continuity is unbroken. They
created the university tradition of the modern world, that common
tradition which belongs to all our institutions of higher learning, the
newest as well as the oldest, and which all college and university
men should know and cherish. The origin and nature of these
earliest universities is the subject of these three lectures. The first
will deal with university institutions, the second with university
instruction, the third with the life of university students.

In recent years the early history of universities has begun to attract the serious attention of historical scholars, and mediaeval institutions of learning have at last been lifted out of the region of myth
and fable where they long lay obscured. We now know that the
foundation of the University of Oxford was not one of the many
virtues which the millennial celebration could properly ascribe to
King Alfred; that Bologna did not go back to the Emperor Theo-
dosius; that the University of Paris did not exist in the time of
Charlemagne, or for nearly four centuries afterward. It is hard, even
for the modern world, to realize that many things had no founder
or fixed date of beginning but instead "just grew," arising slowly
and silently without definite record. This explains why . . . the
beginnings of the oldest universities are obscure and often uncertain,
so that we must content ourselves sometimes with very general statements.

The occasion for the rise of universities was a great revival of learning, not that revival of the fourteenth and fifteenth centuries to which the term is usually applied, but an earlier revival, less known though in its way quite as significant, which historians now call the renaissance of the twelfth century. So long as knowledge was limited to the seven liberal arts of the early Middle Ages, there could be no universities, for there was nothing to teach beyond the bare elements of grammar, rhetoric, logic, and the still barer notions of arithmetic, astronomy, geometry, and music, which did duty for an academic curriculum. Between 1100 and 1200, however, there came a great influx of new knowledge into western Europe, partly through Italy and Sicily, but chiefly through the Arab scholars of Spain—the works of Aristotle, Euclid, Ptolemy, and the Greek physicians, the new arithmetic, and those texts of the Roman law which had lain hidden through the Dark Ages. In addition to the elementary propositions of triangle and circle, Europe now had those books of plane and solid geometry which have done duty in schools and colleges ever since; instead of the painful operations with Roman numerals—how painful one can readily see by trying a simple problem of multiplication or division with these characters—it was now possible to work readily with Arabic figures; in the place of Boethius the "Master of them that know" became the teacher of Europe in logic, metaphysics, and ethics. In law and medicine men now possessed the fulness of ancient learning. This new knowledge burst the bonds of the cathedral and monastery schools and created the learned professions; it drew over mountains and across the narrow seas eager youths who, like Chaucer's Oxford clerk of a later day, "would gladly learn and gladly teach," to form in Paris and Bologna those academic gilds which have given us our first and our best definition of a university, a society of masters and scholars.

To this general statement concerning the twelfth century there is one partial exception, the medical university of Salerno. Here, a day's journey to the south of Naples, in territory at first Lombard and later Norman, but still in close contact with the Greek East, a school of medicine had existed as early as the middle of the eleventh century, and for perhaps two hundred years thereafter it was the most renowned medical centre in Europe. In this "city of Hippocrates" the medical writings of the ancient Greeks were expounded and even developed on the side of anatomy and surgery, while its teachings were condensed into pithy maxims of hygiene which have not yet lost their vogue—"after dinner walk a mile," etc. Of the academic organization of Salerno we know nothing before 1231, and when in this year the standardizing hand of Frederick II regulated its degrees Salerno had already been distanced by newer universities farther north. Important in the history of medicine, it had no influence on the growth of university institutions.

If the University of Salerno is older in time, that of Bologna has a much larger place in the development of higher education. And while Salerno was known only as a school of medicine, Bologna was a many-sided institution, though most noteworthy as the centre of the revival of the Roman law. Contrary to a common impression, the Roman law did not disappear from the West in the early Middle Ages, but its influence was greatly diminished as a result of the Germanic invasions. Side by side with the Germanic codes, Roman law survived as the customary law of the Roman population, known no longer through the great law books of Justinian but in elementary manuals and form-books which grew thinner and more jejune as time went on. The *Digest,* the most important part of the *Corpus Juris Civilis,* disappears from view between 606 and 1076; only two manuscripts survived. . . . Legal study persisted, if at all, merely as an apprenticeship in the drafting of documents, a form of applied rhetoric. Then, late in the eleventh century, and closely connected with the revival of trade and town life, came a revival of law, foreshadowing the renaissance of the century which followed. This revival can be traced at more than one point in Italy, perhaps not first at Bologna, but here it soon found its centre of the geographical reasons which, then as now, made this city the meeting-point of the chief routes of communication in northern Italy. Some time before 1100 we hear of a professor named Pepo, "the bright and shining light of Bologna"; by 1119 we meet with the phrase *Bononia docta.* At Bologna, as at Paris, a great teacher stands at the beginning of university development. The teacher who gave Bologna its reputation was one Irnerius, perhaps the most famous of the many great professors of law in the Middle Ages. Just what he wrote and what he taught are still subjects of dispute among scholars, but he seems to have fixed the method of "glossing" the law texts upon the basis of a comprehensive use of the whole *Corpus Juris*, as contrasted with the meagre epitomes of the preceding centuries, fully and finally separating the Roman law from rhetoric and establishing it firmly as a subject of professional study. Then, about 1140, Gratian, a monk of San Felice, composed the *Decretum* which became the standard text in canon law, thus marked off from theology as a distinct subject of higher study; and the preëminence of Bologna as a law school was fully assured.

A student class had now appeared, expressing itself in correspondence and in poetry, and by 1158 it was sufficiently important in Italy to receive a formal grant of rights and privileges from Emperor Frederick Barbarossa, though no particular town or university is mentioned. By this time Bologna had become the resort of some hundreds of students, not only from Italy but from beyond the Alps. Far from home and undefended, they united for mutual protection and assistance, and this organization of foreign, or Transmontane, students was the beginning of the university. In this union they seem to have followed the example of the gilds already common in Italian cities. Indeed, the word university means originally such a group or corporation in general, and only in time did it come to be limited to gilds of masters and students, *universitas societas magistrorum discipulorumque*. Historically, the word university has no connection with the universe or the universality of learning; it denotes only the totality of a group, whether of barbers, carpenters, or students did not matter. The students of Bologna organized such a university first as a means of protection against the townspeople, for the price of rooms and necessaries rose rapidly with the crowd of new tenants and consumers, and the individual student was helpless against such profiteering. United, the students could bring the town to terms by the threat of departure as a body, secession, for the university, having no buildings, was free to move, and there are many historic examples of such migrations. Better rent one's rooms for less than not rent them at all, and so the student organizations secured the power to fix the prices of lodgings and books through their representatives.

Victorious over the townsmen, the students turned on "their other enemies, the professors." Here the threat was a collective boycott, and as the masters lived at first wholly from the fees of their pupils, this threat was equally effective. The professor was put under bond to live up to a minute set of regulations which guaranteed his students the worth of the money paid by each. We read in the earliest statutes (1317) that a professor might not be absent without leave, even a single day, and if he desired to leave town he had to make a deposit to ensure his return. If he failed to secure an audience of five for a regular lecture, he was fined as if absent—a poor lecture indeed which could not secure five hearers! He must begin with the bell and quit within one minute after the next bell. He was not allowed to skip a chapter in his commentary, or postpone a difficulty to the end of the hour, and he was obliged to cover ground systematically, so much in each specific term of the year. No one might spend the whole year on introduction and bibliography! Coercion of this sort presupposes an effective organization of the student body, and we hear of two and even four universities of students, each composed of "nations" and presided over by a rector. Emphatically Bologna was a student university, and Italian students are still quite apt to demand a voice in university affairs. When I first visited the University of Palermo I found it just recovering from a riot in which the students had broken the front windows in a demand for more frequent, and thus less comprehensive, examinations. At Padua's seventh centenary . . . the students practically took over the town, with a programme of processions and ceremonies quite their own and an amount of noise and tumult which almost broke up the most solemn occasions and did break the windows of the greatest hall in the city.

Excluded from the "universities" of students, the professors also formed a gild or "college," requiring for admission thereto certain qualifications which were ascertained by examination, so that no student could enter save by the gild's consent. And, inasmuch as ability to teach a subject is a good test of knowing it, the student came to seek the professor's license as a certificate of attainment, regardless of his future career. This certificate, the license to teach (*licentia docendi*), thus became the earliest form of academic degree. Our higher degrees still preserve this tradition in the words master (*magister*) and doctor, originally synonymous, while the French even have a *licence*. A Master of Arts was one qualified to teach the liberal arts; a Doctor of Laws, a certified teacher of law. And the ambitious student sought the degree and gave an inaugural lecture, even when he expressly disclaimed all intention of continuing in the teaching profession. Already we recognize at Bologna the standard academic degrees as well as the university organization and well-known officials like the rector.

Other subjects of study appeared in course of time, arts, medicine, and theology, but Bologna was preëminently a school of civil law, and as such it became the model of university organization for Italy, Spain, and southern France, countries where the study of law has always had political and social as well as merely academic significance. Some of these universities became Bologna's competitors, like Montpellier and Orleans as well as the Italian schools near home. Frederick II founded the University of Naples in 1224 so that the students of his Sicilian kingdom could go to a Ghibelline school at home instead of the Guelfic centre in the North. Rival Padua was founded two years earlier as a secession from Bologna. . . . Padua, however, scarcely equalled Bologna in our period, even though at a later age Portia sent thither for legal authority, and though the university still shines with the glory of Galileo.

In northern Europe the origin of universities must be sought at Paris, in the cathedral school of Notre-Dame. By the beginning of the twelfth century in France and the Low Countries learning was no longer confined to monasteries but had its most active centres in the schools attached to cathedrals, of which the most famous were those of Liège, Rheims, Laon, Paris, Orleans, and Chartres. The most notable of these schools of the liberal arts was probably Chartres, distinguished by a canonist like St. Ives and by famous teachers of classics and philosophy like Bernard and Thierry. As early as 991 a monk of Rheims, Richer, describes the hardships of his journey to Chartres in order to study the *Aphorisms* of Hippocrates of Cos; while from the twelfth century John of Salisbury, the leading northern humanist of the age, has left us an account of the masters. . . . Nowhere else today can we drop back more easily

into a cathedral city of the twelfth century, the peaceful town still
dominated by its church and sharing, now as then,

> the minster's vast repose.
> Silent and gray as forest-leaguered cliff
> Left inland by the ocean's slow retreat,
> . . . . patiently remote
> From the great tides of life it breasted once,
> Hearing the noise of men as in a dream.

By the time the cathedral stood complete, with its "dedicated shapes
of saints and kings," it had ceased to be an intellectual centre of the
first importance, overshadowed by Paris fifty-odd miles away, so that
Chartres never became a university.

The advantages of Paris were partly geographical, partly political
as the capital of the new French monarchy, but something must be
set down to the influence of a great teacher in the person of
Abelard. This brilliant young radical, with his persistent questioning
and his scant respect for titled authority, drew students in large
numbers wherever he taught, whether at Paris or in the wilderness.
At Paris he was connected with the church of Mont-Sainte-Geneviève
longer than with the cathedral school, but resort to Paris became a
habit in his time, and in this way he had a significant influence on
the rise of the university. In an institutional sense the university
was a direct outgrowth of the school of Notre-Dame, whose chancellor alone had authority to license teaching in the diocese and thus
kept his control over the granting of university degrees, which here
as at Bologna were originally teachers' certificates. The early schools
were within the cathedral precincts on the Ile de la Cité, that
tangled quarter about Notre-Dame pictured by Victor Hugo which
has long since been demolished. A little later we find masters and
scholars living on the Little Bridge (Petit-Pont) which connected
the island with the Left Bank of the Seine—this bridge gave its
name to a whole school of philosophers, the Parvipontani—but by
the thirteenth century they have overrun the Left Bank, thenceforth
the Latin Quarter of Paris.

At what date Paris ceased to be a cathedral school and became a university, no one can say, though it was certainly before the end of the twelfth century. Universities, however, like to have precise dates to celebrate, and the University of Paris has chosen 1200, the year of its first royal charter. In that year, after certain students had been killed in a town and gown altercation, King Philip Augustus issued a formal privilege which punished his prévôt and recognized the exemption of the students and their servants from lay jurisdiction, thus creating that special position of students before the courts which has not yet wholly disappeared from the world's practice, though generally from its law. More specific was the first papal privilege, the bull *Parens scientiarum* of 1231, issued after a two years' cessation of lectures growing out of a riot in which a band of students, having found "wine that was good and sweet to drink," beat up the tavern keeper and his friends till they in turn suffered from the prévôt and his men, a dissension in which the thirteenth century clearly saw the hand of the devil. Confirming the existing exemptions, the Pope goes on to regulate the discretion of the chancellor in conferring the license, at the same time that he recognizes the right of the masters and students "to make constitutions and ordinances regulating the manner and time of lectures and disputations, the costume to be worn," attendance at masters' funerals, the lectures of bachelors, necessarily more limited than those of fully fledged masters, the price of lodgings, and the coercion of members. Students must not carry arms, and only those who frequent the schools regularly are to enjoy the exemptions of students, the interpretation in practice being attendance at not less than two lectures a week.

While the word university does not appear in these documents, it is taken for granted. A university in the sense of an organized body of masters existed already in the twelfth century; by 1231 it had developed into a corporation, for Paris, in contrast to Bologna, was a university of masters. There were now four faculties, each under a dean: arts, canon law (civil law was forbidden at Paris after 1219), medicine, and theology. The masters of arts, much more numerous than the others, were grouped into four "nations": the French, including the Latin peoples; the Norman; the Picard, including also the Low Countries; and the English, comprising England, Germany, and the North and East of Europe. These four nations chose the head of the university, the rector, as he is still generally styled on the Continent, whose term, however, was short, being later only three months. If we may judge from such minutes as have survived, much of the time of the nations was devoted to consuming the fees collected from new members and new officers, or, as it was called, drinking up the surplus—at the Two Swords near the Petit-Pont, at the sign of Our Lady in the Rue S.-Jacques, at the Swan, the Falcon, the Arms of France, and scores of similar places. A learned monograph on the taverns of mediaeval Paris has been written from the records of the English nation alone. The artificial constitution of the nations seems to have encouraged rather than diminished the feuds and rivalries between the various regions represented at Paris, of which Jacques de Vitry has left a classic description:

"They wrangled and disputed not merely about the various sects or about some discussions; but the differences between the countries also caused dissensions, hatreds, and virulent animosities amng them, and they impudently uttered all kinds of affronts and insults against one another. They affirmed that the English were drunkards and had tails; the sons of France proud, effeminate, and carefully adorned like women. They said that the Germans were furious and obscene at their feasts; the Normans, vain and boastful; the Poitevins, traitors and always adventurers. The Burgundians they considered vulgar and stupid. The Bretons were reputed to be fickle and changeable, and were often reproached for the death of Arthur. The Lombards were called avaricious, vicious, and cowardly; the Romans, seditious, turbulent, and slanderous; the Sicilians, tyrannical and cruel; the inhabitants of Brabant, men of blood, incendiaries, brigands, and ravishers; the Flemish, fickle, prodigal, gluttonous, yielding as butter, and slothful. After such insults, from words they often came to blows."

Another university institution which goes back to twelfth-century Paris is the college. Originally merely an endowed hospice or hall of residence, the college early became an established unit of academic life at many universities. "The object of the earliest college-founders was simply to secure board and lodging for poor scholars who could not pay for it themselves"; but in course of time the colleges became normal centres of life and teaching, absorbing into themselves much of the activity of the university. The colleges had buildings and endowments, if the university had not. There was a college at Paris as early as 1180; there were sixty-eight by 1500, and the system survived until the Revolution, to leave behind it only fragments of buildings or local names like the Sorbonne of today, sole memento of that Collège de la Sorbonne founded for theologians by a confessor of St. Louis in the thirteenth century. Many other continental universities had their colleges, one of which, the ancient College of Spain at Bologna, still survives for the delectation of the few Spanish youths who reach its quiet courtyard. But of course the ultimate home of the college was Oxford and Cambridge, where it came to be the most characteristic feature of university life, arrogating to itself practically all teaching as well as direction of social life, until the university became merely an examining and degree-conferring body. Here the older colleges like Balliol, Merton, and Peterhouse date from the thirteenth century.

Paris was preëminent in the Middle Ages as a school of theology, and, as theology was the supreme subject of mediaeval study, "Madame la haute science" it was called, this means that it was preëminent as a university. "The Italians have the Papacy, the Germans have the Empire, and the French have Learning," ran the old saying; and the chosen abode of learning was Paris. Quite naturally Paris became the source and the model for northern universities. Oxford branched off from this parent stem late in the twelfth century, likewise with no definite date of foundation; Cambridge began somewhat later. The German universities, none of them older than the fourteenth century, were confessed imitations of Paris. Thus the Elector Palatine, Ruprecht, in founding the University of Heidelberg in 1386— for these later universities were founded at specific dates—provides that it "shall be ruled, disposed, and regulated according to the modes and matters accustomed to be observed in the University of Paris, and that as a handmaid of Paris—a worthy one let us hope—it shall imitate the steps of Paris in every way possible, so that there shall be four faculties," four nations and a rector, exemptions for students and their servants, and even caps and gowns for the several faculties "as has been observed at Paris."

By the end of the Middle Ages at least eighty universities had been founded in different parts of Europe. Some of these were short-lived, many were of only local importance, others like Salerno flourished only to die, but some like Paris and Montpellier, Bologna and Padua, Oxford and Cambridge, Vienna and Prague and Leipzig, Coimbra and Salamanca, Cracow and Louvain, have an unbroken history of many centuries of distinction. And the great European universities of more recent foundation, like Berlin, Strasbourg, Edinburgh, Manchester, and London, follow in their organization the ancient models. In America the earliest institutions of higher learning reproduced the type of the contemporary English college at a time when the university in England was eclipsed by its constituent colleges; but in the creation of universities in the later nineteenth century, America turned to the universities of the Continent and thus entered once more into the ancient inheritance. Even in the colonial period a sense of the general university tradition survived, for the charter of Rhode Island College in 1764 grants "the same privileges, dignities, and immunities enjoyed by the American colleges, and European universities."

What then is our inheritance from the oldest of universities? In the first place it is not buildings or a type of architecture, for the early universities had no buildings of their own, but on occasion used private halls and neighboring churches. After all, as late as 1775 the First Baptist Church in Providence was built "for the publick worship of Almighty God, and also for holding Commencement in"! Indeed one who seeks to reconstruct the life of ancient universities will find little aid in their existing remains. Salerno retains no monuments of its university, though its rare old cathedral, where Hildebrand lies buried, must have seen the passing of many generations of would-be physicians. In the halls and coats of arms of "many-domed Padua proud" we behold the Renaissance, not the Middle Ages. Even Bologna, *Bononia docta,* with its leaning towers and cool arcades, has no remains of university architecture earlier than the fourteenth century, from which date the oldest monuments of its professors of law gathered now into the municipal museum. Montpellier and Orleans preserve nothing from this period. Paris, too often careless of its storied past, can show today only the ancient church of Saint-Julien-le-Pauvre, where university meetings were often held, unless we count, as we should, the great cathedral in the Cité whence the university originally sprang. The oldest Cambridge college, Peterhouse, has only a fragment of its earliest buildings; the finest Cambridge monument, King's College chapel, is of the late fifteenth century. More than all others Oxford gives the deepest impression of continuity with an ancient past, Matthew Arnold's Oxford, "so venerable, so lovely . . . steeped in sentiment as she lies, spreading her gardens to the moonlight, and whispering from her towers the last enchantments of the Middle Age"; yet so far as the actual college buildings are concerned they have much more of sentiment than of the Middle Ages. Only at Merton, which fixed the college type, at Oxford, do any of the present structures carry us back of 1300, and nowhere is there much of the fourteenth century. Those venerable glories of Oxford, the Bodleian library, the tower of Magdalen, and the hall of Christ Church, belong to a much later age, the period of the Tudors, and thus by ordinary reckoning to modern times. When we say how very mediaeval, we often mean how very Tudor!

Neither does the continuity lie in academic form and ceremony, in spite of occasional survivals, like the conferring of degrees by the ring or the kiss of peace, or the timing of examinations by the hour glass as I have seen it at Portuguese Coimbra. Academic costume has in it some element of tradition where it is a daily dress as at Oxford, Cambridge, and Coimbra, but in America the tradition was broken by our ancestors, and the formal cap and gown current in the United States today are a product of modern Albany rather than of mediaeval Paris and Bologna. Even in their ancient homes the costumes have changed. "It is probable," says Rashdall, "that no gown now worn in Oxford has much resemblance to its mediaeval ancestor." A student of mediaeval Padua would not recognize the variegated procession which wound through its streets last summer; Robert de Sorbon would rub his eyes at the non-mediaeval styles of the gorgeous gowns which were massed on the stage of the great hall of the Sorbonne when President Wilson received his honorary degree in 1918.

It is, then, in institutions that the university tradition is most direct. First, the very name university, as an association of masters and scholars leading the common life of learning. Characteristic of the Middle Ages as such a corporation is, the individualistic modern world has found nothing to take its place. Next, the notion of a curriculum of study, definitely laid down as regards time and subjects, tested by an examination and leading to a degree, as well as many of the degrees themselves—bachelor, as a stage toward the mastership, master, doctor, in arts, law, medicine, and theology. Then the faculties, four or more, with their deans, and the higher officers such as chancellors and rectors, not to mention the college, wherever the residential college still survives. The essentials of university organization are clear and unmistakable, and they have been handed down in unbroken continuity. They have lasted more than seven hundred years—what form of government has lasted so long? Very likely all this is not final—nothing is in this world of flux—but it is singularly tough and persistent, suited to use and also to abuse, like Bryce's university with a faculty "consisting of Mrs. Johnson and myself," or the "eleven leading universities" of a certain state of the Middle West! Universities are at times criticised for their aloofness or their devotion to vocationalism, for being too easy or too severe, and drastic efforts have been made to reform them by abolishing entrance requirements or eliminating all that does not lead directly to bread and butter; but no substitute has been found for the university in its main business, the training of scholars and the maintenance of the tradition of learning and investigation. The glory of the mediaeval university, says Rashdall, was "the consecration of Learning," and the glory and the vision have not yet perished from the earth. "The mediaeval university," it has been said, "was the school of the modern spirit. . . ."

2

Violence, according to this essay, was an accepted part of evolving university life. Oxford University's early history is filled with accounts of town-and-gown riots. Although violence originated from both sides, surviving accounts are more favorable to the students than to the townsfolk because they were written from the standpoint of the academic community; from the town of Oxford, however, come tales of assaults by the University community.

Town and Gown

Robert S. Rait

The violence which marked medieval life as a whole was not likely to be absent in towns where numbers of young clerks were members of a corporation at variance with the authorities of the city. University records are full of injuries done to masters and students by the townsfolk, and of privileges and immunities obtained from Pope or King or Bishop at the expense of the burgesses. When a new University was founded, it was sometimes taken for granted that these conflicts must arise, and that the townsmen were certain to be in the wrong. Thus, when Duke Rudolf IV. founded the University of Vienna in 1365, he provided beforehand for such contingencies by ordaining that an attack on a student leading to the loss of a limb or other member of the body was to be punished by the removal of the same member from the body of the assailant, and that for a lesser injury the offender's hand was to be wounded ("debet manus pugione transfigi"). The criminal might redeem his person by a fine of a hundred silver marks for a serious injury and of forty marks for slighter damages, the victim to receive half of the fine. Assailants of students were not to have benefit of sanctuary. Oxford history abounds in town and gown riots, the most famous of which is the battle of St Scholastica's Day (10th February) 1354. The riot originated in a tavern quarrel; some clerks disapproved of the wine at an inn near Carfax, and (in Antony Wood's words) "the vintner

From Robert S. Rait, *Life in the Medieval University* (Cambridge, 1931), pp. 124–132. Reprinted by permission of the Cambridge University Press.

giving them stubborn and saucy language, they threw the wine and
vessel at his head." His friends urged the inn-keeper "not to put up
with the abuse," and rang the bell of St Martin's Church. A mob at
once assembled, armed with bows and arrows and other weapons;
they attacked every scholar who passed, and even fired at the Chancellor when he attempted to allay the tumult. The justly indignant
Chancellor retorted by ringing St Mary's bell and a mob of students
assembled, also armed (in spite of many statutes to the contrary). A
battle royal raged till nightfall, at which time the fray ceased, "no one
scholar or townsman being killed or mortally wounded or maimed."
If the matter had ended then, little would have been heard of the
story, but next day the townsmen stationed eighty armed men in
St Giles's Church, who sallied out upon "certain scholars walking
after dinner in Beaumont, killed one of them, and wounded others."
A second battle followed, in which the citizens, aided by some countrymen, defeated the scholars, and ravaged their halls, slaying and
wounding. Night interrupted their operations, but on the following
day, "with hideous noises and clamours they came and invaded the
scholars' houses . . . and those that resisted them and stood upon
their defence (particularly some chaplains) they killed or else in a
grievous sort wounded. . . . The crowns of some chaplains, that is,
all the skin so far as the tonsure went, these diabolical imps flayed off
in scorn of their clergy."

The injured University was fully avenged. The King granted it
jurisdiction over the city, and, especially, control of the market, and
the Bishop of Lincoln placed the townsmen under an interdict which
was removed only on condition that the Mayor and Bailiffs, for the
time being, and "three-score of the chiefest Burghers, should personally appear" every St Scholastica's Day in St Mary's Church, to
attend a mass for the souls of the slain. The tradition that they were
to wear halters or silken cords has no authority, but they were each
"to offer at the altar one penny, of which oblation forty pence should
be distributed to forty poor scholars of the University." The custom,
with some modifications, survived the Reformation, and it was not
till the nineteenth century that the Mayor of Oxford ceased to have
cause to regret the battle of St Scholastica's Day.

The accounts of St Scholastica's Day and of most other riots which

have come down to us are written from the standpoint of the
scholars, but the records of the city of Oxford give less detailed but
not less credible instances of assaults by members of the University.
On the eve of St John Baptist's Day in 1306, for example, the tailors
of Oxford were celebrating Midsummer "cum Cytharis Viellis et
aliis diversis instrumentis." After midnight, they went out "de
shoppis suis" and danced and sang in the streets. A clerk, irritated by
the noise, attacked them with a drawn sword, wounded one of them,
and was himself mortally wounded in the skirmish. Of twenty-nine
coroners' inquests which have been preserved for the period 1297–
1322, thirteen are murders committed by scholars. Attacks on townsmen were not mere undergraduate follies, but were countenanced
and even led by officials of the University, *e.g.* on a March night in
1526 one of the proctors "sate uppon a blocke in the streete afore the
shoppe of one Robert Jermyns, a barber, having a pole axe in his
hand, a black cloake on his backe, and a hatt on his head," and or-
ganised a riot in which many townsmen were "striken downe and
sore beaten." Citizens' houses were attacked and "the saide Proctour
and his company . . . called for fire," threatening to burn the
houses, and insulting the inmates with opprobrious names. When
such an incident as this was possible, it was of little use for the University to issue regulations or even to punish less exalted sinners, and
the town must have suffered much from the outrages of scholars and
of the "chamberdekens" or pretended scholars of the University, who
were responsible for much of the mischief. At Paris things became so
bad that the Parlement had to issue a series of police regulations to
suppress the bands of scholars, or pretended scholars, who wandered
about the streets at night, disguised and armed. They attacked
passers-by, and if they were wounded in the affray, their medical
friends, we are told, dressed their wounds, so that they eluded dis-
covery in the morning. The history of every University town provides
instances of street conflicts—the records of Orleans and Toulouse
abound in them—but we must be content with a tale from Leipsic.

The pages of the "Acta Rectorum" at Leipsic are full of illustra-
tions of the wilder side of student life, from which we extract the
story of one unhappy year. The year 1545 opened very badly, says
the "Rector's Chronicle," with three homicides. On Holy Innocents'

Day, a bachelor was murdered by a skinner in a street riot, and the murderer, though he was seen by some respectable citizens, was allowed to escape. A student who killed a man on the night of the Sunday after the Epiphany was punished by the University in accordance with its statutes (*i.e.* by imprisonment for life in the bishop's prison). The third murder was that of a young bachelor who was walking outside the city, when two sons of rustics in the neighbourhood fell on him and killed him. Their names were known, but the city authorities refused to take action, and the populace, believing that they would not be punished, pursued the members of the University with continued insults and threats. After an unusually serious attack *cum bombardis,* (in which, "by the divine clemency," a young mechanic was wounded), the University, failing to obtain redress, appealed to Prince Maurice of Saxony, who promised to protect the University. A conference between the University and the city authorities took place, and edicts against carrying arms were published, but the skinners immediately indulged in another outrage. One of them, Hans von Buntzell, on Whitsunday, attacked with a drawn sword, the son of a doctor of medicine, "a youth (as all agree) most guiltless," and wounded him in the arm, and if another student had not unexpectedly appeared, "would without doubt have killed this excellent boy." The criminal was pursued to the house of a skinner called Meysen, where he took refuge. The city authorities, inspired by the Prince's intervention, offered to impose three alternative sentences, and the University was asked to say whether Hans von Buntzell should lose one of his hands, or be publicly whipped and banished for ten years, or should have a certain stigma ("quod esset manus amittendae signum") burned in his hand and be banished. The University replied that it was for the city to carry out the commands of the Prince, and declined to select the penalty. On the following Monday a scaffold was erected in the market-place, on which were placed rods and a knife for cutting off the hand, "which apparatus was thought by the skinners to be much too fierce and cruel, and a concourse began from all parts, composed not of skinners alone, but of mechanics of every kind, interceding with the Council for the criminal." The pleadings of the multitude gained the day, and all the preparations were removed from the market-place amid the murmurs of the students. After supper, three senior members of the skinners came to the Rector, begging for a commutation of the punishment, and offering to beat Hans themselves in presence of representatives of the University and the Town Council, with greater ferocity than the public executioner could do if he were to whip him three times in public. The Rector replied that he must consult the University, and the proposal was thrown out in Congregation. On the Saturday after the Feast of Trinity, the stigma was burned on the criminal's hand, and as a necessary consequence he was banished.

Town riots do not complete the tale of violence. There were struggles with Jews, and a Jewish row at Oxford in 1268 resulted in the erection of a cross with the following inscription:—

Quis meus auctor erat? Judaei. Quomodo? Sumptu Quis jussit? Regnans. Quo procurante? Magistri. Cur? Cruce pro fracta ligni. Quo tempore? Festo Ascensus Domini. Quis est locus? Hic ubi sisto.

Clerks' enemies were not always beyond their own household. The history of Paris, the earlier history of Oxford, and the record of many another University give us instances of mortal combats between the Nations. The scholars of Paris, in the thirteenth and fourteenth centuries, had to face the mortal enmity of the monks of the Abbey of St Germain, the meadow in front of which was claimed by the Faculty of Arts. The sight of Paris students walking or playing on the Pré-aux-clercs had much the same effect upon the Abbot and monks as the famous donkeys had upon the strong-minded aunt of David Copperfield, but the measures they took for suppressing the nuisance were less exactly proportioned to the offence. One summer day in 1278, masters and scholars went for recreation to the meadow, when the Abbot sent out armed servants and retainers of the monastery to attack them. They came shouting "Ad mortem clericorum," death to the clerks, "verbis crudelibus, *ad mortem ad mortem,* inhumaniter pluries repetitis." A "famous Bachelor of Arts" and other clerks were seriously wounded and thrown into horrible dungeons; another victim lost an eye. The retreat into the city was cut off, and fugitives were pursued far into the country. Blood flowed freely, and the scholars who escaped returned to their halls with broken heads and limbs and their clothes torn to fragments. Some of the victims died of their wounds, and the monks were punished by King and Pope, the Abbot being pensioned off and the Abbey compelled to endow two chaplains to say masses for scholars. Forty years later the University had again to appeal to the Pope to avenge assaults by retainers of the Abbey upon scholars who were fishing in the moat outside the Abbey walls. The monks, of course, may have given a different version of the incidents.

While this essay is a study of student life in general in several universities, note the instances in which town and gown confronted each other in rivalry. Student turbulence in the fifteenth century had various causes, but the privileged status of scholars was an always present source of conflict with those outside the academic community. The violence reflected class tension.

3

Scottish Student Life in the Fifteenth Century

Annie I. Dunlop

The fifteenth century Scottish student belonged to the great ranks of the Church. When he matriculated at a University he was incorporated, as the phrase ran, in a *studium generale*—a place of general study, whose doors were thrown open to students of Latin Christendom without respect to nationality. A fifteenth century university was, in fact, a privileged corporation, enjoying bulls of foundation or of confirmation from the Pope, by virtue of which it could grant degrees in arts and the higher faculties and confer the master's licence of teaching anywhere. Thus, whether our Scottish scholar studied in one of the struggling young universities at home or went overseas among the schools of Europe, he was a freeman of the vast, cosmopolitan republic of letters.

At the beginning of our period, indeed, he had perforce to go abroad in pursuit of a degree, because Scotland itself possessed no university until 1413, and even after the foundation of St. Andrews in that year, followed by Glasgow in 1451 and Aberdeen in 1494, the older and more influential European schools continued to attract intellectual and ambitious students. To them a degree meant much more than a licence to teach. On the contrary, this obligation was more often considered a liability than an asset. To the average graduate a university degree was chiefly valuable as a passport towards ecclesiastical preferment and a qualification for holding administrative posts

From Annie I. Dunlop, "Scottish Student Life in the Fifteenth Century," *Scottish Historical Review*, 26 (1947), 47–63. Reprinted by permission of the Company of Scottish History Ltd.

in Church and State. The medieval equivalent of the modern Civil Service was in fact supplied from the ranks of the men of letters.

In general, therefore, the acquisition of knowledge was considered as a means to an end rather than an end in itself. On the whole, the "study of the seven liberal arts" was less attractive for its own sake than for the benefits which a degree conferred. A graduate "desirous of ecclesiastical stipends" enjoyed certain privileges and priorities in the pursuit of his ambition—on the ground that "exalted and lettered persons ought to be honoured with greater benefices" than their less fortunate brethren.

There were, of course, exceptions. In the fifteenth century, as in all ages, a few choice spirits yearned to drink of the pure waters of the fountain of knowledge. If they were willing to teach in the Faculty of Arts, or if they aspired to study in the higher Faculties, it was possible for them to spend a lifetime within academic walls; and some of them helped to mould university life and have left their names in the history of literature and education. But our present purpose is not so much with the teachers as with the taught. Let us try, therefore, from the scanty material at our disposal to recreate a picture of the life of the student in the Faculty of Arts, which was the keystone of the medieval university structure.

The child to fifteenth century eyes was the man writ small. Adult minds did not stoop to seek comprehension of the child mind, but treated it as essentially mature. Education began, therefore, at an early age; and boys of fifteen were commonly incorporated as matriculated students, or supposts, of a university. At Cologne freshmen had frequently to be dispensed from the statutory oath on the ground that they were minors under fourteen years. There is no evidence that any preliminary standard of education was compulsory for matriculation, but a certain proficiency in Latin grammar and facility of reading and writing must obviously have been necessary; and in 1495 St. Andrews did indeed enact that no scholar should be admitted unless, in presence of the Dean, he had first been examined by four regents and the master of the grammar school and had been found sufficient in grammar.

These essentials he could acquire in grammar schools or in the song schools attached to cathedrals, monasteries and churches, or in the

houses of the Friars Preachers. We know, for example, that Hugh
Kennedy of the Dunure family was educated at the Friars Preachers'
Monastery at Ayr; that in 1464 the magistrates of Peebles granted to
"Schyr Wylyam Blaklok to haf the scule and to be sculmaster and
tyll teche the chylder, and to tak the prophet of the scoule"; and that
in 1494 the Chancellor of Glasgow complained that a certain Mr.
David Dwne had "actually set himself to teach and instruct scholars
in grammar and boys in the rudiments of learning within the said
City and University without leave of the Chancellor." The standard
of education must have varied greatly from place to place, and sometimes have been far from high.

At St. Andrews, however, learning undoubtedly flourished at the
beginning of the century, and it was out of the existing schools that
the University developed when Scotland found herself isolated in
Europe through her dogged adherence to the Anti-Pope, Benedict
XIII. Political and ecclesiastical differences had already cut her off
from England; and when France renounced obedience to Benedict,
Scots students were also debarred from Paris University, their most
popular place of resort. In an effort to keep these wandering scholars
at home, Bishop Wardlaw therefore erected a university in his episco-
pal city of St. Andrews. Henry Ogilvie, who brought back the papal
bulls of foundation, was welcomed by the pealing of Church bells,
and the occasion was celebrated with solemn thanksgiving to God
and much festivity.

When the acclamation had died down, however, it was soon seen
that an anti-papal university had no future. The aged Pontiff at
Peniscola could not make the rewards of knowledge attractive
through grants of rich livings and privileges and preferences. Self-
interest therefore made the young University lead the nation in trans-
ferring allegiance from the setting to the rising sun; and within six
years Martin V, the Roman Pope, was asked to confirm the foundation of his rival, Peter de Luna, "calling himself Benedict XIII in
his obedience." St. Andrews then took its place in the international
system of papal universities of Latin Christendom.

In theory it was founded for the study of Theology, Canon and
Civil Law, Arts and Medicine and all other lawful Faculties, with
the power of granting degrees and conferring the master's licence of

teaching anywhere. Its constitution was modelled on Paris and the
lesser French universities, and at a later date the influence of Cologne
was felt both at St. Andrews and Glasgow. These were known as
"Master" universities in contrast with the "Student" universities of
Italy, especially the great law school of Bologna. This meant that in
northern Europe the masters, representing a brotherhood of teachers,
formed the pivot of academic life, whereas south of the Alps the pre-
ponderating influence was that of the rather tyrannical student body.
It is significant that although at first scholars and masters at St.
Andrews had alike a voice in the election of the Rector, the undergraduates were soon excluded from participation. This, however, was
no disadvantage in view of the need for strict discipline and good
teaching.

The St. Andrews curriculum was based on that of Paris, while
Glasgow adopted features from both St. Andrews and Paris with
modifications from Cologne. Lack of evidence prevents us from
forming a precise picture of the examination system, but certain
salient features do stand out. The first step in the undergraduate's
path towards the master's degree was determination, which took
place some eighteen months after his incorporation as a matriculated
student, or suppost. Scholars had to hear certain prescribed books on
Logic and Philosophy under teaching masters known as regents,
whose duty it was to present pupils for determination at the beginning of October. Both teachers and candidates then testified that all
the requisite conditions had been fulfilled. We read that in 1445
the regents at St. Andrews took oath in face of the Faculty of Arts,
and that in 1454 the Dean ordered the scholars to come to his room
to fulfil this formality, while in 1455 two candidates were excused
from presenting themselves because they had gone home to see about
their expenses and other necessary business.

The test itself took the form of an oral dissertation in which the
candidate had to maintain a thesis in public debate, summing up in
his determination. No description has come down to us, and the system in general underwent developments during the course of the
century. It is clear, however, that it was divided after the fashion of
Paris into two parts, known as Responsions and Determination, and
that it was a protracted series of debates by way of question, argu-

ment and conclusion, the whole process culminating in the attainment of the baccalaureate in the following Lent. Originally the act of determination took place in winter, usually before Christmas and not later than St. Valentine's Day; and this was followed by Lenten debates, leading up to baccalaureation. During the course of the century, however, both stages came to be concentrated in the season of Lent.

This may have marked an approximation to the Glasgow system, based upon the practice of Cologne. The Glasgow statutes required scholars to be presented in a General Congregation of the Faculty of Arts on the first lawful day after All Saints, and if found fully qualified they were subjected to an examination by four masters as a preliminary to determination. They were obliged upon oath to dispute three times a week in gown and furred hood during Lent upon a thesis which had been duly advertised on a schedule nailed to the school door, and which was threshed out in debate with an opponent who had been licensed beforehand to take up the challenge. After the examination the Dean and examiners together drew up a pass list and named a day for determination, when the successful candidates were pronounced bachelors.

The ceremony of determination was a protracted affair, because not more than four rich scholars at St. Andrews and five at Glasgow might determine on the same day, although in both cases they might associate two poor students with them. Where numbers were small and all academic functions were social occasions it was doubtless found profitable to spin out festivities. The outlay, indeed, tended to become excessive, so that the Faculty had to regulate the expenditure, the number of guests and the customary distribution of gloves among the Masters. It also fixed the fees, but commonly granted remission to poor students upon their promise to pay when they came to a fairer fortune.

Much the same process was repeated at the next stage, when the bachelor was submitted for his licence. When he was presented at the beginning of Lent he had to produce a certificate to the effect that he had attained the age of twenty years and had satisfied all the necessary conditions. This included not only four years of study and the hearing of the prescribed books, but also the making of three responsions. Dispensations, however, were lavishly granted. Thus at St. Andrews in 1448 two scholars who had not completed four years of study were given dispensation for the remainder of the fourth year, while in 1455 two months' extension was allowed to certain bachelors who had not fulfilled all the *formalia*. From this time onward dispensations from the third responsion became common, usually on the payment of five shillings on the part of rich students, with remission of the fine to the poor.

When the candidates had been duly presented and accepted by the Dean with the customary taking of oaths, four examiners were appointed to submit them to a two-fold test, of which the separate parts were known as *temptamen* and *examen* (trial and examination). At St. Andrews, bachelors were presented for trial in Lent, and until 1485 proceedings were privately conducted, but, apparently to obviate abuses, it was enacted in that year that the *temptamen* should be held openly in presence of all the candidates. It was at this stage that the students sat before their examiners on the famous black stone, although when the custom originated the records do not tell.

Lists were then drawn up with a rough attempt at grading the candidates; but although the examiners were required upon oath to accept the worthy and reject the unworthy, this delicate business was rendered still more difficult by the fact that social qualifications were taken into account. Though in theory poverty was honourable when it walked in a scholar's gown, and to give alms to a poor scholar was reckoned a work of piety, yet in practice wealth and rank were keys that opened many doors in the republic of letters. It would be interesting, therefore, to discover on what principle the examiners classified the candidates who had been tried in their *temptamen*. All that we know is that they were graded in batches for their *examen in cameris*. No account of this examination has come down to us, but it appears to have consisted of disputations lasting for three weeks, except in cases of dispensation. On 12 May 1452, the bachelors *in cameris* had their term shortened by eight days; three years later five bachelors were exempted from six days *in cameris;* and in 1464 the King petitioned the Dean to grant a similar dispensation on the morrow after the Feast of Corpus Christi.

Sometimes the students themselves protested against the grading of the examiners. In 1459 three St. Andrews bachelors, "duly tried and placed, refused to enter *in cameris,*" and made a formal, legal protest against the alleged "unjust calling and placing." On second thoughts, however, one of them wrote begging to be pardoned, and the Faculty of Arts asked him to come in person and reinstated him after receiving his submission. Another of the recalcitrants, John of Ireland, cast the dust of St. Andrews off his feet and betook himself to Paris to make his name illustrious.

A pass list of the bachelors was drawn up by the examiners and presented to the Chancellor. It was then sealed by him and handed over to be kept intact until the day of licence, when it was the beadle's duty to read out the names in a clear voice.

At Glasgow, which followed the custom of Cologne, the four examiners "tried" the bachelors in groups of six or eight at a time and presented the passmen to the Chancellor or Vice-Chancellor, who commanded the Dean and examiners to grade them strictly according to merit. As at St. Andrews, the names were then listed in a sealed schedule and not made public until the day of licence. Great importance was laid upon the order of placing, because on it depended future rank and precedence in the academic world. An oath of obedience was imposed upon the licentiands by the beadle, and finally the licence itself was granted by the Chancellor or Vice-Chancellor to the successful candidates on bended knees. The licence carried the right of reading and disputing in the Faculty of Arts and of exercising all the prerogatives of a licentiate therein and anywhere in the world.

To complete his Arts career it still remained, however, for the licentiate to ascend the master's chair and so to be technically incorporated into membership of the Faculty of Arts. Both at St. Andrews and at Glasgow it was enacted for the honour of the Faculty that only two rich licentiates might be created masters on the same day, but two of the poor might be associated with each of them. The master's act (as the technical term ran) could be performed only on certain days—Thursday, Friday and Monday, after eight o'clock in the morning. Before the *biretta* was placed upon their heads the magistrands promised on oath to show due "reverence and honour" to the Dean and Faculty and to promote peace and concord within the

University. The actual ceremony included the giving of a cap of specified value and other customary thank-offerings to the examiners, and the providing of a feast to a certain number of masters and other guests, all of whom were entitled to a pair of gloves of good quality.

When these expensive formalities had been fulfilled and the fees paid or remitted, the newly created master was received into the Faculty of Arts under the obligation of reading lectures for two years. This duty of *lectura* must have mounted to little more than the dictation of texts to supply the want of the prescribed books. From the beginning it was distasteful work, and with the passing of time it became more and more neglected. It is doubtful if *lectura* was ever systematically imposed at Glasgow, and at St. Andrews even the imposition of a graded scale of fines completely failed to have the desired effect. In 1457 Patrick Graham, afterwards Archbishop and Chancellor of the University, presided as Dean over a meeting in which he himself was reported as a defaulter. Some licentiates took the masterate and went down; others escaped the difficulty by declining to ascend the master's chair.

Those who did remain in the University as lecturers might at the same time be themselves students in the higher Faculties or they might become Regents, that is, professional teachers endowed with tutorial functions and powers of discipline. Both regent and non-regent masters had a voice in the General Congregations of the University and both had to do duty as examiners. Of the four masters appointed to examine bachelors for their licence, two were regents and two non-regents.

Aspirants for a regency petitioned the Faculty of Arts and took oath in presence of the Dean to expound the text of Aristotle faithfully, to rule their scholars without fear or favour, not to lure scholars away from another master, not to receive debt-laden or insubordinate scholars until they had made satisfaction to their former masters; not to become too familiar with their scholars in games or at table and not to take them out at nights to haunts of ill repute. These conditions reflect upon some of the most essential aspects of academic life—teaching, discipline and recreation.

On the educational side, the Arts curriculum at all medieval universities was based upon the text of Aristotle and commentaries thereon, comprising books on grammar, logic and philosophy. Some of these, known as Ordinary books, were considered indispensable, while others—the Extraordinary books—were optional and additional. At the beginning of a new session regents chose their books in full Faculty. Unfortunately the St. Andrews minutes never condescend to mention the titles of the books chosen, although in 1425 they stated that the Faculty appointed Mr. John Wricht to read Ethics on Feast Days; and in 1439 the regulations stipulated that the regents should teach their scholars with all zeal and diligence, speaking slowly and deliberately.

About this time St. Andrews University was rent by an academic controversy that was raging throughout Europe. In 1417 it was decided by a majority vote that "the doctrine of Albert should not be read, but Buridan," and again, in 1438, that "the doctrine of Albert should not be read in Logic nor the *Summulae* of Peter Hispanus, but Buridan." Certain influential voices, however, made a vigorous protest, and a month later it was unanimously agreed that "the doctrine of Albert or any others not containing errors in logic and philosophy might be taught at the discretion of the masters." Albert (1193–1280), the author of the disputed doctrine, was a great Dominican teacher, who based his work on Aristotle, tinged with Christian thought. The *Summulae* of Peter Hispanus (afterwards Pope John XXI, 1276–7) were standard text books of Logic which influenced John Buridan, a celebrated French schoolman of the fourteenth century. Buridan's text book on Physics had been popularised at St. Andrews through the lectures of Laurence of Lindores, one of the founders of the University. Although the philosophic and academic issues may now seem to us to be arid and futile, yet the controversy throws an interesting gleam of light upon the dark subject of the fifteenth century curriculum.

Of the Extraordinary books we know still less than of the others. The extent to which they were read must have depended largely upon the numbers of young masters available for *lectura* and on the development of the tutorial system of teaching with the foundation of St. Salvator's College in 1450. Certain lectures, considered fundamental, were delivered in the public school, and these were augmented by the teaching of college tutors and regent masters.

At Glasgow, where numbers were small, Master Duncan Bunch, the first Principal, bequeathed to the University certain books on Philosophy, Logic and Metaphysics, on which he had probably himself lectured. These consisted of treatises on Aristotle, Porphyry and other Aristotelians; and, finally, "one Bible, on parchment, complete in one small volume, beautifully written." At St. Andrews, St. Salvator's College at an early date possessed a fine collection of "books for the choir," and the beginnings of a University library were made in 1456 when "a wooden reading-desk" was ordered to be constructed for keeping the books. Master David Cant, Chancellor of St. Andrews and Dean of the Chapel Royal, presented a "notable book" on the Magna Moralia, and Master John Dunnyn, Vicar of Perth, gave a text of Aristotle on Logic and books on Ethic.

The fifteenth century conception of education was, however, wider than the mere acquisition of learning. It comprised the inculcation of morals as well as of knowledge. The schedules of the *formalia* of candidates submitted for examination contained certificates not only of books read but also a testimonial of character. Any student convicted of insubordination or of debt was disqualified; and we have seen that the functions of a regent included the oversight of morals.

At St. Andrews a root cause of turbulence was the lack of endowment and the consequent competition between masters to procure fee-paying students. From the earliest times masters were forbidden by statute to tout for scholars. In 1450 a master formally protested that a certain student should not be allowed to determine because he had transferred to another house. On craving pardon, however, and pleading ignorance, the defaulter was accepted, although it was decided that the statute should be rigorously enforced in future in order to strike terror into others.

There is, indeed, ample evidence that the existence of rival pedagogies tended to a loosening of discipline. Thus we find frequent complaints about the growing licentiousness of scholars. In 1457, for example, it was necessary to forbid students to carry arms under pain of confiscation; and in 1460 the authorities were gravely concerned about the vagabondage of scholars in the public streets by day and by night, and their addiction to idleness, games and shows. The fact that not only students themselves, but also their servants and dependants, enjoyed special privileges and immunities, aggravated the tendency towards riot and excess, and led to trouble with the university authorities as well as to clashes between town and gown. In 1443 the friction between the University and the burgh had reached such a point that the magistrates sent a deputation to Cologne to enquire into the conditions which prevailed there. In the following year both sides brought their case for arbitration before the Bishop-Chancellor, who composed the quarrel by a "contract of peace." Insubordination, however, was still rampant; and it was in an effort to cut at the root of the evil that Bishop Kennedy in 1450 introduced the College system of tutorial teaching under salaried masters endowed with powers of discipline.

In Glasgow, where the University grew up more immediately under the control of the Bishop-Chancellor, there was never more than one pedagogy or college. Public lectures were delivered in a schoolroom in the Dominican monastery; and the students resided with the masters in a single house, where the rich scholars boarded at a common table with the regents, and the poor rented separate rooms. Nevertheless even the students of Glasgow were exhorted to abstain from the sins of the flesh, such as greed, luxury, carousing, gaming and immoral night life.

Not unnaturally, decency of dress was enjoined along with gravity of manners. University students, as clerks, were bound to wear ecclesiastical garb, except by special exemption. Thus in 1448 a certain student of St. Andrews was dispensed to wear secular clothes on payment of twenty shillings and on condition that he would never in future attend any academic function unless in suitable clerical dress.

On the other hand games and recreation did hold an important place, both officially and unofficially, in university life. Academic feasts were the chief source of official social intercourse; and foremost amongst these at St. Andrews ranked the annual Feast of the Faculty of Arts on St. John the Baptist's Day, celebrated on 6 May to do honour to the Mother Faculty and to promote the spirit of unity and good fellowship. Stewards (known as provisors) were appointed to make the necessary arrangements, and expenses were met partly by a levy upon the students and partly from the money derived from fines and dispensations. Thus, the bachelors being examined *in cameris* in 1453 had remission of eight days on payment of twenty shillings for the expenses of the Feast.

No description of an actual celebration at St. Andrews has survived, but Glasgow has preserved an account of the arrangements made there for celebrating the Feast of the Translation of St. Nicholas on 9 May 1462. At eight in the morning the whole academic body was to assemble at the chapel of St. Thomas the Martyr, after which each was gravely and solemnly to receive flowers and branches, procured beforehand by the stewards from the common funds, and they were then to proceed in orderly array on horseback to the market cross, returning to the College for dinner. This was to be a meal of gaiety and good will, when quarrels were to be mediated and the Prince of Peace to be honoured. After dinner the company should proceed to a suitable place of recreation where masters or students with the approval of the regents were to present some interlude or any other such pastime for the amusement of the populace and the honour of the Faculty. In such a stern and rude and violent age it was a natural impulse to make merry when occasion offered and to drown cares in the flowing bowl.

Apart from these recognised activities the scholars also indulged their own unofficial amusements, which the University might discountenance but could not suppress. When the freshman, or bejaunt, first came up he was initiated into undergraduate life by a ceremony which involved both feasting and buffoonery. No description has come down to us of a "Jocund Advent" to a Scottish University, but at Paris in 1438 Andrew de Durisdar (later Bishop of Glasgow) was mulcted in two francs *pro jocunda adventu,* and in 1445 another Scot sued the University for damages because he had been called a bejaunt in presence of the Rector. It has been suggested that the modern St. Andrews custom for a bejaunt to give raisins to his senior may be a relic of these old rites of initiation, just as the procession of Kate Kennedy's Day may be a survival from the pageantry of medieval folk drama.

As early as 1414 St. Andrews enacted that on the Feast of the Translation of St. Nicholas (9 May) the grammar scholars should not go with the Boy Bishop begging money from house to house on the way from the castle to the monastery and back. Similarly a statute of

1432 declared that on the Feast of the Kings at Epiphany masters and scholars going to Church and returning with the King of the Bean should wear their own clothes, with the sole exception that the King of the Bean might don a costume suitable to his part. Masters and scholars were also forbidden to bring in May as guisers wearing clothing or *insignia* or riding on horses borrowed from knights or lords, feigning to be kings, nobles or emperors.

In addition, the University frowned with disfavour upon football and especially on the popular Lenten pastime of cock-fighting, which distracted the attention of students duirng the examination period and lured their minds from the pursuit of wisdom. It was therefore enacted in 1414 that whereas they had formerly spent two or three weeks during Lent in procuring birds for cock fights, that sport was in future to be limited to two or three days before Easter. The censors of morals might be excused if they made allowance for the natural exuberance of youth during these old traditional festivals, which were admittedly a time of special licence; but they had to exercise constant vigilance in supervising the ordinary recreation of the students.

From the earliest times the scholars at St. Andrews were required when going to the fields for recreation to proceed in marching order under some master or tutor who should compel them to talk in Latin. In 1432 it was added that they should wear their proper academic dress and hear Mass on their return to town, setting aside all superfluities and vanities.

Religious ordinances had thus their essential place, as was to be expected, in the curriculum of the medieval university. According to the bull of foundation, St. Andrews University was expressly erected both for the study of the liberal arts and also for the strengthening of the true religion against heresy and schism; and Laurence of Lindores, its dominating personality, was also Inquisitor of Heretical Pravity. Again, St. Salvator's College was founded and endowed to fulfil the two-fold function of a college within the University for the teaching of Theology and Arts and of a collegiate church for the daily observance of religious worship; and the charter of erection provided for the celebration of an annual Mass to the memory of the founder. Similarly, Lord Hamilton, a benefactor of Glasgow University, stipulated in 1460 that twice a day at the close of the noontide and evening meals the regents and students should rise and pray for the souls of himself, his wife and family, and should sing the *Ave Maria* every Saturday after vespers.

Almost all the teachers and many of the students were beneficed clergy. Canon Law expressly sanctioned non-residence in the interests of education so that church livings could legitimately be diverted to serve the purpose of modern bursaries. Thus Patrick Graham, who succeeded his uncle as Bishop-Chancellor of the University, was a canon of Aberdeen and Moray during his undergraduate days at St. Andrews. His income from these two rich benefices no doubt stood him in good stead when he proceeded thereafter to pursue the higher studies at Paris.

Like many another ambitious Scot he went abroad with an eye to his own advancement. It was, for example, a well-known fact that the doctors and masters of Paris University enjoyed certain prerogatives in the obtaining of benefices. The University regularly sent to the Pope a schedule containing names of graduates recommended for provision. In 1413 Mr. John Crannach (afterwards Bishop successively of Caithness and Brechin) paid £1 because he was elected envoy to carry this roll to the papal court, but if he did not go the money was to be refunded to him.

As for the relative attractions of other universities, it was expressly stated in 1461 that "students at Rome have more opportunity of obtaining a benefice than students at Bologna," and Thomas Muirhead, nephew of the Bishop of Glasgow, was painfully conscious that as a student at Bologna he suffered a disability in the race for preferment. Obviously, ambitious men selected their university for other considerations than mere scholarship.

At the beginning of our period, Paris and Cologne were the schools most frequented by the Scots, and although Paris was debarred to them for a generation, it regained its popularity after the expulsion of the English from France in 1450. The founders of Aberdeen University, for example, had been students and teachers there. Bishop Elphinstone himself was a Bachelor of Decreets of Paris, while Hector Boece, the first Principal, and William Hay, his colleague, had both studied and taught in that "nobil universite" of their affectionate remembrance. Moreover, these men had felt the influence of the printing press when in France and came home to be patrons of that revolutionary art in Scotland. Further, about 1493 a certain Mr. James Liddell of Aberdeen diocese, a regent at Paris, published a students' text book which is noteworthy as the first work printed by a Scotsman, although published abroad.

The experiences of this Mr. James Liddell in many ways illustrate the life of the Scottish student at Paris. In 1485 he formally petitioned for a "school" and awaited a vacancy to teach as a regent master. In 1484 he was proctor of the German Nation—that is, the master elected by the Nation as its official representative on the Faculty of Arts, whose duty it was to keep the minutes of proceedings affecting the Nation. As the German Nation comprised such diverse elements as Poles, Finns, Bohemians and Swiss, it is clear that Mr. James Liddell and his fellow-countrymen belonged to a very heterogeneous company.

For the rest, the official records of the continental universities are as tantalisingly defective as our own with regard to the details of student life. The amount of a scholar's *bursa* (or weekly board) is noted in cases where matriculation or graduation rolls have survived, as at Paris and Cologne. Fees were reckoned on this basis, but it is uncertain how things worked out in practice. It is clear, however, that charges were heavy, and that it needed a full purse if a man aspired to hold academic offices, or at least to keep the state demanded of him. As a result there was a constant temptation for even wealthy students to feign poverty.

Thus in 1445 John Kennedy, on the plea that he was more or less a pauper, had his *bursa* at Paris assessed at fourpence a week. The Nation learned, however, that he was in truth of noble race, a bishop's nephew, and provost of "a certain venerable Church" (Maybole); and that, moreover, he had brought with him "a good hundred crowns and had afterwards received another fifty crowns and twenty nobles." Even then, however, Kennedy was recalcitrant, and had to be compelled to pay at a higher rate under threat of deprivation and expulsion. How the instalments of his income were transmitted the record does not state. No doubt the bankers acted as convenient middlemen; and Paris, at least, had recognised officials, known as messengers, who were elected by the students to transact their financial business. When money failed, valuables might be given in pledge. Thus, in 1417 a breviary according to the Scottish use, handsomely ornamented with gilded silver work and oriental pearls, was pawned for twelve crowns.

Little as we know about the cost of living, we may be sure of one thing: the expense was no deterrent to the impecunious lad of parts or to the ambitious climber. Thus John of Ireland, who quarrelled with his examiners at St. Andrews in 1459, was a *pauper* or poor student, yet he spent "neire the tyme of thretty zere" and filled many important posts at Paris University before he returned home to win a place of distinction in the great world of letters and diplomacy.

In Cologne the majority of Scottish students were sworn *pauperes* to whom their matriculation fees were accordingly remitted. It is more surprising to find that remission was also granted in favour of men of exalted birth or influential connections. Thus it is noted in 1443 that James Douglas, "illustrious son of the Earl of Douglas, paid nothing"—at a time, moreover, when the proud and arrogant Black Douglas bestrode Scotland like a devastating Colossus.

Doubtless, however, those who could afford to do so were constrained to provide in other ways for the maintenance of the University. Even the poor students who were exempted from the payment of fees were expected to contribute towards the salary of the beadles and other officials. Of one, John Zhoman, we read that he paid nothing, "but will pray for the good of the University." Peter Davidson, again, was an "utterly poor" student, yet he maintained himself for many years at Cologne before he found his way to Copenhagen in 1478, while his two contemporaries who afterwards migrated to Tubingen and Ingolstadt were also classed as *pauperes*.

Poverty certainly did not clip the wings of men who were fired with the love of travel and adventure or burned with a scholar's zeal for letters. Such as these had the pioneer spirit that animated all Scots who fared overseas in the fifteenth century in search of profit and adventure. The student abroad, were he secular or regular, rich or poor, old or young, pedant or careerist, brushed shoulders with his fellows in a cosmopolitan world. Some lived and died on foreign shores, some came home to a life of obscurity, and some added lustre to the name of Scotland in the medieval commonwealth of letters.

Modern minds may tend to despise them as mere schoolmen, beating the idle air and wasting their energies upon hair splittings and useless dialectic subtleties; but in truth they belonged to a period of transition when a new age was being born out of the ashes of the old. Hector Boece, for example, was part schoolman and part humanist, rooted in scholasticism as to his matter but bearing the foliage of the Renaissance in his Latin prose style. We may take him, therefore, as typical of the continuity between medieval and modern University life.

Since then, much has changed. At times St. Andrews and Glasgow had a stern struggle for mere existence, and if their founders were to return today they would rub their eyes at first in sheer bewilderment; but when they had grown accustomed to the light they would realise that the mighty tree of modern knowledge, with its far-spreading branches, had grown from the tender sapling which they planted, and that the students who now eat of the fruits of the tree are come of the same stock as their fifteenth century predecessors.

II

Student Movements
in
Western Europe

This essay analyzes student involvement in national issues. It shows how German students, many of them from middle-class rather than upper-class backgrounds, gave the revolutionary cause support and even a flag of national unity. Note how they demanded a voice in the governing of universities, and how in Vienna they started a revolution that the army had to quell.

4

Students on the Barricades:
Germany and Austria, 1848

Priscilla Robertson

German students in the nineteenth century, like Americans in the twentieth, had periods when serious study was fashionable, other periods when the great thing was collegiate life, rare ones of military enthusiasm, less rare times of romantic artiness, and occasional violent periods of social concern. They went through moods of academic exclusiveness and moods of devotion to the rights of man. Sometimes their reforming zeal was turned toward their own institutions, and sometimes they were out to change the wide world. Sometimes these moods seem to have succeeded each other almost at random, but it is possible to trace a pattern leading up to their highest moment of political involvement, in 1848. It turned out to be the last such moment before 1918, but it was one in which all their passion for liberty and for solidarity with the underprivileged reached a tremendous climax.

I

Perhaps this process began when Fichte addressed his class at the University of Berlin on February 19, 1813: "This course will be suspended until the close of the campaign, when we will resume it

From Priscilla Robertson, "Students on the Barricades: Germany and Austria, 1848," *Political Science Quarterly,* 84 (June 1969), 367–378. Reprinted by permission of *Political Science Quarterly.*

in a free fatherland or reconquer our liberty by death." We are told that the young men streamed out of the classroom to join the forces fighting to get Napoleon out of German territory; many of them fought and fell in the triumphant battle of Leipzig the following October.

When the survivors came home to their free fatherland, they were in a high state of exhilaration, but, as often happens after wars, the peace failed to live up to their dreams. They found themselves still subjects of thirty separate sovereigns; liberal institutions, though promised, were slow to materialize.

In this mood the *Burschenschaft* was founded. This was to be a widespread student association seeking the elusive ideal of a unified German state with representative institutions. The plan originated at Jena University, in a territory where the Grand Duke allowed free discussion, and by 1816 it had spread to sixteen campuses. The *Burschenschaft* groups emphatically rejected the snobbery of the old student fraternities and proclaimed that they were in favor of democratic integration of all social classes, and they hoped their practice would be a model for all German citizens. They proposed to further this aim by a strict code of personal morality. All foreign observers commented on their sexual continence, and the by-laws of some of their groups called chastity "a national and truly German virtue." They also hoped to turn the duel from an aristocratic rite to a purifying "human" ordeal. A modern sociologist would probably note that these students were, in actual fact, mainly middle class, seeking equality with their social betters under the rubric of equality for all men. (In this they were copying French Revolutionary models.) At this time they did not yet identify with the workers. But they did feel a clear call to discuss public affairs, and explained that in this way they could partly compensate for the lack of proper legislative chambers in their governments.

On October 17, 1817, they put on a memorable festival at the Wartburg, a mountain famed for Luther's stay there, so that it was an appropriate place to commemorate the Reformation as well as the Battle of Leipzig. Four hundred students from a dozen institutions enjoyed a torchlight parade and a huge bonfire in which they burned symbols both of foreign domination and domestic repression—

a corporal's cane, a wig, a copy of the *Code Napoléon*. They were forging a new brand of liberalism, different from French revolutionary and old German feudal notions.

In 1819 a mediocre poet named Kotzebue, who wrote conservative plays and was thought to be an agent of the Czar, was murdered by an unusually excitable student. Though the assassin is commonly called mad in the textbooks, his fellow students saw him in an aura of exalted idealism, as an exemplar of direct action and of a policy of violence against unheeding government.

To the reactionaries waiting in the wings, this act was all that was needed to justify bringing out the apparatus of repression. Metternich, who had more or less arranged Europe and particularly the German states to suit himself, clamped down previously unheard-of political controls on all universities in the German-speaking world. (These measures were embodied in the Carlsbad decrees.) Each institution was to have a special official in residence, to sit in on lectures and watch the spirit in which classes were taught, without of course interfering in scholarship or in the methods of instruction. But all teachers with the wrong spirit, especially those who had been close to the *Burschenschaft,* were removed and blacklisted. The General *Burschenschaft* itself was suppressed as an inter-university association, and, although separate clubs continued to carry the name, they were forbidden to communicate with similar groups at other institutions.

It is generally agreed that a mood of romantic conservatism followed. This was the period when Stendhal commented that civilization was arrested in Germany, by the universities first of all, where the students drank and dueled instead of studying; and he thought this practice was encouraged by the various governments to build up German sentiment. The judgment of a contemporary Englishman, William Howitt, is more credible as to the motive, that when the students tried to throw off their club life and adopt enlightened ideals, they were violently forced back and reduced to merely drinking toasts to freedom.

At this time the old fraternities, now called *corps,* were reinstituted for the rich and nobly-born students, while the *Burschenschaft* societies served the same needs for the middle-class boys who were sons

of Lutheran ministers, small tradesmen, and well-to-do peasant pro-
prietors. Naturally some students remained unaffiliated, a group
which was (somewhat later in the century) characterized as consisting of "Poles, Jews, often disreputable types, the type that drifts into
socialism." In other words, not the sort the *Burschenschaft* members
wished to be equal to. Still, the *Burschenschaft* cherished the feeling that it was still devoted to some ideals, and that the corps represented "a type of base life among students, animated by no sense
of patriotism." But even the *Burschenschaften* were conservative at
this time.

The first new liberal group, called Germania, founded at Erlangen
in 1827, soon put out feelers to other universities in spite of the ban.
This liberalism of the thirties, never adopted by a majority, was a
romantic international cosmopolitan liberalism; this was the time
when a high-minded student would wish to fight for Poland. It was
also a time of another big festival, at Hambach, in 1832, where
students demanded a German republic even if they had to get it by
violence.

Gradually this mood, too, wore off, and a more intense, popular,
and nationalistic movement for "Progress" began among the unin-
corporated students at Göttingen. This was taken up by a part of
the *Burschenschaft* which now split into a liberal and a conservative
wing. Once more the call went out to break down the barriers between German citizens. Poland did not count. A special faction called
the *Burgkeller,* at Jena, urged communication among students of different universities and with different classes of citizens.

About this time the Duke of Wellington remarked that it was
"curious that all the mischief of Germany seems to have its rise in
the universities, while in [England] we look to [them] and to the
state of feeling there as one of our main sources of security." The
good duke was inclined to blame the mischief on the neglect of
religion, the dependence of German professors on their lecture fees,
and the absence of residential colleges. We, looking back, might
feel the political condition of Germany was at least equally responsible, together with the different social class from which German
students came.

Academic freedom received lip service in increasing measure, but often seemed hollow when incidents which violated it abounded. For instance, when the Grimm brothers, having been dismissed from Hanover for political reasons, were called to Berlin, the Berlin students organized a torchlight procession on one of their birthdays. The Grimms happened to have as a guest Hoffmann von Fallersleben, author of "Deutschland über Alles," and the students cheered him loudly. A number of students were expelled for this *faux pas*—the government of Prussia did not take kindly to this demonstration in favor of a united Germany—and they were sickened to hear that the Grimms had apologized to the *government.*

The situation was obviously working up to a climax, which came in March 1848, when, following an outbreak at Paris, there were revolutions in nearly every German state. The *Burschenschaft* colors of black, red, and gold became the colors of German unity everywhere, and the newly elected parliament of the German people at Frankfort contained 150 members of the old *Burschenschaft*. So the young students rushed into the fray feeling equal to any opportunity that the crisis should open up. In fact, they created "March demands" themselves.

II

Their first clashes were with the police; in some university towns such as Göttingen, the bitterness of these led to a cry that the students be armed. Since this was part of a general liberal demand, continent-wide, for the arming of citizens and the creation of national or civic guards, the students' wish was nearly always gratified. Carl Schurz gives the impression that at Bonn, where he was a student, the affair amounted to little more than a chance to joke, drink, and clank their swords along the pavement, and if possible face down their adult co-guardsmen.

They also seized the chance to try to update their own universities; the first measure that came to mind was to arrange a new "Wartburg" festival. The call went out originally from the conservative wing of the *Burschenschaft* at Jena, but after it had been picked up by the liberal *Burgkeller* it took a more serious tone. This time there were to be no fine speeches, no oaths, no freedom songs, no tears, no bonfires, only sober parliamentary discussion of specific demands. The agenda had three planks: the universities should no longer be tied to their separate states but should be under a national authority; unconditional freedom of learning and teaching; and the elimination of the special legal code for students which "separates the people from its educated youth." This code allowed for dueling, but other provisions had often been used against students because of their political opinions. The conference was to meet at Eisenach, in June 1848.

The Jena students had expected to dominate the conference, but had not reckoned with the railroads which had so changed the face of Germany since 1817 that large numbers of Austrians and students from the east were able to get there. The heroes of the occasion were actually fresh from barricades, in Berlin—or Vienna. The conference consisted of about 1,200 delegates from all but three German universities, and also from Vienna.

The first item for debate was almost equally a matter of politics and of education. Like nearly all intellectuals at the time, the students were eager for the various small states to be united into a single fatherland; even if this political consummation did not come about, they wanted a central educational authority which would allow them to be *German* students at *German* universities, instead of, for example, Saxon students at a Bavarian university. Since, paralleling their own conference, a big democratically elected Parliament of the German People was sitting at Frankfort to consider precisely the formation of a liberal and democratic Germany, they had reasonable ground to hope they were not talking in a vacuum.

Before 1806 the German universities had enjoyed considerable autonomy; eighteenth-century professors could call whom they would to their chairs, and then they might freely teach. Under this system, Kant's ideal of the university as a place where even the state could be criticized was possible. Since the Napoleonic wars, however, the schools had been under strict political control. In 1848 there were few to advocate the restoration of the old self-limited freedoms of

universities, since most were so in love with the ideal of a new democratic and powerful state that they did not imagine it could possibly
threaten academic freedom. On the other hand, they saw in separate
corporations and separate autonomies a violation of the principle of
a society that was supposed to consist of equals. They did not realize
that precisely these chartered institutions are often guardians of liberty against the tyranny of equality. The students voted for national
control, for free movement to any school of a student's choice, and for
the government to pay some larger share of the bill than formerly—
particularly, that it should pay the fees of the lowest grade of faculty
members, the *Privatdozenten,* hitherto living from the attendance
fees at their lectures.

By "freedom of learning" the students meant free admissions policies and more representation for themselves in the governance of
universities. They wished to abolish totally the strict state-adminis-
tered examination of graduates of *gymnasien,* which controlled entrance to the higher schools and which they felt made university
entrance a kind of rat race. They pointed out that it could be used
to punish heretical thinking in candidates. While they were about it,
they also voted to abolish semester exams and the administration of
civil service examinations by the schools. They also wanted new
subjects such as political economy to be taught, and recommended
that the faculties have less rigid dividing lines. Lastly, they demanded
student representation in the choice of the rector and the governing
committees.

As regards the special legal code for students, its abolition was the
key point in the "Progress" movement at this Eisenach convention.
Its majority was significantly smaller than that for the nationalism
clause, but it did pass. Closest to the hearts of most students was the
right to duel, a special privilege allowed to no other civilians. (The
fencing master at Jena received a higher salary than the head professor.) But since they were committed to a society of equals, and
since the special jurisdiction had in fact often been used against students for their political opinions, they voted to ask the Frankfort
Parliament, which was drawing up a draft constitution for a German
empire, to include a clause abolishing the student exceptions. The

Frankfort constitution, in the end, came out for academic freedom in a bland way, but said nothing whatsoever about financing universities or about abolishing the special jurisdiction.

It is interesting to compare the student convention at Eisenach with one held for university faculty members at Jena in September of the same year. The professors, too, were concerned with the problem of democracy inside their institutions; especially the bright young scientists and the *Privatdozenten* wanted to break the stranglehold which the full professors and their academic senates had on all university decisions. Young men were often kept for years from promotion. In the spring of 1848 a hundred low-ranking faculty members at Berlin had petitioned for representation on their academic senate; the government, working together with high-ranking faculty who were paid by the state, issued a decree forbidding any Prussian university from sending official delegates to Jena. Still, eighteen other universities were represented.

Just as the students had scrutinized the question of university autonomy from national control, and in spite of the fact that it seemed far more doubtful than it had in June that the new big state would be liberal, the professors, like the students, voted against restoration of the ancient university autonomy. Only the Prussians (for some Prussian faculty members had attended as observers) cast doubt on this resolution, with a sharper look at the possibility that arbitrariness might be a function of any government, not only of the small officious tyrannies the men from the smaller states were thinking of. The faculty did *not* favor having the state pay the *Privatdozenten,* and they did not favor having students on the governing committees of the university, though they made an ambiguous plea for wider representation of lower-ranking professors. When the Jena Academic Senate issued the final report of the convention, they watered down the clauses that had been voted for representation of associate professors and *Privatdozenten* in electing the rector and committees. The academic senates, however much opposed to special privileges for students or corporations, kept a very tight grip on their own reins of power.

At the same time that students were trying to get some democracy into their own universities, their real heroes were those students who had fought on the barricades to get democracy into their governments.

Although less organized than many students into corps or *Burschenschaften,* Berlin university men were sharply divided into democratic and reactionary political groups. The democrats, the smaller fraction, had made a point of befriending the workers, and had made serious efforts to get gifted proletarians admitted to the university, so that they could become cultivated and well-rounded human beings. When the barricades went up on March 19, at least a hundred students were on them, although legend has exaggerated the number. To get support, these students went to fetch the workers out of the machine shops; the workers, after carefully collecting their weeks' wages, came back cheerfully with their young friends.

The Berlin workers were better organized and more radical than in many other German towns, but a few Berlin students went so far beyond them that in the long run they lost the workers' confidence. Probably the most radical of all the students in the 1848 revolutions was Gustav Adolf Schöffel. Perhaps he should be called a non-student, since he had been expelled from Heidelberg in February for distributing Communist literature to the Odenwald peasants. Arriving in Berlin with the intent to matriculate there, he was overtaken by the revolution and immediately set to organizing in the fashion suggested to him by history. He got out a paper in imitation of Marat's of 1792, entitled *Volksfreund* (compare *Ami du Peuple*) and dated it "Year One of Freedom." Next he tried to organize a march on the palace, hoping that sixty thousand demonstrators would appear for it, but when only 1,500 showed up he decided the workers were too indolent to respond to his program to destroy capital, to unite as brothers, and to "clear away the bayonets of the middle class citizens guard." Then, when he suffered six months' imprisonment without any notable expression of support from his fellow students, his disillusionment was complete. He went off to the last revolutionary battles in Baden, where he was killed the following year.

III

In Vienna the students were not so sophisticated nor so radical as the extreme Berliners, but they had a more sustained and successful period of power. They took over management of the whole city for months, and the organization they created was defeated only by an army, for regular troops were sent to besiege the city.

Vienna was the only town where the revolution was actually started by student action; elsewhere the students tagged on to a movement begun by others. A group of Viennese medical students conceived the idea of sending a petition to the sovereign after they heard of the overthrow of Louis Philippe in Paris. It was a delicate matter to pick exactly the right tone, since petitions were a rarity under the Hapsburgs; some expressions they considered too bold, some too grovelling, but at last they hit on a "manly" one that seemed just right, and told the Emperor that freedom is the strongest bond between a monarch and his people. Their ideology was liberal, not radical, and they asked for the standard liberal demands of the period, free press, free speech, a constitution, and, of course, academic freedom.

Realizing that the situation was explosive, the police, instead of going after the young men themselves, called upon the professors and ordered them to make the "criminal youth" come to terms. By this time enthusiasm in all the schools was too great to be curbed by anybody; as the students swarmed into the hall where the petition was to be signed, one remarked that this was the first time students had given orders to faculty. The professors, he added ironically, thought the world had come to an end and that they would now be expected to give high grades all around.

The petition was not answered, so it was decided to have a demonstration. According to the poet Grillparzer, the students were put at the head of the demonstration because they were the only citizens willing to pull hot chestnuts out of the fire.

When some troops fired on the mob, killing as their first victim an eighteen-year-old mathematician, the students cried out that they must have arms or they would tear down the armory to get them. The weakening government gave in, and ordered arms issued to anyone who could prove himself a *bona fide* student by answering in Latin.

Thus was formed the Academic Legion, in the words of their chaplain, "the finest youth that ever walked the earth."

As the government abdicated its functions, and eventually the imperial family fled, the administration of the city of Vienna fell into the hands of a committee largely consisting of members elected by various companies of the Legion. It is true that in May conservative Viennese were demanding that the whole university should be closed and the students sent home, but this only led the students to a new determination to defend themselves. The chaplain went out and brought ten thousand workers from outside the city walls to aid them, and when the National Guard went over to the students, all resistance ceased and for the rest of the summer the students had their own way.

In the great hall of the university, the Aula, they set up headquarters where students, exhausted by their patrol duties, could find food and drink and where they "extended fraternization to girls," as a shocked member of what would now be called the Old Left, a member of the previous puritanical generation, noted. The food, drink, and parties were paid for by sympathetic citizens, many of whom volunteered as foster parents for young men whose own parents had cut off their allowances.

Besides keeping order in the city by their patrols, the students offered all kinds of services to their worker friends—medical students setting up a program of medical care, legal students offering their help in labor arbitration and in other legal matters, other students delivering welfare services and taking up collections. The workers responded with touching devotion. A group of the poorest offered to contribute a *kreutzer* a day out of their wages to help maintain the Legion; later on they acted as body guards. "If one of our men falls, it is no matter, but for one of the fine young student gentlemen, to whom we owe our freedom, it would be a great pity."

The problem the young administrators could not solve was the economic crisis, and by fall there was a distinct falling off of the Legion as the more conservative students resigned. At the end of September the Legion was divided, undisciplined, and had turned into something of a mob. Nevertheless, when the army came against the city in October, it organized a stiff defense and fought bravely against hopeless odds.

IV

At Munich in 1848 things were different, partly because Bavaria was Catholic and reactionary and partly because of the role of the King's mistress, Lola Montez. A year earlier, a group of professors had been dismissed for opposing the system of government, and Lola is said to have interceded for some of them. But she was seen wearing a student cap from one of the corps (the corps, rather than the *Burschenschaft,* had been encouraged at Munich as part of the conservative tone); the young men caught in the cap-episode were expelled from their corps, Palatia. They immediately formed a new, anti-traditional corps, Alemannia. Lola bought uniforms for them and, it was whispered, got their relatives good jobs in the civil service. This was intolerable to the old established corps, who rioted and harassed the Alemannia students in and out of the classrooms. Finally the other corps told the rector they would rather be dissolved themselves than have Alemannia continue on campus. The situation got so bad that the King ordered the university closed, but many students lacked funds to get home, and the citizens who lived off student boarding and lodging fees were desperate. The order was at last rescinded, the King yielded, and Lola fled—and all this happened just in time for the Munich students to take part in the general excitements of March 1848.

They proved their basic conservatism, however, in their lack of sympathy for the workers who appealed for their help. The *Schusterbuben* of Munich wanted to place themselves under student protection in demanding better working conditions from their masters, and were stiffly refused.

V

The *Burschenschaften* disappeared in the fifties, and students lost their taste for rebellion. The student association created at Eisenach disappeared; one explanation was that such a large body failed to yield the satisfactions that small fraternal groups did. Academic freedom did prosper mightily to be sure, but at the same time state control became more subtle. Later on a Frenchman who visited German universities commented that from all the academic freedom of Germany came the most docile group of students he had ever seen, and that he never caught a skeptical smile on the face of any of them at any lecture.

For a general opening up of the freedom fought for in 1848, Germans had to wait until the twentieth century.

This essay is written by a man who had personal experience in leadership in the UNEF, a part of the French student movement, while a student at the Sorbonne. Note how student associations were at first mainly social, how change came with the influx of lower-middle-class children into the universities, how and why students opposed the Algerian war, and how the ideals of French students compare to those of Americans.

5

The French Student Movement

Jean-Pierre Worms

This chapter attempts to apply an historical perspective to the analysis of the French student movement since 1900. It concentrates on the history of the *Union Nationale des Étudiants de France* (UNEF). The UNEF is not the only channel for French students' political action. Indeed, it is constitutionally non-political, although this has come to mean that it is not affiliated with any political party rather than not concerned with political issues. Until recently, the UNEF was by far the most influential student organization in the French political sphere.

From 1900 to 1914: The Golden Era of Student Folklore

The rise of a national organization of French students expressing a sense of collective identity is a relatively new phenomenon in France. In 1877 the first local student organization (*Association d'Étudiants*) was founded—that is, the first organization in which "studenthood" was the only criterion for membership as opposed to the previous organizations, which recruited on the basis of religious or political affiliation. By 1900, such non-political and non-religious student associations existed in all French university towns. In 1907 these associations were federated in a single "National Union" of students

From Jean-Pierre Worms, "The French Student Movement," in Seymour Martin Lipset, ed., *Student Politics* (New York: Basic Books, Inc., 1967), pp. 267–279. © 1967 by Basic Books, Inc. Reprinted by permission.

which marks the birth of the *Union Nationale des Étudiants de France*. Until the end of World War I, however, the UNEF played no significant role on campus or in society.

The pre-World War I student population was a very small elite (29,000 in 1900). Students came almost exclusively from the upper bourgeoisie and prepared themselves for professional careers which were assured them. They enjoyed almost complete financial and future professional security. The time at the university was "the good life"—the prelude to an elite position in society. Their position rendered them completely indifferent to social or political issues. They went through university as through an initiation rite. Determined to "enjoy life," they had wild drinking and singing parties, outings on the town, and generally participated in the kind of expected and benevolently tolerated student folklore described as "sowing wild oats." The student associations presided over such recreational activities. In many ways they resembled the American fraternities: high membership fees, a system of recommendation by alumni, and strong school traditions. There was very little unity in the UNEF, no feeling of general solidarity, no nationally organized action, and a great deal of energy spent in traditional local school rivalry.

1914 to 1945: The Corporate Orientation

The thirty years that separated the beginning of World War I from the end of the second signaled important changes in French higher education: the highly elitist model disappeared with its small number of upper class students secure in their status, self-indulgent, and indifferent to the world. Increasing numbers of middle class students entered the university with greater economic and professional worries. With a new style of studenthood and with different ties to society, the student organization, the UNEF, assumed new functions.

The 1914–1918 war was, of course, the first gigantic shock to traumatize the "happy-go-lucky" student body. One figure tells the whole story: two out of three students were called up. Another effect of the devastation of war was the undermining of confidence and economic well-being of the upper and middle classes. As a result, postwar students lost their carefree attitude and were strongly motivated to terminate their studies as rapidly as possible and proceed with the business of making a living.

Moreover, the universities had begun to recruit students from a wider section of the population. By 1926, there were 58,000 students in France—twice the 1900 figure. The result of significant reform in the educational system was added to this general effect of technological change: all secondary education became free in 1930. Subsequently, many children of the *petite bourgeoisie* continued their schooling up to the *baccalauréat* (terminal examination of the secondary cycle) and demanded entry to the universities. The French student population had grown to 80,000 by 1939.

However, access to universities of social classes hitherto excluded was not the only factor to affect the economic security of the student population. With the 1930's came the depression and ensuing unemployment and economic hardship. Students became absorbed in solving their material problems; their local associations and the UNEF assumed an essentially new function of pooling efforts to solve them. Grants were to be obtained from the government, subsidized housing for the increased student population and various other needs had to be taken care of: health, restaurants, sports.

The UNEF undertook to secure these benefits but the methods used to do so were influenced by its past experience. The organization had been built as a federation of fraternal or friendship societies, not as a mass movement. There was little internal democracy in the selection of leaders and the determination of policies. The national level of leadership had little power and was most reticent to use its limited power for planning mass demonstrations which might have shaken the "nepotic" structure of the UNEF. There was no national "doctrine," no sense of responsibility for future student generations or for the university system as a whole, with the result that the UNEF handled problems with piecemeal action and generally at the local level.

A few demands were coordinated at a national level such as tuition fees, grants, and social aid, but they never erupted into mass demonstrations, student strikes, or the like. Instead, the most important work was done by the local association which also acted as a charitable, mutual aid organization. Students turned to their local association for financial loans, help with housing, etc. But their most important contribution was the soliciting of help from outside with great reliance on the alumni. Thus, a number of charitable organizations, private or semi-private, were created *for* the students, like the *Cité Universitaire* in Paris, university restaurants in the provinces, and sanatoria. The local associations which had often played an important role in the instigation of such endeavors rapidly lost control. And as these charities developed they were federated on a national level either through private foundations (e.g., the Sanatoria Foundation) or through semi-public "offices" or "services" such as the *Service de Médecine Préventive,* the *Office du Tourisme Universitaire,* the *Office du Sport Universitaire,* the *Bureau Universitaire des Statistiques* (which, among other services, advised on future careers), and, most important of all, the *Centre National des Oeuvres* which dealt with the building and administration of student housing and food services.

It is obvious that politics played only a minor role in these activities. Indeed, the UNEF adhered to the most restrictive interpretation of its "non-political" constitution. Each problem was seen as practical and limited, to be faced separately from all others—without political ramifications. To do otherwise, to elaborate a global set of demands or strategy would have called for a different type of organization and a sense of some collective identity on the part of the students, a different conception of "studenthood."

The lack of militant action by the UNEF, its uninvolvement in political issues, and its inherent respect for the established political order can probably be explained in part by its structure and history and, in part, by the urgency of material problems students had to face—their economic difficulties and uncertainty of their future led them to strive for individual benefits without "rocking the boat." However, another factor seems relevant: the political atmosphere of the society at large.

This was not a time of political quiescence. The Left increased its power to the point of winning an electoral majority and forming a Popular Front government while the Fascist *ligues* (under the

leadership of Maurras) became a real threat. The students participated in the political battles and growing ideological strife. Violent
fist fights between students of the Left and Right became frequent
in the Latin Quarter.

Two comments should, however, be made: these demonstrations
were not specifically student political manifestations, but participation in national "adult" political movements. Secondly, the level at
which the political confrontation took place was so "ideological" in
terms of a clash between total theories of society that the current
demands of the students pertaining to their more immediate basic
needs could hardly be introduced into the debate. In other words,
there was a dichotomy between the political involvement of students
and their involvement in everyday preoccupations. This also explains
why the UNEF was able to remain so aloof from raging political
battles.

This describes the situation when World War II broke out. The
UNEF continued to function as if nothing had changed. It established "normal" relations with the new Vichy government and even
went as far as collaborating with its program of compulsory youth
work camps in Germany (*Service du Travail Obligatoire*). The university suffered less from World War II than it had from the first. In
1940 the number of students had dropped from 80,000 to 55,000, but
it soon increased again and reached a peak of 106,000 in 1943. Students then began to join the *maquis* in greater number—others were
taken to German work camps.

There again the fact that the UNEF ignored the war was not indicative of the lack of French student involvement in political problems of the day but only of their organization's narrow corporate
orientation. In fact, the first demonstration organized against the German occupation was a student agitation on the Champs-Elysées on
November 11, 1940, which resulted in some hundred dead and many
more sent to Germany. Subsequently, an increasing number of students participated in the Resistance movement. However, when the
war ended, it was obvious that whatever students had contributed to
the fight against Hitler had been done outside their own organization.
In postwar France, when the Resistance spirit was the focal point of

national identity, the UNEF was discredited and could no longer
be considered to represent French students.

1945 to the Present: Student "Syndicalism"

1. *The Resistance heritage: 1945–1950.* When the French universities resumed normal peace-time activities a large minority of students
had been directly involved in the war. Of 123,000 students in 1946,
approximately a quarter emerged from the *maquis* or from Germany.
France had been greatly damaged by the war and it was conceivable
that students might primarily be concerned with their studies and un-
interested in anything else—a phenomenon which seems to have
taken place in postwar America. However this was impossible in view
of the enormous intellectual and moral influence of the "Resistance
spirit." Unlike America, where the war had tended to unify the
country and dissolve most of the political battles in the common effort, France had suffered the war as a divided nation. The Resistance
had led the fight as much against the Vichy Government as against
the German occupation. The war had been a partial civil war and a
highly ideological one at that. Political choice was a basic factor of
the French involvement during the war, and France emerged highly
politicized from the war.

Three "lessons" learned by the new generation of students in the
Resistance were particularly relevant to the future of the UNEF.
First, no representative organization, no group in society can stand
aloof, indifferent to others and to national political issues, without
"losing its soul." Second, the old political parties had failed to rise to
the challenge of the times and were attributed great responsibility for
the French debacle. In addition, rigid ideologies were highly suspect.
Third, fundamental solidarities should not be forgotten between intellectuals and the working class in a country, and between all countries including those under colonial rule.

These were the main guide lines along which the "heirs" of the
Resistance chose to organize student participation in the reconstruction of postwar France. A national organization was needed with a

window on the world at large and its problems, and yet independent of political parties, truly representative of the specific interests and aspirations of students. A doctrine was also needed to reconcile these two potentially divergent aims.

In the Resistance, students had been affiliated to a variety of political, social, educational, cultural, and religious organizations. They federated into one single *Union Patriotique des Organisations Étudiantes* (UPOE). Should this organization assume all the tasks which the old UNEF had handled with the risk of endless faction fights inherent in this form of student "parliament," or should the slower process of "capturing" the UNEF and changing it from within be tried? The second course was finally adopted. In one year "Resistance" candidates for leadership of local associations affiliated to the UNEF had stood for most elections and had won against the old discredited leaders. The Easter 1946 annual convention in Grenoble ratified their majority.

A way had to be found for reconciling the old defense of students' corporate interest with the new ideology of social and political responsibility. This was done through a remarkable "charter" which first attempted to define "studenthood" in socially meaningful terms ("Students are young intellectual workers") and then elaborated on the ensuring "rights and duties." Despite the rather grandiloquent style indicative of the time it was written, this document deserves to be quoted extensively:

La Cherte de Grenoble

> *Preamble.* The representatives of French students legally assembled at a national congress in Grenoble on April 24, 1946, aware of the historic significance of the times,
>
> When the French Union is elaborating the new declaration of the rights of man and of the citizen,
>
> When a pacific Statute of Nations is being drawn up,
>
> When Labor and youth are elucidating the bases for a social and economic revolution at the service of man,
>
> Assert their willingness to participate in the unanimous effort of reconstruction.

True to the example of the best of them who died in the fight for freedom of the French people,

True to the traditional aims of French students when they were at the peak of awareness of their aims,

Recognizing the outdated character of the institutions that govern them,

Declare their decision to be in the vanguard of French youth as often in the past by freely defining the following principles as the bases for their action and demands;

Article I: The student is a young intellectual worker.

Rights and duties of the student as a young person

Article II: As a young person the student has a right to particular consideration from society from the physical, intellectual and moral standpoints.

Article III: As a young person, the student has a duty toward national and world youth.

Rights and duties of the student as a worker

Article IV: As a worker, the student has a right to work and live in the best possible conditions, to be independent, both personally and socially, as guaranteed by the free exercise of Union rights.

Article V: As a worker the student has a duty to acquire the highest competence possible.

Rights and duties of the student as an intellectual

Article VI: As an intellectual, the student has a right to the pursuit of truth, freedom being the first condition thereof.

Article VII: As an intellectual, the student has a duty:

— to define, spread and defend truth which comprises the duty to propagate and enrich culture and to assess the meaning of history.

—to defend freedom against all oppression which is the foremost consideration for an intellectual.

Thenceforth, the UNEF became a mass, democratic organization both in style and action with little resemblance to the prewar era.

The first national student strike was organized in 1947 for reduction of university fees and increased government grants. It was a total success. In 1948, after demonstrations and another strike, students won the right to a special health service financed by the National Health Service and administered by their own elected representatives. Student sanatoria, mental hospitals, clinics and medical care without cost still remain the most important achievement of the UNEF. In 1950, after three years of intensive campaigning among students, the National Convention, with a near unanimous vote, adopted the principle of a student "salary," which is still on the books of the UNEF, but not yet granted by the government. The reasoning behind this last claim is that the work of the student will ultimately be of benefit to the national community. They therefore have as much right to material independence and moral dignity of a salary as any other group of workers. Such a salary would be but a long-term investment for society. This demand is interesting in that it constitutes a paradox: along with other demands such as educational reform and financial aid to working class families putting children through university, it aims at democratizing the university and is, therefore, the expression of a privileged group contriving to abolish its privilege. And as such, it is a direct consequence of the new doctrine of solidarity elaborated at Grenoble in 1946.

Solidarity was, however, also to be applied on an international basis. Difficulties in this field were to bring the downfall of the Resistance generation of leaders. The International Union of Students had been founded in Prague in August 1946, following one year of preparatory work by a committee representing students from the U.S.A., U.S.S.R., Great Britain, France, Denmark, Belgium, Czechoslovakia, Yugoslavia, Poland, India, China, and Australia. However, international student unity could not resist the Cold War. After the Prague conference in 1948, Canada and the U.S.A. withdrew from the International Union, soon followed by most other Western countries, and the Communist delegations gained a clear majority. The UNEF remained a member trying, with increasing difficulty, to save its ideal of international cooperation. However, in France itself, the Communist party no longer formed part of the government and became increasingly isolated from the rest of public opinion. Any collaboration with the Communists was stigmatized as collaboration with the enemy in the Cold War atmosphere. The president of the UNEF was voted out of office upon his return from an international conference in 1950.

2. *A new "corporate" interlude: 1950–1956.* In the France of the 1950's the Cold War was only one aspect of significant changes in the political atmosphere which made a Left-oriented militant student organization obsolete. The enthusiasm with which the political leaders, born of the Resistance, had faced the reconstruction of postwar France had been short lived. First, de Gaulle had taken away most of their powers and then the old-style politicians entered the scene with the familiar political games. With the abandonment of a militant mobilization of energies, the economic hardship of the postwar years was beginning to tell, to which was added the moral and economic cost of a spreading war in Indochina. It is not surprising that most students returned to a conception of unionism which emphasized narrower corporate needs to the detriment of a greater involvement in national or international issues, taxed with being "political." As is often the case, such a rigid non-political doctrine was in many instances a cover for conservative political values: many of the leaders of this period were later deeply involved in right-wing or even neo-Fascist groups. For five years French students and their union were mainly concerned with fighting for better material conditions, graduating quickly and obtaining jobs.

The left wing of the movement was, however, still in control of large student associations such as Lyon and Grenoble and was a sufficiently strong minority to influence the decisions of the majority. Thus, they succeeded in retaining the movement's militant mass tactics (e.g., street demonstrations and sometimes a strike when the Education budget was before Parliament) and avoiding a piecemeal approach to problems of student welfare. During this period, a reorganization of the *Oeuvres* (student housing and restaurants) was achieved which rationalized the entire structure in a single organization administered jointly by the Ministry of Education and elected student delegates—each wielding an equal number of votes. It was only in the fields of international cooperation and anti-colonialism that the "a-political" majority refused to be influenced.

Eviction from office taught the left that defense of student welfare could not be neglected with impunity and that a long educational effort at the grass roots level had to be maintained if the students were to accept greater social and political responsibility. Realizing the strength of a unified single student organization, they set about to recapture a majority in the UNEF. Working at the local association level, they campaigned on well-defined corporate platforms, organized a number of practical "services" for students, and generally won the respect of their electorate as efficient administrators and defenders of student welfare. Involvement in politics was advocated not on "ideological" grounds but for a limited number of issues presented as a direct outgrowth of such corporate interests or even as a precondition to the satisfaction of the immediate demands of the students (e.g., how can the state finance the necessary reforms of the university when such a high proportion of the national budget goes to the war effort?). By 1956, the left was again in the majority, but with a more solid platform and a more "educated" rank and file.

Three factors seem to have played a particularly important role in the return of the left:

a. *The improving economic situation.* Despite the game of political musical chairs, the Fourth Republic had done a remarkable job of restoring France to economic progress. In the same way that deteriorating economic conditions seem to have fostered a withdrawal into an attitude of narrow self-interest, a rise in material well-being and a glimmer of hope seem to afford the individual liberty for involvement in altruistic and long-term political action.

b. *The political situation.* Contrary to its success in the economic field, the Fourth Republic had failed politically to solve the gigantic challenge of the emancipation of the colonies. The election of Pierre Mendés-France in 1954 was a marked change in style as well as in content of political leadership and demonstrated the bankruptcy of previous governments. The need for "change" was felt throughout the country and the electorate returned a left majority to the 1956 National Assembly. The student left undoubtedly benefited from this general shift in public opinion.

c. *The political student organizations.* With the Communists as isolated among students as they were in the "adult" world, two organizations rose to prominence in the non-Communist left: the Socialist students and the Young Christian Students (JEC). The former enjoyed a high degree of independence from the Socialist party and accordingly took on a specifically "student orientation." The student world was their immediate field of political action. They provided a number of leaders for the UNEF. Similarly, the JEC was the militant student organization of the *Action Catholique* which emphasized complete immersion in the "milieu" for educational and social action. Thus they trained another important contingent of UNEF leaders. These two organizations worked in close collaboration to re-establish a left majority in the UNEF.

3. *From "issues syndicalism" to "revolutionary syndicalism": 1956–1960's.* From 1956 to 1961, the Algerian war was the main preoccupation of the UNEF, although action on corporate issues remained the basis for a large part of its student support. The UNEF involvement in the Algerian problem was indicative of the new educational and issue-oriented approach elaborated by the new leadership during the six years of their opposition. Rather than advocating outright independence for Algeria, an intensive educational campaign was launched. Within four years student opinion was ready to support a strong political stand in favor of Algeria's independence. These were some of the intermediate problems emphasized by the UNEF leadership: the suppression of Algerian "culture" under French colonial rule, the discrimination against Algerians in the French educational system and the special responsibility of the academic community in both matters, the methods used by the French army and the moral responsibility of the academic community; the cost of the war and its effect on the budget of the university and, closer to home, the restrictions on student deferments. The UNEF was able to mobilize vast numbers of students and play an important political role in bringing

together the more reluctant labor unions when the time came for effective public pressure on the government in favor of a negotiated settlement for Algerian independence.

However, when the Algerian war ended, so did this particular type of student approach to politics. "Decolonization" had greatly favored such a practical, issue-oriented political involvement. It was a highly political problem in the broadest sense of the term and not only a moral one: if a "meaning of history" had to be discovered, the rise to independence of previously dependent nations offered a clear example; yet it was a problem with obvious practical consequences in the everyday life of all and thus allowed for a practical educational approach and not an exclusively ideological one. When the Algerian problem disappeared, the UNEF, which had concentrated all its political energy on it, was left with a highly politicized rank and file but with no clear issue on which such political energy could be spent. Consequently, it suffered a deep re-orientation crisis as was the case with other left-wing political organizations and labor unions.

With no clear issue at hand, the involvement in politics of some students has become more abstract and theoretical. This trend has, in recent years, profoundly affected the leadership and policies of the UNEF and has, for the moment, resulted in a drastic reduction in its membership.

This new trend has been qualified as revolutionary syndicalism. Before analyzing its content, I should cite other factors which seem to have played a role in bringing it about.

The Gaullist regime. De Gaulle acceded to power in 1958 after a military coup d'état in Algeria thereby estranging most of the university community and particularly the UNEF. He never forgave their dissent. His government cracked down on the UNEF with a number of measures: a subsidy justified by the various services directly run by the students was abolished; the number of student representatives on the various boards where the UNEF had gained equal number of seats with the government was reduced; a rival student union was established and heavily financed by the UNR (the Gaullist party) thereby destroying the unified student representation which UNEF had established. Contact with Government officials became increasingly tense and devoid of meaning—a trend which was accentuated by the Gaullist doctrine: any representative organization was suspect and branded as standing between the leader and "his" people. At any rate, the delicate balance between militant action and constructive cooperation with the government in certain fields was broken.

Changes in the student political sub-stratum. The Catholic student organization (JEC) had encountered the wrath of the Catholic Church hierarchy who had imposed authoritative change in the leadership and policies of the organization. The Socialist students' conflict with the policies of the discredited Guy Mollet (head of the French Socialist party and largely responsible for the conduct of the Algerian war) had led them to withdraw from the Socialist party and lose most of their political influence on national policies. Thus, the two political "training grounds" which had proved so fertile in the emergence of the new issue syndicalism had vanished from the scene. In their place, the more aggressive Communist student organization (UEC) and the new-left organizations advocated a different approach to student unionism. They encountered wide support among students in a political situation where de Gaulle allowed little room for "constructive opposition."

Demographic changes. The birth rate which had stagnated before 1945 picked up tremendously from 1945 on. By 1961–1962, the effect was felt on the universities. The increase in the student population from 1950 to 1960 had been approximately 75,000 (25,000 in the first five years and 50,000 in the following five years as a result of the improved economic situation). A 300,000 increase has been predicted between 1960 and 1970.

Very little has been done in recent years in the way of university construction, student housing, and restaurants, and recruitment of professors to prepare for such an explosion of the student population. The crisis calls for radical "revolutionary" measures—not moderate reforms. Consequently, it is not difficult to understand that many students turn to what they term "revolutionary syndicalism."

The new revolutionary student ideology seems to have the following characteristics:

Suspicion of traditional "representative" democracy, in their own organization as well as in government and emphasis on "participatory democracy."

A search for a new ideology which emphasizes concepts such as student and intellectual "alienation."

As to the university, a special emphasis on grass roots participatory educational processes as a way to democratization in contrast to the previous approach which advocated structural reforms.

This new trend offers obvious similarities to the ideals of some American students. This chapter has not explained how such convergence came about. However, knowledge of the historical development behind the evolution of the French student movement might afford some insight for understanding divergent student movements. This may be useful in future comparative studies.

6

While this essay shows the elements Italian activism has in common with other contemporary student movements in Western Europe, it stresses the distinctive features of that movement. Italian students, for instance, do not want a voice in the running of universities, but instead demand "direct democracy." Despite its ostensibly leftist ideology, Mancini claims, the Italian movement is basically bourgeois. Note why he thinks it will not lead to revolution.

Italy: From Reform to Adventure

Federico Mancini

Rebellion in the Italian universities was already detectable in 1966. The crucible of the student movement, however, was the month-long occupation of the Turin campus in November 1967. From Turin the rebellion spread throughout the country, making a clean sweep of the old party-controlled organizations. Soon its unique traits began to take shape.

First of all, there is a flat refusal to participate in university decision-making. While the German SDS has sometimes laid claim to *Drittelparität* arrangements and some SDS people sit on student-faculty committees, though with the purpose that Lenin assigned to Communists in bourgeois parliaments, the Italian students oppose codetermination. They "don't want to run the pigsty" with the professors, lest they be coopted and corrupted. One reason they fight the government-sponsored university reform bill is that it aims to "cage" them by student participation in university governing bodies.

Besides, running the pigsty together implies the election of representatives, and disavowal of the principle of representation is a second trait of the Italian student movement. Nowhere has "direct democracy" been so uncompromisingly espoused as in Italy, though its original purism now seems in decline. Student assemblies are still held and lip service is paid to the sovereign authority of the direct voice of the people, but such assemblies have proved time-consuming

From Federico Mancini, "From Reform to Adventure," *Dissent,* 15 (July–August 1969), 413–422. Reprinted by permission of the author and the publisher.

and unwieldy. Hence, more and more emphasis is laid on a new form of organization, the "grass-roots committees" (*comitati di base*), which are small and geared to specific problems and obviously more effective. An even more significant departure from the careless spontaneity of old is the progressive transformation of an open and constantly changing leadership into a semipermanent steering committee. This self-appointed Jacobin elite already shows all the symptoms of bureaucratic degeneration.

The third distinctive feature of the Italian student movement has been its remarkable ability to map out and implement a common strategy for the major campuses. Of course, this has been made easier by the highly centralized nature of the Italian university system: the rector of Palermo will respond to a student challenge in much the same fashion as his colleague of Milan, because both are responding to the same ministerial circular. But, granted that the student movement has been lucky in not having to deal with a Hayakawa here and a Perkins there, the primary reason for its success in coordinating activities at various universities has been its own internal cohesion. The hard core of the movement is composed of Communists who find themselves at the extreme left of their party, Anarchists, Trotskyites, Maoists of various persuasions, and members of *Potere operaio* (Worker Power), a group with aspirations resembling those of the old revolutionary syndicalists. These sects have always expended considerable energy in internecine wrangles but, until a few months ago, have also managed to patch up their differences and rally dissenters to the general line. The moral tension of the militants, rather than their adhesion to the Leninist doctrine of "democratic centralism," and especially the undiscriminating character of police busts have contributed to this extraordinary achievement.

The strategy of the Italian student movement has varied with circumstances. In broad outline, its development falls into three phases: the last months of 1967, spring and autumn of 1968, and the winter of 1969.

1. The first phase was characterized by a harsh critique of the university as an authoritarian "class" institution, but also by a determination to make use of it. Future economic exploitation is anticipated

in the university which is, indeed, often compared to a factory (a graffito at the Liberal Arts Faculty in Rome reads: *"FIAT is our university, the university is our FIAT")*. But the men and the facilities of the university can be turned to account with a view to producing new values, to laying the cultural foundations of the coming revolution. To achieve this goal, the student movement demanded a "restructuring" of courses: no more lectures delivered *ex cathedra* or teacher-dominated seminars but egalitarian "study groups" where professors, now called "experts," would cooperate with the students in approaching the subject matter (any subject matter) from more "relevant" angles and, above all, in debunking the myth of the neutrality of science (any science).

The study groups were conceived as models of a nongovernmental university and, for their most daring advocates, a nongovernmental society. These notions, which resemble the schemes of a pragmatic anarchist like Paul Goodman, were often expressed in Che Guevara's phrase: "Society as a whole will have to be a gigantic school." Less loftily, the study groups were also supposed to provide activists with an opportunity to influence the inchoate mass. "Campus" and "college life" are meaningless terms in Italian universities where, except for a usually squalid cafeteria, students have no place to get together. Students meet "on the job," in the classrooms. Classrooms being the only places where new proselytes could be made, it was imperative for the militants to change the conditions of classroom work in order to insert the preaching of their gospel and legitimate it.

Those were the days. . . . How many are the professors who look back in anger to the "study-groups period"? Surely not those—a huge majority—who turned down the students' offer (at that time offers were not always accompanied by threats and it was easy to show some backbone), nor the very few who agreed to participate in the experiment. Actually, the excitement of the latter—mostly liberals—was boundless. In Italy one becomes a tenured professor (a "baron") through cooptation by one's peers. To wield academic (baronial) power one must enjoy their confidence. But is there a more exalting experience for a liberal liege lord than seeing his power recognized, nay legitimized *also* from below? Indeed, the above-below relation remained by and large untouched. Being referred to as an "expert" was for the leftist professor not unlike the pleasure Count Honoré Riqueti de Mirabeau must have experienced when addressed as *citoyen:* in the study group it was he who did most of the talking and the replies of the radical students were still very much within the rules of the old game.

Besides, many a progressive member of the faculty felt that by agreeing to join the study groups they were contributing to a self-regeneration of the university, of whose wretched conditions they were agonizingly aware. The student-movement leaders did not conceal their revolutionary intentions; but the liberal professors hoped that, while theory remained revolutionary, practice could be steered along reformist lines. In time, they thought, the dross (the inordinate politicizing, the lack of interest in cool research) would be jettisoned; the substance (more vivid seminars and fewer drab lecture courses, more contact between teachers and students) would stick. Such delusions were soon exposed, but for once it is not the students who should be blamed for the liberals' defeat.

2. The blame lay on Academe as a whole. The university might have taken up the student challenge by working to reform itself. It would have required patience, political skill, and some knowledge of adolescent psychology; at that stage, when only a few student chieftains really knew their own mind, efforts might have yielded fruit. Or the university might have counterattacked. Against the portrait that the radicals drew—a center entrusted by the capitalist system with the task of training its future slaves—it might have put forward a different image: a center of free inquiry and criticism, whose aims should be realized in a climate of political neutrality. But in Italy we had practically none of this; we had none of the soul-searching of the French professors after May or of American professors after Columbia. Cynical shrugs, condescending conversation, or vindictive indignation at "those cranks" were the reactions of most Italian faculty members.

Which, in turn, had a number of consequences. It radicalized many students who still hesitated at all-out confrontation. It persuaded the student leadership that the university could be neither relied on nor exploited. It brought grist to the mill of the fringe (left-Maoists and *operaisti*) who had been contending that the movement's only chance of survival was in an alliance with the revolutionary agents *par excellence:* the industrial workers in the north, the land-less peasants in the south. In the history of the student movement, this was a major turning point. Until then most militants had thought that in revolutionizing the universities they were touching the jugu-lar vein of the system; from that moment on, they knew this was not true. In order to revolutionize the universities, they had to get out of them—and, in the words of Rudi Dutschke, embark on "a long march through the institutions."

The study groups were given up. They were no longer useful; they entangled energies needed elsewhere: in winning over the high-school children (high schools were an obvious first choice among the "outside" institutions to be attacked); in helping the workers on picket lines; in organizing the slum dwellers of the large cities, and so forth. But what was to be done with the universities? Surely, they could not be left alone, for there the movement found its strength, its "masses" (not an ironical expression: Italian students number about 600,000). Nor could they be captured. The student movement under-stood in practice Lenin's critique of Blanquism. Besides, its leaders were not yet certain about their ability to mobilize a large enough number of recruits, or about the measure of the authorities' tolerance.

Therefore, a proposal was made by Vittorio Rieser—possibly the movement's cleverest strategist—to break the universities in two parts. On the one side, a section should be left to the academic authorities for routine activities (courses, examinations, etc.); on the other, an "autonomous space" should be created to be controlled by the stu-dents for such initiatives as political meetings, workshops, and "anti-courses." Rieser's scheme obviously echoed foreign experiences: e.g. the American free universities, the German *kritische Universität*. But it also served a practical purpose. The professors' university would play the role of a *Gegenvolk;* it would be the tangible incarnation of Evil. Its inbred authoritarianism and irrelevance would continuously beget frustration and dissent. The "autonomous space" would ensure the presence of the movement in the university and enable it to reap what the enemy had sown: in other words, it would be the move-ment's sanctuary.

The battle for "autonomous space" took place during the Easter holidays and ended in May after a number of "stiff" occupations. In June, having secured their rear, the students of Turin, Milan, Trento, Padua, Bologna, Pisa, and Rome were ready to start their long-planned "operation working class."

3. The summer of 1968 was spent in analyses of the French May, in attempts at establishing contacts with fellow movements abroad (especially the Germans, whom the Italian students admire for their superiority in matters of theory) and, above all, in the search for ways to form a student-worker alliance. But this period of relative inactivity did not last long: a new tumultuous phase was beginning in Italy. First the chemical industry near Venice, later the tire industry in Turin and Milan, and the sugar refineries of Ferrara were upset by a powerful wave of strikes, often of the wildcat variety. The workers' decisions often bypassed or ran counter to union policy. Reminiscent of the factory councils (*consigli di fabbrica*) the young Gramsci had advocated in 1920, these workers' meetings invented or rediscovered tough forms of struggle—slowdowns, sit-ins, "staggered" walkouts, short and repeated (or "hiccup") stoppages. When they put forward a claim, they made it clear that it was nonnegotiable.

In November and December the crisis became acute. Hundreds of thousands of high-school students supported demands for freedom of assembly in the schools. Two Sicilian farmhands were killed by the police during a labor dispute and the emotions aroused in the public were violent. Normally sedate social groups, such as white-collar employees, higher government officials, school teachers, resident physicians in hospitals, began to display an unprecedented aggressiveness in their demands for better working conditions. Not even the courtrooms, where left-wing and right-wing judges engaged in incredible brawls, escaped the contagion of *contestazione*. The whole country seemed to be in a frenzy; the government seemed at a loss for solutions, and the Communist party—the Great Sphinx of Italian politics —was about to hold a congress that everybody expected to be crucial.

It must have been at this point that the leaders of the student movement decided to cross the Rubicon. This "objectively pre-revolutionary situation" could be helped to blow up through a few "voluntarist pushes," in their words, through some *lotta leggera urbana* (light urban struggle). As [Antonio] Gramsci would have said, Italian society had grown "gelatinous" enough for a resolute vanguard to storm it. If it could be brought home to the Communist bureaucrats that power was within reach, even *they* might awaken from their 25-year-long sleep.

All this, however, was bound to take time. The student movement needed bases in which its commandos could prepare their expeditions into the cities and seek shelter afterwards: it needed its Sierra Maestra or—an even more alluring reference—its Yenan. For this, the "autonomous space" conquered in May was no longer sufficient. The universities had to be seized and kept under absolute control; in other words, they had to be destroyed as centers of teaching and research. It was a dramatic decision, even for people much toughened by a year of conflict and hard bargaining. New slogans appeared. The old graffiti were turgid, bombastic, at times sophomoric, but one could smile while reading them—or feel sympathetic. In January 1969 they acquired a sinister, anti-intellectual, even fascistic dimension: "When class warfare becomes acute, culture is of no use"; "To be a spectator means to be a traitor"; "Rape your Alma Mater"; etc. A brilliant scholar, who counts himself a fellow traveler of the movement and had just finished a thousand-page book on the use of analogy in philosophy and science, told me without flinching that the burning of the Alexandrian library by Amr Ibn al-As was the first example of a successful cultural revolution.

The new tactics consisted in keeping the universities occupied as long as possible and, during the brief lulls between occupations, in making demands which, if accepted by the faculties (and they often were), would make serious work impossible. Thus, the Bologna Faculty of Liberal Arts was requested to suppress the written test in Italian; most universities were forced to accept an arrangement under which students were entitled to refuse failing marks and take the same examination, month after month, until they passed.

It was bedlam, but the uproar remained largely confined to the campuses. One after the other, the delegates at the Bologna Communist Congress censured the "adventurism" of the student vanguards. The government finally moved. The truth at last dawned upon the students' leaders: *there would be no revolution in Italy in the foreseeable future*. At the end of March the police broke into the occupied universities, with a tremendous deployment of men and weapons. In Rome they found five students asleep, no students in Bologna, and everywhere garbage, anti-Communist writings, broken furnishings and, oddly enough, a number of clogged toilets. Today, a rather lugubrious order reigns again in the groves of Italian Academe.

So far narrative, now interpretation.

Last year, it already seemed clear that, despite Marxist jargon, the Italian student movement had little in common with socialism. At least in its Italian version, I wrote, the New Left might be the legatee not of the Old Left, but of the *Older* Left, the *philosophes* and particularly Rousseau. Today, this seems even more evident. The student movement—or, more precisely, the non-Communist part of it, is *a characteristically bourgeois movement*. First, in the obvious sense that its militants are of bourgeois extraction (only 13 per cent of the Italian students have a lower-class background and these are very scantily represented in the rank and file of the movement, let alone its leadership). But also in the far more important sense, despite the movement's self-image, its traits fall into a familiar bourgeois pattern. This is not to deny the radical character of its protest; the contrary is true. Indeed, must all revolutionary critiques of the capitalist system be Marxist-inspired and Marxist-orientated?

One should not attach an excessive importance to words, even when they sound convincing. Any project can be adorned with suitable quotations from Marx, Lenin, or the most recent patron saint of the movement, Rosa Luxemburg. It is equally easy to coin slogans with a Guevarist or a palaeo-Bolshevist ring, and to write articles explaining why and how one should love Chairman Mao, particularly when the authors operate in a cultural context (the Italian intelligentsia) which has been imbued with Marxist ideology for half a century.

Nor should one overrate the students' insistence on the leading role of the working class and their almost obsessive wooing of the working man. Bourgeois movements, too, have tried to involve the working class in their own enterprises. Italy has a long tradition of such movements. Obvious cases in point are Mazzini, Arturo Labriola, Gaetano

Salvemini and, more recently, Carlo Rosselli and Piero Gobetti, Gramsci's liberal friend who saw in the automobile workers of Turin the emerging aristocracy of modern Italy.

Let us forget the words and consider the deeds; let us go back to the trajectory of the movement and try to break through the screen of its own rationalizations. The university appears to the student both as a Leviathan and a Juggernaut: a huge, clumsy and crushing monster which *represses* him, *atomizes* him, stuffs him with an enormous amount of *irrelevant* information and eventually flings him—a badly-packaged marketable product—into the world of business, the civil service, or the professions. His first reaction is a critique of the university in strictly liberal terms. Against the alienation he suffers, the student advances such characteristic "bourgeois" values as the right to resist indoctrination (why should we law students be taught that legal science must be insulated against the intrusion of value judgments and social facts? What kind of lawyers do they want us to become?); the right to inquire beyond the unreasonably stiff limits of the studies program (why should we students of government be offered but one course in Afro-Asian institutions, and none on Latin America? And why should the subject of this course be confined to the legal systems of a few "safe" Afro-Asian countries?); freedom of speech (why are questions in class frowned upon by most professors?); freedom of assembly and association (why are our requests for classrooms for political meetings usually rejected?).

Hence, the proposal to set up "study groups": these, despite the many catchwords in which they were couched, basically amounted to a new, *nonauthoritarian* way of studying *together* things *more relevant*. But this attempt, naïve or impractical though it might have been, ran into a wall, which allowed no room for future student initiative. On the other side, students found opposition—not of ideas —but of ossified structures (the universities) and of other institutions more violent (the police) or obtuse (the judiciary). Grievances that at the outset had been fundamentally cultural became political. The students embarked on an anti-institutional struggle (Dutschke's "long march") that manifested itself first as a refusal of, later as an all-out assault on, the institutions, above all the university.

But even this struggle, for all its harshness and the anger it revealed, is not founded on a "class" analysis of the university and the system that supports it. The university may be hell, it may stifle the students, deprive them of their power of self-determination and emancipation. *But it does not technically exploit them, it does not extract from them any surplus value.* In spite of the Roman graffito, the university will never be the students' FIAT; students *qua* students will never be part of the working class, and their protest is bound to be superstructural, that is, at bottom, vain or inadequate. This appraisal, of course, will not be shared by people like Herbert Read, who wrote that, since institutions in the modern world "legalise tyranny and spread its invisible tentacles into every cell of life," it is at their breakdown that one should primarily aim. But Sir Herbert was an avowed anarchist: namely, as any Marxist would tell you, a petty-bourgeois radical day-dreamer.

A number of marginal elements confirm the irredeemably nonsocialist nature of the student movement. First of all, the "style" of its protest, which is impulsive, nervous, some say epileptic; at any rate, very different from that, as a rule patient and robust, of worker actions, when they are carried out under the leadership of the Communist party or the Communist-oriented trade unions. Second, the character of its literature, which is basically sociological (sociology, the bourgeois science!) and clearly eschews historic-economic analyses in the Marxist tradition. Third, its reaction to the developments in the Iron Curtain countries. The Italian revolutionary students have no sympathy whatever for the Yugoslav experiment. They took no interest in the Prague spring. When the Russians invaded Czechoslovakia, they accepted without turning a hair the Chinese view that the whole incident amounted to a rift between two revisionist cliques. When Jan Palach burned himself, they remained unperturbed. As a matter of fact, on the front of the Commercio Hotel in Milan, which the students occupied last November and still keep under control, a huge inscription appeared: *"Down with Palach!"*

At first glance, this attitude seems outrageous and contradictory. In reality, it simply proves that the student radicals don't care about socialism. To say, as they do, that socialism has nothing in common with the systems of Eastern Europe and to point to their models of the just society by rhythmically chanting, *Cina - Cuba - Corea - Vietnam,* may be amusing but is also shallow. By hook or crook, "socialism" is there too: between the Elbe and the Ussuri. It is a tangle of contradictions, failures and successes; it has brought emancipation to some, slavery to others. Probably, on balance, the liabilities outweigh the assets. Yet those who do not feel—no, not sympathetic to that mess, that toilsome and bloody human venture but just—involved in it, have no right to count themselves socialists. I hazard the guess that the students and the metalworkers of Prague would agree.

The above interpretation suggests that the Italian student movement is bound not to attain its long-range goal. In other words, no revolution is in sight, no "new-left"-inspired mass movement is likely to take root.

The reason is clear enough. The causes of the nation's present malaise and recurrent crises have been pointed out a thousand times: a parliament apparently unable to legislate, an inept central and local bureaucracy, a judiciary still thinking of Italy as a basically agrarian society, the most expensive and least efficient social security system in the Common Market area, a shameful health and welfare system, a wretched school system—in brief, a decrepit social structure that does not allow a more equitable distribution of the benefits accruing from the tremendous economic and technical progress of the last decade. The Italian problem, therefore, is to create efficient institutions, not to deny them. The Communist party, for one, knows all this perfectly well. Thus, while it demands "structural" or "strategic" reforms—reforms not assimilable by the system and hence potentially subversive—it concretely goads the government into taking such measures as would help streamline the system.

Why this is happening is not a question to be discussed here. For this analysis, two facts matter: (*a*) during the last few years the issues which the PCI has most agitated have been decentralization of the legislative power, pension reform, hospital reform, town planning, high-school reform; (*b*) their remarkable electoral gains in May 1968 prove that in doing so the Communists have correctly interpreted the character and the direction of the protest spreading in Italian society.

It is precisely these facts—the interest of the PCI in the rationaliza-

tion of the system and its ability to represent the dissatisfied segment
of the electorate—that makes the position of the student movement
hopeless. The movement actually had but one real chance: to force
upon the PCI a process of revolutionary hardening, that is, to stir up
such unrest among the masses as to convince the Communist leaders
that, by pursuing their previous strategy, they would have lost a considerable slice of their following. Considering the experience and the
organizational strength of the two movements, the possibilities of the
student movement were infinitesimal; in fact, they did not materialize.

The reverse took place: it was the Communists who turned the
student revolt to advantage by beating the young radicals at their
own game. Whereas the French C P was compelled by circumstances
to commit itself right away on the issue of student extremism, the
Italian C P was so lucky as to have time to reflect. Its leaders realized
that the campus war and the spontaneous stepping up of class struggle in the nation at large were a gift of providence in two respects.

First, these events would force the parties in power (Christian
Democrats, Socialists, Republicans) to draft far-reaching measures,
and especially a university reform bill—that is, to tackle a number of
burning problems which were bound to make mischief among them
and inside each of them. The Communists, of course, would be able
to profit from such differences by playing one faction against another,
or taking up the cause of underprivileged groups (e.g. the junior faculty in their conflict with the tenured professors), so as to weaken
the government coalition.

Second, the PCI felt that it might capitalize on the creeping chaos,
the *chienlit rampant* which the students were spreading throughout
the country. Not that the Italian Communists have any fondness for
chienlit: like their French comrades or, for that matter, General de
Gaulle, they hate the sight of it. But a little *chienlit* would enable
the party, if it managed to have it stopped at the right time, to present
itself as the guarantor of social peace, thus enhancing its prestige.

Consequently, the Communists beat their breasts in self-criticism
for not having immediately understood the "deep roots" of the student revolt and stated that the latter had opened "a new front in
class warfare" (which wasn't quite the same thing as saying that

students were part of the working class, but came pretty close to it). In the autumn of 1968 they vigorously supported the high-school insurrection and in January 1969 they harshly attacked the police for shooting at the students who—in what should probably be regarded as their most futile action—had thrown tomatoes at the customers of a plush nightclub in that Italian Miami Beach, Viareggio. Having realized, however, that a frenzy of adult backlash was building up, particularly in the lower class, the C P drastically reversed its course. It did not approve of the February–March wave of occupations and, when the police broke into the campuses, its protests were mild and mixed with reproaches about student "vandalism."

At the outset Communists and extremists managed to coexist in the student movement, though with some difficulty. The charismatic leaders were all self-styled Maoists, but the Communists made up the bulk of the intermediate echelons and were no less belligerent than the others. In folklore (attire, hair style, rhetoric, songs etc.), the two groups were so similar as to make it impossible for an outsider to tell them apart. Then, toward the beginning of this year, the Communist "university sections," which had always been regarded as part and parcel of the movement, appeared to seek the status of autonomous units. Conflicts broke out on policy, which were less furious but far more serious than the mostly theoretic wrangles of old. During the sit-ins of the late winter, the two factions clearly pursued diverging policies; today, on many campuses, they have proceeded to a formal rupture.

A couple of weeks ago, I saw in Bologna a *dazibao* (Italianized Chinese for "hand-written poster") calling a meeting of the "red-line comrades" for the next morning. It was an ominous sign. In the jargon of the revolutionary sects, the notion of "red line" implies that of "black line," where "black" stands for ugly, devious, nocturnal; and the black-line fellows are no longer comrades but renegades.

The strength and the prestige of the Italian student movement appear to be, at this moment, at an all-time low. The price the movement is paying for last winter's blunder is very high. Apparently, its strategists had mistaken nationwide disturbances for an imminent revolution and had concluded that the advent of the revolution might be speeded up by turning the nation's major universities into "red bases." Now, many militants are in jail, others—the Communists— are hastily abandoning ship, and most rank-and-file students no longer respond to the old slogans. The government reform bill, a far-from-daring piece of legislation which grants the students a *Drittel-parität* in the university decision-making bodies, has been drafted and laid before the Senate. The movement's last fortress, the Commercio Hotel in Milan, still holds out, but its days appear numbered. The occupiers have already been ordered by the bailiff to leave, and the bailiff is usually soon followed by the police.

Of course, there is no assurance that the present calm will last. The crucial question is whether and how the reform bill is enacted. If the government manages to promulgate it by the start of the next academic year, the situation will not greatly differ from that of France after the coming into force of the Faure *loi d'orientation*. The Communists will lay aside their largely verbal bias against co-determination, form some front organization and enter lists of candidates for the new mixed student-faculty committees. The left-radicals of the student movement will boycott the election of student delegates and stir up riots wherever they can, but they will suffer a definite retrenchment. In other words, they will be reduced to the status of a small and not particularly fascinating extra-parliamentary opposition, whose main function will be to train the leaders of the future Italian United Revolutionary party, if indeed the *groupuscules* of the extreme left ever coalesce to form such a party.

But if the reform bill is not enacted or undergoes a further emasculation, a very different development is to be expected. The moderate or reform-minded groups which are beginning to fill the present power vacuum in the student body would collapse and the student movement could easily capitalize on the students' rage. Moreover, under such circumstances, the movement would certainly regain the support, though itself tactical, of the Communist party: and past events have shown how explosive this mixture can be.

The universities, which have practically not functioned for two years, would become impossible places to live and work in. The despondency of the younger professors would reach a climax and support already strong inclinations to seek shelter in private research

centers and foreign seats of learning. The contention of the radicals
that the role assigned to Italy in the international division of labor
is to import patents and export brains would be confirmed. It would
be a disgrace and, in the long run, a tragedy. Do the men who in government and the opposition command the allegiance of the Italians
realize what is at stake?

This essay shows that the historic role of the university in Spain as a coherent center of political influence persists even under dictatorship, and that student activism, though illegal, exerts pressure on the regime. The student protest movement, concerned at first mainly with economic conditions, took up political questions and in effect challenged the totalitarian structure of the government.

7

Students' Opposition in Spain

Enrique Tierno Galván

The Facts and the Author (Editorial Note)

For some years now Spanish university students have been drawing attention to themselves by their political activity in a regime in which political activity is not legal. The conflict has since 1962 taken the form of a demand by the students to set up an autonomous Students Union in the place of the officially sponsored SEU (Sindicato Español Universitario). A new wave of student disturbances occurred in the winter of 1965, sparked off by the exclusion of a student who had attended a meeting of students who refused to join in the activities of the official union in January 1965. The students throughout the country began to demand autonomy, both for the rectors of the universities and for the students' union, and supported demands by workers on 27 January who were also demonstrating in favour of free trade unions. On 6 February demonstrations took place again in Madrid and Barcelona, and a number of arrests were made. Further demonstrations of students against the obligatory SEU took place on 12 February in both cities. A number of students were beaten-up and arrested in Madrid; in Barcelona 1000 students met in the Faculty of Law, with the permission of the dean. Faculties in Bilbao and Madrid were closed for a while by the authorities, but the students

From Enrique Tierno Galván, "Students' Opposition in Spain," *Government and Opposition*, 1 (May–August, 1966), 467–486. Reprinted by permission of the author and the publisher.

continued to hold unofficial assemblies at which they demanded "free unions," and refused to cooperate with representatives of the official union. On 19 February some 2000 students in Madrid demonstrated in favour of university autonomy, and carried on with their protest for three days.

The main demonstration occurred on 25 February 1965, when at a meeting of students and staff, a number of demands were put forward: an autonomous union, amnesty for the students, freedom of expression within the university, freedom of association, exemption from obligatory membership of the SEU, and aid to students from poor families. Some 5000 students headed by Professors Aranguren, Montero Díaz, García Calvo, Tierno Galván and García de Vercher, marched silently to the rector's office, but were met by police. The procession stopped and offered no resistance, even when the police brought up fire engines and played jets of cold water on them. In spite of the assurance of the professors that the demonstration would disperse quietly the police attacked and some 100 students were injured, some critically. Fighting lasted some hours. The next day the five professors were suspended from their posts pending investigation. Two thousand students now assembled and called for a strike in all Spanish universities, to take the form of attending classes but ignoring the lecturers, in order not to justify the authorities in closing the universities. Further unauthorized meetings took place on 26 and 27 February, when 3000 students went on strike in Madrid. At their "free" meetings the students repeated all their previous demands as well as their demand for the re-instatement of the suspended professors; they pressed for freedom of information, if only to counter the alleged official distortion in the press of their own activities. On 1 March a meeting of 1500 students in Madrid determined to constitute themselves a constituent body of a new, free syndicate pending its creation. These meetings were attended by the suspended professors as well as by other staff. The meeting ended in a demonstration in the streets of Madrid which was attacked by the police. Support for the movement developed all over the country, notably in Granada, Valencia, Bilbao, Saragossa and Oviedo. In Bilbao 12,000 students went on strike, and at Salamanca Professor Enrique

Tierno Galván spoke to a large meeting of students. In Barcelona some 17,500 out of a total of 19,000 refused to attend classes for a week from 1 March.

In the meantime the future of the SEU had been under discussion between the Ministry of Education and the Falangist movement, to determine whether the students union should remain under the control of a ministry, and if so which, or under the control of the Falangist movement, or whether it should be allowed some degree of autonomy, or some representational element. On 5 March the government agreed to see a delegation of students to discuss changes in the structure of the SEU. For a while the protest movement ran parallel with a series of unofficial talks, and unofficial promises made by officials of the Falange movement, and the leaders of the official students union began also to declare their agreement with the necessity for a change. Tension and uncertainty prevailed, owing to the suspension of the professors, the unconciliatory speeches of the Minister of Information, Fraga Iribarne, and the fear that reforms would only amount to the SEU in a remodelled form. Towards the end of March there were fresh and vigorous student demonstrations, including a sit-down strike by teachers and students in the Faculty of Political Science and Economics, on 26 March. In Barcelona the Ministry of Education cancelled the registrations for examinations as a reprisal against student demonstrations.

By 31 March the SEU itself came out openly in favour of a reform, stating that it would disclaim responsibility if the students took matters into their own hands. It also opposed the suspension of grants to students and the inquiry into the teachers' conduct. Finally on 8 April the government decision was announced. The students unions were to be organized on a national basis according to faculties, and into unions within faculties in universities. These would jointly constitute the new SEU, which would still however be the sole union, of which membership would be obligatory. Representatives would however be elected instead of appointed as at present, and a commissioner would be appointed to undertake liaison between the students, the government and the Falangist movement. This solution by no means satisfied all the demands of the students, and it was rejected by the students of the Economics Faculty of Bilbao on 23

April, and later by the students of Madrid and Barcelona. Further
details of the government reform programme were published on 5
June, and seemed to take back some of the concessions made previously, notably the union was to remain under the "control" of the
Falange movement and the Minister of Education; limits were also
placed on those eligible as representatives, of a kind which would
have barred all those who had led the protest movement; even the
leaders of the old SEU dissociated themselves from the "new pattern"
of the SEU. Student agitation died down during the summer, but it
has recently flared up again, notably in Catalonia, and disturbances
have continued ever since both in Madrid and Barcelona.

Meanwhile government action against the five professors suspended from their chairs for their participation in the demonstration
of 24 February 1965 was announced on 21 August 1965. Professors
Aranguren, García Calvo and Tierno Galván were dismissed from
their chairs for life; Professors Montero Díaz and Aguilar Navarro
were suspended for two years, for breaches of the regulations covering academic discipline promulgated on 8 September 1954.

(End of Editorial Note)

Forces and Trends of Opposition

The Spanish Labyrinth is the name of a well-known book on Spain,
and the name applies only too well to the country's social, political
and economic reality. Spain is a maze from which the exit leading to
normal political life is very hard to find: there are many forces and
trends, meaning by forces the groups and institutions which can
exert pressure and influence upon the regime, and by trends the
doctrinal orientations in society. One of these institutions is the university, and the main object of this study is to describe its evolution
in the last few years and to assess its future role in this context. But
before discussing the role of the university a word must be said about
the other forces, institutions and political groups which act in Spanish society—and it is necessary to stress that they act *in* rather than
on society—especially the Church, the banking and business interests and the army. These three apparent interest groups can really

be reduced to one, because together they form the oligarchy in contemporary Spanish society. It is an oligarchy which dates from the
post-civil war period, since before the civil war the state was not so
closely interwoven with these three great centres of power. With
the establishment of a totalitarian state after the civil war, the imposition of one single ideology tended to bring about the identification
of state and society, the merging of political and social activities. In
this early post-war period, state, Church, army and finance were all
closely connected and it was not possible to differentiate clearly between them in terms of political purposes. But this is no longer the
case.

To take first the army: the new generations recruited into the
armed forces have, for a number of reasons, given the army more
political and social independence. For one, the new men have no
personal recollection of the civil war. Furthermore, the salaries paid
to all ranks beneath the highest are not sufficient for a life of reasonable comfort. The junior officers must thus have some supplementary
jobs, or indeed professions, and this gives the army a civilian and a
military complexion at the same time. It must also be remembered
that the army is not a closed corps, isolated from society as a whole.
The higher ranks are drawn from the middle classes or the upper
bourgeoisie; but the sons do not necessarily follow their fathers.
Many enter the university or the special schools. The social life of
the family unit influences the character of the army, giving it greater
flexibility and receptivity to new ideas.

But in addition to these social factors, the army has been subjected
also to influences deriving from Spain's international relations. Some
of the armed forces have been in close contact with modern, technical, non-Spanish armed forces. This has helped to wean the soldier
from the idea of the army as a body with a policy of its own. By now
the army, which used to be an offshoot of the ruling class, imbued
with a rigid ideology, has evolved in the direction of greater breadth
of mind. It is the officers with a modern mentality and a sense of
civic values who are now coming forward. If this trend were to continue, the army could become an institution aspiring towards a democratic way of life. The soldier is beginning to think for himself, and
is ceasing to subordinate his political views to military discipline as

was the case previously. It is unlikely therefore that there will be further *pronunciamientos*. The army has a role to play in the future, but it is a moot point whether it will be a reactionary one. Though there is a diminishing number of older officers wedded to more traditional views, the present trends of thought in the army make it unlikely that it will serve as the instrument for re-imposing totalitarianism in Spain—indeed it is more likely to lean towards the democratic solutions.

A similar process of realignment has been taking place in the Church. It too can be seen as divided into a more elderly group, firmly anchored in the theocratic tradition of the post-civil-war period, and a younger generation which has left these traditions behind. This internal contradiction within the Church (which must be seen against the background of the changing attitude of Rome and the recent Vatican Council), has led the Church to move slowly away from the state and to assert itself as an independent institution, less involved with the present political regime. There are indeed striking discrepancies between the decisions of the Vatican Council of 1965 and the provisions of the Spanish Concordat of 1954 with the Holy See, notably with regard to liberty of conscience. Events may move to a denunciation of the Concordat. This would be an important step towards opening up a new phase in relations between the Spanish Church and the state, and might have a great influence on Christian Democracy as a political trend (a matter to which I shall turn later).

Finally the financial circles in Spain have also shown an interesting political evolution. They have tended to undergo a process of ever-increasing concentration on their own purposes within the present political situation. But as they became more concerned with their specific interests, they too have moved away from totalitarian political principles. In the early days of the regime the financial world was closely intertwined with the authoritarian state for its own political and economic interests. This aspect still survives in the close link between the *Opus Dei* and the government; a number of Ministers in the government are members of *Opus Dei*, which, although an organization of religious character with political aims is itself a great financial power, with an undue influence on the economic activities of the regime. But, otherwise, in general terms it is fair to say that the development of the Spanish economy makes more and more Spanish business men and industrialists, in close connection with their European and American opposite numbers, draw the conclusion that a more democratic structure of state and society could not but encourage financial progress. In general terms there is in Spain an evolution towards democracy, arising spontaneously from the evolution of Spanish social forces. This social evolution does not coincide at any point with the existing political institutions. This is the fundamental and characteristic contradiction of the present regime in Spain. The political institutions suffer from the extreme rigidity typical of totalitarian forms, and have been outstripped by social evolution. As the country advances on the road of neo-capitalism, so the survival of antiquated political forms becomes more problematic.

We now come to the question of political tendencies or trends. The social-economic evolution of Spanish society has slowly destroyed the totalitarian unity of the regime established after the civil war. This has necessarily led to the birth of new political trends, and to some extent, to the crystallization of new political groupings. But one must distinguish between political trends and political groups in Spain, because, whereas the political or ideological trends are recent and spontaneous orientations, the political groups, at least in name, refer to organizations which existed before the civil war and have continued since under their old names, such as anarcho-syndicalist, communist, socialist, etc. One of the most important problems for Spain today is that these political groups should adjust themselves to the new political trends, and thus be able to express them more adequately. Their disparity is evident in the case of some of the groups studied below.

Christian Democracy for instance is a trend which appeared after the civil war, and which has endeavoured to formulate its policies and create its organization according to new criteria. It expressed the aspirations of part of the hierarchy of the Spanish church, but reflects also the trend of Roman thinking, as well as that of Christian Democracy as an international doctrine. The cultured minority of Spanish catholics has evolved away from its previous rigidity, prejudices and fanaticism, and a more open-minded catholicism is beginning to spread in Spain. (Here it is worth mentioning in passing that the general assumption that most Spaniards are practising catholics is subject to certain reservations. Such an assumption is not borne out by recent sociological studies of a number of parishes. Many catholics do not in fact practise their religion, and a high percentage of the population is either indifferent or anti-clerical. No nation-wide figures are available, but studies of particular localities give some idea of the general trends. In Madrid only 2 per cent of the population, in Barcelona 4 per cent, in the Basque Provinces 24 per cent, according to recent surveys of parishes, carry out their full religious duties regularly.) The growth of religious indifference has contributed to the more modern approach of the Christian Democratic trend. As a trend it bears no relation to the pre-war organization. It has established itself as a clandestine body and of late has been more successful than other groups in setting up its organization and cadres, formulating its views and policies, and establishing high level international contacts. If this trend succeeds in forming itself into a properly organized political group—even if clandestine—with a definite character of its own, it may prove to be the axis around which the other trends of opposition will gravitate. Indeed the fact that it is a catholic trend allows such a group to progress more rapidly, and for the same reason its existence is to a limited extent tolerated by the regime.

Spanish socialism and Spanish communism have also suffered from a certain fragmentation. Inside Spain, where the influence of the British and German models is particularly strong, the new trend is pressing for the modernization of the old ideology and a reconstruction of the pre-civil-war party organizations. There have been profound changes in the social and economic conditions of the working class and socialism also now appeals to large numbers of the middle class. The survival in exile of some of the pre-war groups of the Spanish socialist movement, whose heroism and tenacity are beyond praise, has nevertheless introduced an element of confusion into this situation, since they have on the whole stood aside from the political trends emerging inside Spain. It is of course almost inevitable that the trends arising inside the country cannot be adequately reflected abroad. Yet these exile groups, which represent to some extent the old cadres and mentalities will not fail to contribute their part to the reorganization of the new orientations of Spanish socialism as detectable in the internal political trends.

Communism has the most limited appeal and recruitment basis in Spanish society as a whole. The very name *communism* still carries grim associations in the memory of Spaniards (which the constant propaganda of the regime helps to keep alive). This cannot but reduce the opportunities for a dialogue between a political organization, which because of its past history has to make greater efforts than any other to adjust itself to present day political trends, and contemporary Spanish society. Time will show whether the communist party will be capable of adapting itself in Spain, as it seems to have done in other countries, to new situations and become the political organization of those social elements which could provide its main supporters. As a political trend it is today more successful in some intellectual quarters, where however its impact is somewhat indeterminate, as it leads mostly to abstract debates and to doctrinal arguments. But, though small, it is strongly entrenched and very effective in some sectors of the working class.

There remains the *Opus Dei,* which is very difficult to define, since though it acts in politics, it appears under a religious label. It is, as mentioned before, financially very powerful, and yet it represents no particular social or political forces. The difficulty with *Opus Dei* and other such bodies is that they are not political in the sense that they represent specific political ideas, nor are they real pressure groups, because they are too closely allied with the present regime and the state. They are ephemeral groups which can best be defined as interest groups, born as opportunity arises, in periods of transition and uninstitutionalized political activity.

The University and Its Political Role in Spain

In Spain the university exercises more effective pressure on state and society, than the state and society on the university. As the university has succeeded, both as the main body of the intellectuals and as the principal institution in the cultural life of the country, in shaking off the control and discipline of the state, it has been able to influence society more effectively than any institutions which remained directly under state control. As an institution, the university has shown itself to be the most responsive and sensitive to the trends developing spontaneously in Spanish society, and it has reflected more clearly the estrangement of Spanish society from totalitarianism. The discrepancy between antiquated political structures with a purely formal character, incapable any longer of regulating the life of the country, and the new models and aspirations of the social forces· has found its clearest expression in the university. Its open and explicit function has thus become to point up the difference in rhythm and vitality between the dynamic society on the one hand and the immobility of the state institutions on the other.

How has the Spanish university succeeded in escaping from state control? Why has it been able to assert itself as an institution which can act as a particularly efficient "pressure group" in Spanish society? One of the main reasons is that as a body, the university kept up intellectually with the changes produced by Spanish neo-capitalism— by which I mean the more rapid evolution of the Spanish economy in recent years towards more enlightened social relations and more active industrial investment and modernization. Both the faculty and the student body thus acquired a more modern mentality within archaic institutional forms, and were able to become in turn the initiators of the movement for the reform and reconstruction of Spanish institutions. That the university was able, after the civil war, to develop a greater awareness of the real changes and of the evolution in national and international society was in turn due to two favourable circumstances. The first was that because of its professional rights and its institutional prestige the university was able, unlike other groups and institutions, to maintain an active and close contact with the European and American intellectual worlds, and to acquire, by means of these contacts, and within its archaic forms and structures, a more democratic attitude and outlook. The other was that the university, as a social body, was less suspect to and less persecuted by the jealous regime.

If the university has reacted with more energy than any other institution to the need for Spanish society to adapt itself to the inevitable and obvious economic and social evolution, it is precisely because it is itself a class institution, and that it reflects the views of the upper middle class and the middle class, that is of those who have been able to read, travel, and alter their outlook. For some time this privileged class composition of the university has served as a cover under which it has been able to carry out its political protest. But now, after the recent open conflict with the regime, relations have reached such a point that the university no longer enjoys any special protection.

The university was able to stand out as the leading force for reform in Spanish society, because in its present state, it is the strongest coherent centre of political influence. Moreover it is carrying on the traditional role of the university in the past. The reaction of the university to the conflict between state and society is not something new. It represents on the contrary a traditional process, characteristic of Spanish intellectual life for at least two centuries.

Since the 18th century at least the Spanish university has been the arena of a struggle between two trends: abstract, academic knowledge, on the one hand, and on the other an attempt at a more concrete, pragmatic approach, which endeavoured to relate university study to the realities of the social forces and the evolution of the economic structure. The university has certainly always been guilty of a tendency towards abstract thinking. As a bourgeois institution it has a double experience of liberty. It has known liberty in fact, since as an institution the university always enjoyed a great degree of liberty. And it has proclaimed liberty as an aim, as the desire for perfection in the moral sphere. In the 19th century and well into the 20th, teachers and students have both enjoyed the freedom belonging to members of the ruling class, and have aspired to an abstract, idealistic conception of freedom. Their political protests in the last quarter of the 19th century had a romantic flavour. They projected and demanded an abstract liberty. Above all they were not related (insofar as this is in fact possible) to the active social and economic forces of the country, notably the workers and trade union elements.

But if the university failed at this stage to develop broader bases for its educational activity, private institutions stepped in to fill the gap. The most notable was the Institución Libre de Enseñanza, which, from the end of the 19th century to the outbreak of the civil war, endeavoured to redress the balance against the abstract and unrealistic thinking of the university. Particularly in the period of Giner de los Ríos, the Institución Libre marked a deliberate effort to correct the Spanish university's tendency to concentrate on abstract *Weltanschauungen,* unrelated to specific national economic and social structures. The generation of '98 reinforced the more empirical trend of the Institución and added the lustre of its prestige to the study of the basic features of Spanish social structure, and the university itself in the 20th century began to reflect this approach. It began to show an increasing interest in the study of social realities, and developed a political inclination towards the left. But the civil war unfortunately interrupted the progress of Spanish intellectuals towards a pragmatic approach to social, economic and political studies. It led to a renewed concentration on abstract concepts, in which facts were distorted to fit in with preconceived ideas, at that time copied from German and Italian Fascist philosophy. Youth was thus submerged in a university living under a monistic ideology, and the prospect of a further development of a liberal, scholarly outlook receded into the distance. As organizations, the university, the teaching staff and the students were incorporated in a totalitarian system, which was perfectly summed up in the preambles to some of the laws governing its activities.

But fortunately the very evolution from within the regime of the social forces and economic structures of the country led to a revival of empiricism. The pendulum has indeed swung so far as to lead the new generations to undervalue the ideas of their forerunners, and to place too much emphasis on a somewhat sterile technicism. Oddly enough, the state itself contributed to this process. Once it had lost its ideological Falangist umbrella, it had to reach a compromise with facts in a pragmatic way. Around 1957, when the financial stabilization plan was launched, and Spain for all intents and purposes entered on the path I described as neo-capitalism, greater stress was laid by the state on the empirical approach, and this was reflected in the vastly increased number of students in theoretical and applied sciences, and in the spate of critical works which appeared on the subject of the past metaphysical tradition and aesthetic value judgments.

The students too started to adopt new ways of life and sought new outlets, often copied from American and European student life which was more in contact with the real world than that of Spanish students. The idea of "working one's way through college" or of travelling "rough" to see the world has caught on. This new conception of life coincided with the introduction in the intellectual realm of the philosophic trends of neo-positivism, existentialism and other similar trends of thought. It also coincided with the introduction of programmes of study which were in open contradiction with the programmes inspired by the totalitarian ideology of the early post-civil war years. Technological progress has gone hand in hand with this new utilitarianism, and has led the new generation to a greater awareness of the needs and conditions of Spanish life. This post-war generation has thus been liberated from the standards and values of the previous generation—the generation which had made the civil war.

By now the swing towards concrete achievements and pragmatic thinking is reflected in the studies pursued in Spain. In the field of science, physics and mathematics are applied to the concrete world through practical science and technology. The state itself, in its effort to train people in the professions and careers needed for the economic development of the country, has furthered the study of economic and social sciences by creating new faculties in Political, Economic and Social Sciences in Madrid and a number of provincial universities. The proliferation of the social studies, which are encouraged also by some private institutes, has led in Spain to an increasing interest in sociology. Sociology is by now replacing philosophy and metaphysics as a first choice for students, and the great expansion in sociological and economic studies has strengthened the positivist trend of thought among students. Another side effect of this concentration on economics and sociology has been to alter the location of the various centres of unrest and ferment in the faculties of the university. Traditionally the Faculty of Law and the Faculty of Medicine were the mainsprings of student protest movements, partly because they were the most numerous, and partly because students in these faculties tended to come from the upper income groups in the bourgeoisie, precisely that class which benefited most from the freedom they demanded. But since the civil war, and particularly since 1957 (although no definitive surveys have been made on this subject) the situation has changed. The centre of political unrest and non-conformity is to be found in the faculties of Political and Economic Sciences, to some extent in the faculties of Philosophy and Letters, and even, and somewhat surprisingly, in the faculties of Sciences. In Madrid, for instance, the Faculty of Science turned out to be one of the most forward in its participation in protest activities. This can again be explained by the increasingly pragmatic approach, which links student protest much more closely with the actual demands of the situation.

The Students' Protest

It is generally assumed by the well-informed that for instance in Madrid, where the student population numbers some 27,000, only some 10 per cent are actively involved in protest movements and are very irregularly distributed in the various faculties. The more general, undifferentiated form of protest may mobilize up to 75 per cent of the student population. In Barcelona, where the Catalan issue has to be taken into account, the number actively involved is perhaps double that in Madrid.

If we try to break the protest movement down and seek its original motives, several questions arise. Is the protest aimed primarily at the fact that the social process and the political institutions are out of step? Is the protest aimed specifically at bad economic organization in the country? Is it directed at lack of opportunities for employment of the students themselves? Does it imply an underlying influence of the evolution of the trade unions and the working class in general, reflected in some way in the university world? Or it is simply a protest against existing political forms?

We can distinguish more active and more passive centres of unrest in the universities throughout the country. The most active are linked to the largest urban concentrations, namely Madrid and Barcelona; the more passive are to be found in country towns, where there are fewer students, or where the faculty, owing to local structural peculiarities, exercises a closer control. If we examine the protest movement as a whole, we can detect two levels of protest, both among staff and students. The first reflects the attitude of those who show concern for the social and political problems of the country above all. At the second level, the protest is based more generally and somewhat vaguely on the concepts of democracy and liberty. This second group is more influenced perhaps by the observation, through reading, travel, films and plays, that the principles of life in other countries and cultures are different from those which the present regime defends as universally valid. There are thus generic, unspecific protests and more specific, identifiable protests. The latter are what will concern us here.

In the non-political sphere, student protest activity is directed primarily at the economic situation in general, and the problem of their own future employment. They are only too aware of the inadequacy of the technical equipment in their universities, and of their general poverty in comparison with European and American universities. They also feel the lack of well-prepared and enthusiastic teachers. Furthermore, they are dissatisfied with their own future prospects and this leads them in turn to adopt a critical view of their country, which seems to them out of step with the rest of Europe. This kind of protest is therefore founded on social grounds insofar as it demands a better organization both of the university and of the student community, and on both social and moral grounds insofar as the poor administration of the university is projected on to a wider national context.

But even this more undifferentiated protest movement, with its moral, social and professional overtones, has of late been evolving towards more concrete political formulations. At first organized political groups exercised but little influence on student protest movements; but this influence has been growing as a result of the indiscriminate repressions of the authorities. The situation is thus now more propitious for the deliberate activities of political groups and organizations. The distinction made previously between political groups and political trends applies in this context also to the university. Political groups as such have emerged as organizations in the universities during the events of 1965, and they correspond by and large to two fairly clear political trends. The FUDE (Federación Universitaria de Estudiantes) represents the left wing, inspired mainly by a socialist trend. CUDE (Confederación Universitaria de Estudiantes) is related more closely to the Christian Democrat trend. Neither of these groups in fact controls the university's protest activities; indeed both may well be fairly ephemeral organizations which in time will either be replaced by others or will reform into a wider front. (Similar groups under different names exist in the regions, notably Catalonia.)

The political character of the students' protest is in fact of very recent origin. Even the events of winter 1965, briefly recapitulated in the introduction to this study, which culminated in the expulsion of three professors from their chairs, the suspension of two, and the expulsion of many students, was in its origins primarily of a moral and social character, with little if any political content of a concrete nature. This is confirmed by the fact that the initial protest of 1965 took place within the framework of the official students' union, SEU, and was protected, encouraged and echoed, up to a point, by the very leadership of the SEU.*

What remains to be seen is the extent to which the political content of the students' protest will grow, or whether it will remain at the moral-social level. Will the protest lose its political overtones if the students are given a certain freedom and better prospects for employment? This question is very difficult to answer since there are certain imponderables at work. One of these imponderables is the continuing influence of political literature on the students. There is a growing interest, even among students in the scientific faculties, in political literature of a somewhat extremist character and a notice-

---

* Membership in the SEU (Sindicato Español Universitario) is compulsory for all students. It is a union organized on the "vertical" principle, typical of the Spanish state, and its leaders must be members of the Falange party. The union organizes student life in the material and cultural spheres and is in charge of such matters as scholarships and grants, discussions regarding lecture notes with the staff, library facilities, publications by the students, film and cultural clubs, sports and canteens.

able increase of discussions among students of such political-social philosophies as Marxism, Leninism, Maoism, etc. This may well lead to a considerable politicization towards the left, aiming at a complete transformation of Spanish society. A second imponderable is the influence of the part played by women students in the protest movement. In the earlier stages of the movement women students were perhaps more concerned with the moral issues, but they too are now feeling their way towards political demands. Their participation has strengthened the zeal of the students in general, and in itself it reflects in part the evolution of Spanish society. Once again the university has responded more speedily to a social change, this time the change in the position of women, though in itself the university may not provide the best framework, nor is such a response in the best interests of the university itself or of the students' protest. The real integration of women in Spanish political life should be achieved by constitutional and social reforms.

Another imponderable is the extent of the contact between the students' protest and working-class protest, or the influence of the proletariat on the university. For the moment the evidence suggests that it is slight, because the university protest movement was initially and is still basically social and professional, directed at achieving the freedom to organize student life. But if and when the university protest movement overflows these banks and acquires an overtly political character, it will inevitably link up with the working-class protest movement. So far there is evidence of a certain mutual sympathy and even occasionally mutual assistance, between the politically conscious students and the workers, though the workers look upon the students as members of a privileged class. (The percentage of students who are the children of manual-workers is about 1%).

But the main bridge between the students' movement and the working-class movement can be found in the nature of their demands. Both are asking for free unions. The "vertical union", as established after the civil war is, in the eyes of the greater part of the intellectuals and the workers, a serious obstacle to the normal evolution of Spanish society. The students have specifically asked for the freedom to organize their own independent union and the government decree of 5 June 1965, intended as a measure of conciliation, in fact amounted to a rejection of these demands since nothing was solved in a decisive way. Nevertheless, in spite of the decree, a curious situation has arisen by which an unofficial "free" union has come into existence *de facto,* side by side with the official union. It may indeed eventually end by being recognized *de jure.* Thus, in spite of government restrictions and reprisals, the movement in favour of free unionism is developing. A free students union exists and is making progress in Barcelona, cutting the ground from under the SEU, and also in Madrid. It seems senseless to remain in this *de facto* position. What is the point of a legal situation to which no one pays any attention and a *de facto* situation which is actually in control of events? At present the government can of course always find legal arguments to justify its repressive measures. But common sense demands that law and reality should be brought together to put an end to the tension created by the divorce between legality, as represented by the law of the state, and actual practice, or the legality recognized by society.

The Teachers and the Protest Movement

To understand the role and attitude of the teachers in the political movement of the students one must remember that scholars and intellectuals as such have their own grievances against the present Spanish social and political system. A Spanish professor does not enjoy academic freedom, and lives in a narrow social framework. There are restrictions on intellectual liberty, social liberty and political liberty, and disciplinary restrictions within academic life. These have combined to turn the average faculty member into a cultured but un-enthusiastic teacher. What is more he is badly paid and usually has to seek outside work as well. (Recently steps have been taken to raise salaries, precisely in order to disarm the teaching staff and to provide some stimulus for intellectual life.) But generally speaking the lack of intellectual interest and the soporific atmosphere of Spanish culture within the limits imposed by the state have tended to transform the teachers into a discontented group living a marginal life in the university. (It may be noted that teachers do not belong to any union. Some belong to the Falange party, but the only condition imposed on teachers is that they should be catholics and that they should be in general agreement with the so called Fundamental Principles of the Falange National Movement.)

Most of the teachers have on the whole stood aside from the students' protest movement; but they have shown a certain tacit sympathy with the causes of the students' discontent. And the fact that professors in almost all faculties throughout Spain have sent letters remonstrating with the government over the suspension of their five colleagues shows a degree of sympathy with the latter as well. (Two cases only have occurred of full backing for the five suspended professors: Professor José María Valverde of Barcelona University, and Professor Federico Gaeta of Zaragoza University, at present in the University of Buffalo, N.Y., both resigned from their chairs.) But this sympathy does not amount to sharing their ideas. It simply expresses the general understanding of most university teachers of the urgent necessity of adjusting the political institutions of the country to its social evolution; and their feeling that the university can scarcely continue to be both the victim and the protagonist in this struggle simply because existing political institutions do not allow it to become the normal expression of this social advance. The teachers are concerned in more than one way to solve the contradiction between the rigid political institutions and the process of social evolution; they suffer from this contradiction not only in their professional lives but in their private lives as well.

One has to remember that since university teachers have to combine their teaching duties with other means of earning their living, their own protest is likely to be somewhat half-hearted. Moreover many of them suffer from mental fear, or from the weakness of submitting to power, a feature characteristic of intellectuals. The teaching staff are not restricted by belonging to a "vertical" syndicate, and though in theory there is some degree of ideological control, in practice it is very weak. Pressure is brought to bear on them not so much by the state as by the social structure itself, and above all by economic factors—by their dependence on outside economic openings to supplement their university emoluments. This increases their dependence on the state as employer.

The relationship between the state and the teaching staff was illustrated by the reprisals against the five professors which were announced in August 1965. (The author of the present article, as one of the professors taking part in the protest movement who has been subjected to reprisals, may of course be lacking in independence of judgment and objectivity in this matter.) Since the events of February–March 1965 were, in the view of most observers, quite spontaneous and not subjected to any specific political leadership, and since most of the professors who intervened did so without any specific political objectives or party attachments, one may well ask what was the point of so drastic a punishment? Under what law were they disciplined and to what extent has such repression forwarded the inevitable process of democratization of Spanish society ?

The law which was invoked in order to discipline the five professors had been passed in 1954. It provided for sanctions of the kind which were in fact imposed, but with reference to a legal offence, not a political situation. This raises the question: was the government's estimate of the political importance of these events a realistic one, or did it swell the political consequences out of all proportion to the actual events?

Conclusion and Perspectives

If we take the events of winter 1965 at their face value, then clearly the reprisals were out of all proportion, since the protest lacked active political content. But if one considers the protest movement in the social context of the Spanish authoritarian state, then evidently such a protest must have serious political repercussions. Liberty is indivisible, and to demand, or obtain freedom for one sector of society is bound to have an impact in other, unfree sectors. Hence the government's reaction, though exaggerated in terms of what actually happened, shows an awareness of the real significance of the students' protest. For what the students' protest amounted to (and in this they have been supported by the attitude of the teachers) was nothing less than a demand for the complete transformation of the union structure throughout the country, which is in turn part of the present system itself. Thus the government was not just punishing a mere breach of public order; it acted as it did because the totalitarian structure of the regime itself had been challenged. Nevertheless the demand that the university should be a free institution, not subject to interference by the executive; that the "vertical" syndicate should be transformed into a free students' association, and that the teaching staff should be freed from their present restrictions, will have in time to be accepted. Such a move would mark the beginning of the institutionalization of democratic processes in Spain, which are at present developing in a spontaneous manner, without being channelled in any way, and which may therefore become unmanageable. In any case the present neo-capitalist economic development in Spain requires to be accompanied by a process of democratization.

What of the future? Facts seem to bear out that the students' protest movement will continue. Incidents are constantly recurring, government repressions are failing to keep the movement within bounds; the disaffection of the teaching staff is increasing, and the appearance of similar protest movements in other sectors of national life justifies and supports the action of the students and the university. A clear parallel arises with the action of the syndicates. Led by the metal-workers, there is a struggle to secure some degree of trade union freedom. And such freedom seems in a certain measure to be tolerated by the authorities, and the struggle may end in some form of legalization of these emerging groups. Indeed it seems that the working-class struggle for union freedom is viewed with less apprehension by the government than they show for the movement in favour of liberty of the students and the intelligentsia. How can this be explained? There appears to be a concerted attitude behind this policy—an attitude based on a theory held seemingly by the Spanish government, and which finds an echo even in some international working-class organizations. The theory runs as follows: working-class liberties do not affect the political situation, indeed up to a point they are necessary for the process of economic and social mobilization. But intellectual freedom can be dangerous; it can lead to ideological tensions, to an attack on the political structure, possibly to a revolutionary situation. As a corollary, the argument goes on: if the standard of living of the workers and of the middle class is raised to the point of producing a pleasant, if somewhat vegetative life, and if the working class is granted some degree of participation in the profits and in the management of business, the intellectuals will have to submit to this new order of things, and their theories and ideas will dwindle into mere academic word spinning. Thus the danger that intellectual ferment might jeopardize the political structure will be avoided, and a working class devoid of ideology would act in such a system as a barrier between the intellectuals and real life, isolating them in a dream world. Government would be a government of technicians, and this would facilitate the preservation of the authoritative structure of power. It is a policy aimed at preventing political evolution by encouraging social *embourgeoisement*.

But if this is indeed the policy planned and pursued at present, then it is ill-conceived. The fostering of the social aims of the working class is bound to have repercussions on an archaic and useless political structure. The intellectuals will always have a decisive part to play, since they give birth to the ideas which may change the world—sometimes change it by violence. It is a fundamental error to believe that intellectuals can be confined to a private academic world. Above all in Spain is such an approach out of place. The tensions between the classes are particularly strong there, and they will not disappear at once as a result of a rise in the standard of living. The workers will demand admission to the universities and to the life of the mind. The state will have to have a cultural policy as well as one concerned with material needs. If there is too big a gap between the intellectual life of the country and the workers a dangerous lack of equilibrium results. Authoritarian regimes have often fallen into the error of assuming that ideas can be controlled by concentrating attention exclusively on questions of material welfare. In itself a perversion of the ideas of the Enlightenment, this can lead to a pre-revolutionary situation. The improvement in material standards of the working class and Spanish society as a whole will make sense only if harmony is achieved by intellectual freedom. Otherwise the rising standard of living will simply become the taking-off ground for protest movements of a far more radical and ideological character, and more dangerously utopian.

The policy put forward by the university demands enough liberty for the intellectuals to enable them to integrate with the neo-capitalist development in such a way as to avoid tensions and to prevent a rupture between the two basic elements in society. If the alternative way is followed, it may well produce a situation similar to pre-1917 Russia: the beginnings of state-protected and state-fostered industrialization, and the extreme radicalization of the intellectuals as a result of the limitations on intellectual freedom.

III

The
Activist Tradition
in
Eastern Europe

Taken from a larger work based on the thesis that educational
policy expresses the character of the government, this selection
shows how Tsarist repression turned students into revolutionaries.
Note the government's use of violence, spies and detectives in
classrooms, and other devices to keep professors and students
under control.

8

Students and Politics in Russia

Nicholas Hans

During this period [1897–1904] student strikes continued to occur
regularly. Hardly a year passed without some "students episode."
The more serious disturbances happened in 1894, 1896, 1899, 1901,
1902 and 1904. Strikes ceased to be sporadic and accidental, they
developed into an organized political movement, which united all
Universities and other Higher Institutions. In every University secret Committees were formed which led the movement. It was a
custom among Russian students to form societies of natives of the
same provinces or cities (*Zemlyachestva*). They resembled to a certain extent the "nations" of the medieval Universities. The most
influential and the best organized unions in the southern universities
were the following four "nations": a) Ukrainians, b) Poles, c)
Georgians, and d) Armenians. These societies were prohibited by
law, but all the efforts of the Government could not annihilate
them. At the beginning they had no political aspirations and were
founded solely with the purpose of mutual aid and friendly intercourse. But the restrictions and persecution turned their opposition
into political channels and compelled them to organize resistance.
Every society elected one representative to a "Coalition Committee,"
which received dictatorial powers and could declare a strike without
a previous vote among students. The Coalition Committees of all
Universities were connected among themselves and could declare a

From Nicholas A. Hans, *History of Russian Educational Policy, 1701–1917*
[1931] (New York: Russell & Russell, 1964), pp. 167–175, 202–204. Reprinted by permission.

"universal strike" throughout Russia. The students followed their own leaders with astonishing loyalty. Such strikes occurred in 1899, 1901, 1902, and 1904, when all the Universities were involved resulting in the expulsion of thousands of students.

It is difficult to estimate the exact number of expelled students in consequence of these strikes during this period, but the total is quite near 10,000. The Moscow Commission of 1901 gives the following figures for Moscow University.

I. expelled by the University authorities.

II. expelled in consequence of arrest and banishment by the police.

	I	II
In April 1881	203.	
In November 1887	57	36.
In March 1890	454	111.
In April 1891	14	16.
In Nov. & Dec. 1894	3	49.
In November 1896	26	91.
In Feb. & March 1899	840	199.
	1,394	502 = 2,099

In Kiev during the nineties not less than 1,700 students were expelled. Petersburg University suffered the following losses: April 1881—13; March 1887—197 (five were executed); December 1887—74; March 1890—22. Kazan University in 1887—90. These data are incomplete, but give an idea of the number of ruined careers. Every expelled student was a potential member of the revolutionary organizations. In this way the Government continuously filled the ranks, depleted by banishment and executions. In March 1899 occurred a universal strike in all Universities which lasted the whole spring. The disturbances began in Petersburg, where three consecutive students Committees were arrested and expelled, in all 43 students. The students of Moscow University followed, and this led to banishment of 222 of them by the police. Kiev, Odessa, Kharkov, Kazan, Tomsk, Riga, Dorpat, Warsaw, and Novo-Alexandria joined the movement. The Government then ordered that all the Universities and other Higher Institutions should be closed and all the students expelled *en masse*. Although the majority of them were taken back during that year, about 3 to 4 thousand students remained unpardoned and were not allowed to live in the university towns. This explains why the figures for 1899 show 1,359 students less than in 1898 in spite of several thousands of new students. Moscow alone lost 1,089 students, and of the fourth year students of Kiev University not less than 244 were expelled without receiving degrees.

The dimensions of the disturbances of 1899 caused the Government to appoint a Commission of Inquiry under General Vannovsky, which published its report on 25 May 1899. Vannovsky indicated the abnormal conditions of the life of a Russian student. The Minister of Public Instruction, Bogolepov, who succeeded Delyanov after his death in February 1898, appointed another Commission, which modified the Rules for the inspection of students on 27 June 1899. The number of subinspectors was increased and the members of the Inspection were instructed to help students in their requirements. The former freedom of choosing the place of study was restricted and a young man was only able to enter the University of his native Educational Region. The conditions of student life and the constant lack of means, in the opinion of Bogolepov, were the chief causes of discontent. Therefore he advised the Emperor to establish hostels for poor students where they could live very cheaply and at the same time could be well supervised. For this purpose the Government assigned 3,262,000 Rubles, but this measure was unsuccessful. Simultaneously repressive measures were introduced. The prohibition of students societies was again emphasized, and on 29 July 1899 the Emperor issued a decree, by which all expelled students were enlisted in the army as private soldiers. They were deprived of all the privileges which usually were enjoyed by students and had to serve on the same conditions as illiterate peasants. Every army detachment (company or squadron) could receive only one expelled student, in order to separate them.

In June 1900 a secret congress of student delegates from all Universities took place in Odessa at which it was decided to continue the struggle. All the delegates were arrested, but the organization was not broken up. On 7 December 1900 in Kiev University a meeting of 700 students took place which was rather unruly. The Rector sentenced the two leaders to four days of solitary confinement in the University. Both students declined to obey, in consequence of which they were expelled from the University the same day. On the following day hundreds of students forced their way into the University Hall and demanded the reversal of the sentence. This the Rector declined, upon which the students resolved to remain in the Hall until it was done. The University was surrounded by police and army detachments, and all the students present were arrested. A Special Commission was appointed by the Government to try the offenders. The Commission announced the following sentence on 31 December 1900: the two students were condemned to three years of military service, five others to two years, and the remaining 385 to one year. Bogolepov confirmed the sentence for 183 students and reprimanded the remaining 202, declaring that the next offence would bring the punishment inflicted on the others. This unduly severe measure led to serious consequences and new outbreaks. On 14 February 1901 Bogolepov was assassinated by Karpovich, and this was followed by disturbances in all the Universities.

The Council of Moscow University, acting on its own initiative appointed a Commission to inquire into the causes of the student disturbances. Among its members were such well-known professors as Vinogradov, Guerrier, and Klyuchevsky. The sole fact of the forming of this Commission on 28 February 1901 stopped the disturbances in Moscow University. The professors performed their task very conscientiously and published a report. The conclusions at which they arrived unanimously were the following: 1) The chief cause of the student disturbances was the natural desire for friendly intercourse in student societies, which is strictly forbidden. 2) The repressive policy had only strengthened these illegal organizations and increased discontent. 3) It was necessary to permit students to form societies authorized by special Statutes. 4) The Inspectors to be restricted in their powers. 5) A special University Court, elected by the professors, should be established to deal with students. 6) Self-government should be restored to the Universities in order to make all the previous measures effective.

The new Minister of Public Instruction General P. S. Vannovsky, appointed on 27 March, decided to act in this direction. On 29 April 1901 he sent 18 questions to all Universities, in which he covered all the details of the University life. Self-government, methods of instruction, system of remuneration, student organizations, the Inspection and other important questions were included. During the autumn of 1901 the answers of the Universities were gradually received. They unanimously declared in favour of the restoration of self-government and for the legalization of student unions. On 22 December 1901 Vannovsky issued new Rules concerning the students organizations. The students received the right of establishing dining clubs, libraries, and societies for mutual aid under the supervision of the university authorities. Students of every faculty and of every "year" were allowed to elect their "elders" whose duty it would be to divide the State and private subsidies among the poorest comrades, to arrange details with the professors as to examinations and deal with similar questions. Even student meetings were permitted under the supervision of the university authorities.

But all these concessions did not satisfy the students, because their traditional societies *zemlyachestva* remained forbidden. The other grievance was the great number of expelled and banished comrades, who could not continue their education. In November 1901 all students of the first year in Kharkov Veterinary Institute and 52 students of Kharkov University were expelled. In February 1902 about 400 students of Moscow University were expelled and banished. The Rules of 22 December were not applied and were modified afterwards by Sänger on 24 August 1904, the rights of the students being curtailed to a great extent. The banishments were carried out without trial by the Ministry of Interior Affairs. A student, Balashov, assassinated the Minister of Interior Affairs Sipyagin and was executed. A new universal strike therefore broke out in the spring of 1902, which led to the banishment to Siberia of 115 Moscow and Petersburg students. This banishment of young men and women to the remotest regions of Russia without any trial or even legal inquiry produced a very unfavourable impression in Russia and abroad. The new Minister of Interior Affairs, von Plehve, wished by this severe measure to stamp out the revolutionary spirit among the students. But even Plehve was abliged to retrace his steps and to repeal his own act.

He sent his Chief of Gendarmes, Prince Svyatopolk-Mirsky, to Siberia to negotiate with banished students and to persuade them to return home and to abstain from taking part in strikes in future. Fifty-six of the students sent telegrams declining even to see Prince Mirsky; the rest consented to meet him, but declined to promise anything for the future. Prince Mirsky returned with empty hands and Plehve advised the Emperor to "pardon" the banished students unconditionally but to forbid them to live in any University town.

At that time Vannovsky was replaced already by Sänger, who was appointed to the post on 10 June 1902. One of the first steps of the new Minister was the formation of a Commission for the elaboration of a new University Statute. The decree was issued on 18 May 1902; the Commission assembled on 30 September and continued its labours up to 18 December. It consisted of elected representatives of all Universities and other Higher Institutions with some officials from the Ministry. By a majority of 34 to 5 the Commission decided in favour of the restoration of self-government. The Government then submitted the following alternatives to the Commission: they were asked either to choose the abolition of the powers of the Curator over the University with the retention of an appointed Rector, or an elected Rector with the retention of the supervision of the Curator. Neither of these combinations was equivalent to self-government, but the professors preferred the lesser evil and voted in favour of the second proposal. The new Statute, however, was not put into practice, because Sänger was obliged to retire in 1904 and give place to General Glazov. This change of Ministers again meant a change of policy. The new tendency was very reactionary and the Government intended to transfer all elementary schools to the Holy Synod and to restore a strict class policy with regard to secondary schools. The time for such measures, however, was inopportune, as the complications in the Far East ended in that year in the Russo-Japanese War. The attention of the Government was diverted into another direction and the university question remained unsolved. . . .

On 11 January 1911 Casso issued another Circular abolishing the Rules of 11 July 1907 concerning student societies and forbade students meetings. On 17 January a meeting was held in Tomsk Technological Institute which led to the arrest and banishment of 375 students. Another mass meeting took place on 31 January in St-Petersburg University, in consequence of which 392 students were arrested and banished. On 3 February a fresh Circular ordered the Universities not to delay in informing the military authorities of all expulsions of students in order that they might be taken into military service. "This is especially necessary," says the Circular, "because of the great number of expelled students." On 15 February Casso himself expelled 75 students of Moscow, 14 of Kharkov, 66 of Odessa and 28 of Kiev. On 17 February he expelled 370 from Moscow University, 98 from Warsaw and 28 from Dorpat. The Rector of Moscow University A. Manuilov and the Prorectors Mensbir and Minakov tendered their resignations of these offices in protest. Casso retaliated by dismissing them altogether from the University, depriving them of their Chairs. This illegal and provocative act was followed by the voluntary resignation of 21 Moscow professors and about 80 lecturers. Several professors were discharged from other Universities. Meanwhile the strike continued with much violence. On 21 February Casso introduced a system of espionage into the Universities and the lecture rooms were filled by detectives in students' uniforms. Armed supporters of the Government, with detectives and police, attended the lectures of reluctant professors, who were afraid to lose their only means of subsistence. The opposition party took recourse to chemical obstruction with poison gases. The lecture rooms were made unworkable for days. Fresh groups of students were arrested and banished. The total number of expelled students amounted to 6,000. This was a wholesale "cassation" of the Universities. On 21 March Casso issued a new Circular, ordering the expulsion of all students, who had been more than 13 semesters at the Universities, notwithstanding the fact that during the 4 semesters of 1904–05 the Universities were closed. All these measures considerably diminished the number of students. Many Chairs remained empty. But Casso was not satisfied. The students of the Medical Institute for Women in Petersburg, in order to avoid persecution, left Petersburg and went home to provincial towns. Casso illegally declared a new semester during the summer and as the students did not return, he expelled all the 1,360 students, with the exception of 28, who happened to be in Petersburg. The State Duma tried to bring the Government to its senses, but to no effect.

Only when the Prime Minister P. A. Stolypin was assassinated on
1 September 1911, did the Government adopt a more moderate
course. The majority of the expelled students were again admitted
into the Universities and a relative calm ensued. Casso, however,
remained Minister of Public Instruction till his death in 1914. The
Great War averted attention from the Universities and no more disturbances occurred. The last demonstrations took place in 1913 and
1914 in connection with the alteration of the Statute of the Military
Medical Academy and with the shooting of workmen in the Lena
gold fields.

The new Minister Count P. N. Ignatiev tried to reconcile public
opinion and introduced liberal measures. From the start he devoted
his energy to the revision of the University Statutes and the abolition
of many restrictions imposed by Casso. Owing to the latter repressive
policy the number of students decreased considerably and many
Chairs were empty. In July 1915 Count Ignatiev granted to the students of Church seminaries the right of admission to the Universities.
On 17 August women were again allowed to enter State Universities.
In September the pupils of Commercial, Real and other secondary
schools, whose programme differed from that of the Gymnasia, were
also granted the same right. The Jewish quota was enlarged and all
Jews in some way connected with the War activities were admitted
in excess of the legal percentage. The Petersburg University alone
admitted 600 Jews in 1915 in accordance with this decree. The pupils
of the Polish private schools and pupils of Slavonic origin from
Austria-Hungary were allowed to enter Russian Universities after
an examination in Russian. All these measures greatly increased the
number of freshmen in spite of the War and mobilization of young
people.

9

This selection deals with one incident, the student riots in Warsaw in 1957, but its historical significance goes far beyond this episode. The author advances the hypothesis that social-class tension has always been an important element in town-and-gown antagonism, and that it contributed to what was basically a political disturbance between students and police. This hypothesis appears to hold true even in the theoretically classless society of a communist state.

Social Cleavage: Warsaw

George Z. F. Bereday

Social class is an important source of student antagonism and one of its expressions is the pattern of hostilities based on interuniversity prestige. The celebrated relationship between the English Oxbridge and Redbrick universities has been dramatized. . . . The difference in prestige between the University of Tokyo and other Japanese universities is also well known and colors the style of student demonstrations by the Zengakuren. In the U.S., the rivalries around the Harvard-Yale or Army-Navy football games are only a faint reflection of more deep-seated divisions. In 1965, for instance, the Harvard Chapter of the Students for a Democratic Society (SDS) did not vote in favor of civil disobedience while the Berkeley and Michigan groups did. In reverse, Irish-Catholic boys from Boston College resent, even hate, Harvard, but their favorite week-end hangout is the Oxford Grill in Harvard Square; Harvard students stay away from the Grill preferring Jim Cronin's, a little off the Square.

We quote the Warsaw riots in 1957 following the suspension of the magazine *Po Prostu* as illustration of such cleavages. Poland, for centuries a society of virtual castes, emerged into modernity as a strongly class-conscious country. The richest *szlachta*, the land-owning gentry, was not entirely dispossessed until the Communist takeover. Poorer gentry in alliance with the rising professionals from

From George Z. F. Bereday, "Student Unrest on Four Continents: Montreal, Ibadan, Warsaw, and Rangoon," in Seymour Martin Lipset, ed., *Student Politics* (New York: Basic Books, Inc., 1967), pp. 108–113. © 1967 by Basic Books, Inc. Reprinted by permission.

other classes quickly became an alloy, a bourgeois intelligentsia to use the appellation of Poland's present sociologists. This socio-intellectual class administered Poland between the wars. It attempted to meet but on the whole it postponed the growth of the aspirations of the expanding working class and of the enormous landed peasantry. The Communist takeover has changed things, but not entirely. Poland remains past rather than future oriented, hence old buildings are lovingly reconstructed, museums assiduously visited, heraldry and knowledge of the lines of descent and blood relationships discreetly but persistently maintained. The intelligentsia of Poland continue to evince an almost built-in dislike of manual labor, in spite of the fact that it is being revolutionized by the accession of the able sons of workers and peasants. Marxist philosophy *à la polonaise,* in contrast to the Russian, encourages a lively and sociologically scientific interest in social classes and class behavior. Things are being talked about freely and *eo ipso* consciousness of class exists and persists.

In education, the major weapon of equalization, the social class situation reflects itself, by prewar standards, somewhat strangely. Emphasis is, as in all Communist countries, on social rise and equal opportunity for the underprivileged classes. But Poland is one of the first countries in the world to be also affected by a reverse phenomenon: a refusal by many sons of peasants and workers to take advantage of that opportunity. Education is still influenced by the traditions of the old intelligentsia and academic standards remain conservative and exacting. An unusually large proportion of the almost forcibly impressed sons of workers and peasants become thus discouraged and quit long before graduation.

Within the world of the educated a re-evaluation of the distinction between scientists and humanists is taking place in favor of the former. The Soviet vogue for science was passed on to Poland, further reinforcing an older tradition. In most prewar European countries there was a recognizable prestige distinction between humanists trained as civil servants, publicists and literati, and those in sciences and technical skills who ranked somewhat below. By contrast, in Poland, similar to Germany, there was always less social distinction between the humanists and the technologists. The tradition of the *Politechnische Hochschule* meant that technological occupations enjoyed equivalent, if not equal, prestige. Under Communist tutelage the prestige of the scientists has tended to soar even further. This has forced the humanists to adopt techniques and defenses characteristic of the underprivileged groups.

Given these atypical features, the "usual" class structure in Polish society and education cannot be denied. The basis of it is ascription rather than achievement. What matters is not so much what a person does or even what his income is, but indirectly his blood line and circumstance of birth and directly his life style as a cultivated even more than as an educated man. Set in this way the field of higher education is ripe for a strong operation of intellectual snobberies. Feelings of inferiority and superiority persist in spite of the communization of the country. It is the contention of this discussion that social class tensions, especially illustrated by the relation between the two leading higher education institutions in Warsaw, were present on the occasion of the October 1957 riot, which followed upon the suspension of the magazine *Po Prostu*.

The basic theme of the riots was, of course, political. After the October unrest of 1956 Poland became the scene of a bid for power by two groups of Communist leaders. One, known as the Natolin group, advocated the modernization of Polish Communism, de-Stalinization and greater accommodation to the historical heritage of Polish freedom. The other group, supported by old-line Stalinists and later known as "Pulawianie," attempted to maintain Poland on more conservative Communist lines. The key person in this struggle was, of course, Gomulka, who was brought into power thanks to the pressure of the Natolin group, but who within a year found himself forced to make more and more concessions to the "Pulawianie." The weekly magazine, *Po Prostu*, an organ of youth and university students, was one of the main weapons in the hands of Natolin. On its pages a young and idealistic editorial committee over and over again expressed its concern for what they regarded as an uncontaminated liberal construction of the Communist experiment. As time went on their voice became steadily more critical and in the first days of October, a year after the Polish October Revolution, *Po Prostu* was suspended, causing a four-day outbreak of major youth riots.

The details of the riots are fairly well known. On October 3 the rumor of the suspension of the magazine caused a group of students from Warsaw Polytechnic, numbering about two thousand, to assemble for a protest meeting in Warsaw's Narutowicz Square, outside the largest student hostel in the city. Before any speeches were made the students were charged by police armed with sticks and tear gas. For the space of some three hours, the police battled the students. Some bystanders coming out of the nearby church service also became involved, causing an even greater public outcry against police action and forcing the Commissioner of Police, a few days later, to issue a public apology. Late in the evening the government requested directors of all the institutions of higher education in Warsaw to issue a communiqué warning the students "against too hasty efforts" and bidding them to refrain from illegal action.

A new rally was scheduled for the next evening, October 4, in the Central Courtyard of the Warsaw Polytechnic, the same place where the protest meetings in 1956 had been held. Four thousand students appeared and were addressed by a member of Parliament, who was elected not as a Communist, but as an Independent. An attempt was made by the speaker to pacify the students by declaring that the suspension of *Po Prostu* was only temporary. Following the address a resolution was drawn up requesting the government to order the continuation of the magazine. The leader of the meeting, having conferred with officers of the police massed outside, assured the students of safe conduct upon leaving. When the students streamed out of the building, however, new outbreaks and police violence occurred and again lasted for several hours. About twenty students were injured and thirty student leaders were arrested. All but eight were released the next morning.

On that morning, October 5, *Trybuna Ludu* (People's Forum), the official organ of the United Workers' party, published its decision to close *Po Prostu*. The statement indicated

> that its editorial team, including party members working on it, for many months acted counter to the resolutions undertaken by the Central Party organ and thus sank to the level of barren negation, representing falsely the political and economic reality of the coun-

try, disseminating lack of faith in the feasibility of building Socialism, and in many cases advocating bourgeois concepts.

The events of the previous two days were later described as defensive
action of the police being forced to tackle some "adventuresome students who yelled anti-government slogans."

On that day and on the following day, October 6, the riots broad-
ened to include working class youths and others described as "hooli-
gans and dregs of society." A motorized police column was attacked
during the afternoon of October 6 in the center of town. The attack
was fought off, reputedly, by three battalions of police. In other parts
of town, militia cars were attacked and stones were thrown at cars
and at house windows. A sign "Freedom of Word" was placed on the
student hostel building where the earliest disturbances occurred, but
was later taken down. Earlier that same day, a three-member student
delegation called on Prime Minister Gomulka to present its petition.
That student delegation was later arrested at the student hostel. Disturbances continued for another day but became almost entirely non-
student in character. The issue of the magazine *Po Prostu* was forgotten, and one by one different intellectual groups disassociated
themselves from the riots. In one of the statements issued by the
House Committee of the Narutowicz Square student hostel, the following was stated by the Polytechnic students: "We want to stress
that the large majority of academic youth did not take part in the
incidents, nor did they instigate any demonstrations that would dis-
honor the name of the students."

It is the disassociation of the intellectuals from the demonstrations
once they became working class in character that is a significant social class component in an otherwise political riot. At the height of
the student disturbances during the first and second day, factory
meetings of workers were held to condemn "street brawls." Now
that the lower class youths appeared in the riots the intelligentsia in
turn were in retreat. The journal *Sztandar Mlodych* (The Banner of
Youth) published an article on October 7 entitled "Enough," demanding that the authorities put an end to the disturbances. Even
more interesting was the fact that the students of the University of

Warsaw had not taken part in the demonstration at all and according to one source, actually assisted the police in quelling the riots. On the subject of the intellectuals' withdrawal one eyewitness has written as follows:

> Beginning with the third day, the riots became unpopular. The participation of the intelligentsia in the two last demonstrations was minimal and even those who took an active part in previous ones, from the third day, stayed aloof and condemned further demonstrations. . . . I will not forget a conversation with a man who at the outbreak of the demonstrations took a vital part and who told me later that the demonstration in Constitution Square was a "raid of hoolligans from Targowka, Mlocin, and Powisle" (working class districts of Warsaw). He probably was of the opinion that the revolution was good only as long as it was led by the intelligentsia. The reader may not know that on Constitution Square are located the most luxurious shops of Warsaw among them two large jewelry stores. It is a fact that during the entire demonstration not one window in these shops was broken, not one person could be found coveting the gold and diamonds and thus giving the reactionary press a chance for a display of moral indignation. The stones flew only at the policemen.

The internal social class tensions within the groups of intellectuals can be stated in this case only in the form of a hypothesis. They are analogous to the broader animosities between the intelligentsia and workers. There is class tension in a political contest in which the Natolin group refers to the "Pulawianie" as "Zydy" (Jews) and is in turn referred to as "Chamy" (Peasants). These terms are hard to translate into English because in Polish they carry definitely derisive social class connotations, implying perverse intellectualism or cleverness on one side and vulgarity and uncouthness on the other. But these analogies do not adequately answer the question why the students of the University of Warsaw refrained from participation in the riots. One can only offer conjectures. Both the University of Warsaw and Warsaw Polytechnic are modern creations with a system of respective ranking that is not distinctly drawn. The University concentrates on humanities and thus enjoys cultural pre-eminence. The

Polytechnic on the other hand, as already indicated, has an old and respected German tradition. Still there is a distinction made between the arts and the sciences, between the Latin and the German. It is accentuated by the fact that in Communist Poland the Polytechnic, which trains engineers, guarantees better salaries and a better share of power and voice in the management of government enterprises. It thus creates envy toward and rejection of the Polytechnic students by the students of Warsaw University. It is interesting to note that the oldest Polish university, Cracow, where Copernicus studied, prides itself as much on its scientific as on its humanistic tradition. Cracow students are reported to have staged a demonstration in favor of the Warsaw rioters after the *Po Prostu* suspension.

That social divisions between the University of Warsaw and Warsaw Polytechnic exist can be further deduced from different attitudes which the students at these two institutions display toward economic equality. According to a series of studies carried out by a group of Polish sociologists, it appears that, taken as a whole, for students of all the institutions of higher learning in Warsaw "acceptance of social ideological values is to be found more often in the lower regions of social stratification." If we break down that group into respective universities the students of the University of Warsaw show themselves consistently more egalitarian. In a manner reminiscent of the reversed prestige between the French universities and the *Grandes Écoles,* the students at the University of Warsaw appear now to be of humbler origin, more careful as to the chances of future employment. Open rioting, as indeed any excessive activity of a political nature, is considered less appropriate by these more academic and economically less privileged students. It is at the more self-assured and more independent Polytechnic that reform movements crowned by the October 1956 revolution arose. And it is students of this institution that set out to keep and to consolidate the political relaxations and achievements then won. The device of the *Stodola* (Barn) has been used not only to provide places for dancing and social gatherings, but also to present the now famous student political skits which became the major conveyors of political caricature. Another device was the magazine *Po Prostu.* Its demise had goaded the Polytechnic students to fury.

Just as the participation of non-students put the riots beyond the pale of any university student, so the participation in the riots by students in technology put them beyond the pale of students in the academic faculties. We see here a parallel to the animosities between academic and technological students in Montreal resulting in the burning of the student journal *Le Quartier Latin*. . . . It is a rare educational system that can escape reflecting the distinctions of social class prevailing in society. Even in the heat of political struggle for and against Stalinist communism the students of Polish universities prove to be no exception.

In this essay note how the government made use of students to build lasting support for its program in a single-party state. The authors explain historically how, when, and why student activism later became a powerful political force in Turkey.

10

Students and Politics in Turkey

Leslie L. Roos, Jr., Noralou P. Roos, and Gary R. Field

In Turkey, as in other countries, the role of students in politics has varied from historical period to historical period, from one political regime to another, and from one university to another. Turkish students have been associated with both arch-conservative causes and radical movements. They have rioted against politically repressive regimes and demonstrated in opposition to moderately progressive ones.

The place of students in Turkish political life also varies widely according to the period being studied. During the last century of the Ottoman Empire, particularly between 1850 and 1920, students were frequently the most active and effective political force. They deposed sultans and plotted revolutions. On the other hand, student political activity was much less important during the years between the founding of the Republic in 1923 and the beginning of multiparty politics in 1946. Students were so inactive during this period that it is difficult to find even a mention of them in any of the standard historical accounts.

Since the beginning of the multiparty period, students have shown a new interest in politics. This involvement reached its peak in the days before the 1960 military coup with riots at the Law and Political Science Faculties and a march demonstrating the antigovernmental

From Leslie L. Roos, Jr., Noralou P. Roos, and Gary R. Field, "Students and Politics in Turkey," *Daedalus,* 97, no. 1 (Winter 1968), 184–200. Reprinted by permission from *Daedalus,* Journal of the American Academy of Arts and Sciences, Boston, Mass.

sentiments of cadets at the Army War College. The students' moment of glory was, however, shortlived, and although students have remained more active than they were during the long single-party era, the level and importance of student political involvement would seem to be much less in present-day Turkey than in many other developing countries.

Students and Politics in the Late Ottoman Empire

By the nineteenth century, the deterioration of the Ottoman religion-based education system was almost complete. The *ulema* who served the Empire as both judges and teachers were ignorant of conditions in their own empire and, especially, of events in the outside world. They stressed the unquestioned superiority of Islam and an absolute rejection of anything foreign. The *ulema* and the students whom they were training to follow them were both threatened by any change in the traditional Islamic system and well situated to block reforms, since they and the military caste of Janissaries held the balance of power against the sultan in his own capital city. Thus, it is not surprising that when Selim III, the first sultan who could be accused of imitating Frankish ways, was faced with a Janissary revolt in Rumelia and an *ulema*-organized mob in the capital, the infidel reforms were quickly suspended. Although Selim's successors were very effective in undermining the power of the religious and military opposition to reform, they were not able to neutralize the theological students' opposition to change. It finally became necessary to ward off conspiracies by limiting the number of theological students in the capital.

In 1876, the political activity of the students was more direct. A student strike was called and spread from one *medrese* (religious school) in Istanbul to another. In addition to buying arms, the students organized mass meetings at the mosques and heard inflammatory speeches about the weakness of the government in the face of rebellion by its subject populace and threats from Russian influence. The students prepared a petition calling for the dismissal of the grand vezir and the head of the religious establishment (*şeyhülislam*). In direct response to the student agitation, the offending officials were dismissed.

Although political activities of the theological students were usually associated with extremely reactionary causes, one should note that the riots in 1876 were in sympathy with the aims of the reforming Young Ottomans. Members of this Western-educated group were intent on limiting the powers of an incompetent sultan, Abdülaziz. Since the Young Ottomans were committed to saving traditional Ottoman values, they were at times able to enlist the support of certain theological students who also revered these values, even if from a slightly different perspective.

Unfortunately, the perspective of the theological students was narrow, and they found many of the Young Ottoman reform efforts, such as agitation for a constitution and parliament, totally unacceptable. The continuing political unrest of the theological students during the late-nineteenth and early-twentieth centuries was, however, understandable in their terms. They were observing the progressive deterioration of the Empire and blamed it on the Westernized reforms that were changing the traditional basis of the Ottoman state. The Young Ottomans and their successors interpreted the Empire's troubles in a quite different way. These students came from the newly Westernized schools and felt that the reforms had not gone far enough. They objected both to the lack of implementation of a constitution and to the arbitrary power exerted by the sultan.

Westernized education was brought into Turkey in the late-eighteenth century by sultans intent upon their armies' learning the secrets of the West in order to save the Ottomans from increasingly disastrous defeats. Although these secular schools met outspoken hostility from the conservative Janissaries and the traditional religious educational structure, they were so obviously successful that many other secular institutions were added over the following years. The contact with Western culture that instruction in French allowed had a predictable impact on this new elite group. Feelings of sensitivity to Turkish cultural and political backwardness led to an intense commitment to structural changes which the students felt necessary to revitalize the Ottoman Empire. Overt political activity by these students was slow to develop because at first they were few in number and operating in a potentially hostile environment. In addition, the most promising graduates of these new schools were so welcomed by the reformist sultans that they had unique opportunities for wielding influence at the highest military and governmental levels.

The results of the graduates' participation within the system were, however, so disappointing in actual practice that a new form of covert revolutionary planning began in many of the new schools. According to one source, the first organized opposition was formed in 1889 by four medical students in the garden of the military's medical college. The new group won support in all the higher schools in Istanbul, eventually taking the name of the Society of Union and Progress. The Society unsuccessfully attempted a coup in 1896, and despite the failure of this effort, the Society continued to attract adherents, particularly among the military cadets. One writer describes the military academy at this time as a "hotbed of sedition" where "every officer seemed to be a revolutionary." The strategic positions assumed by these students made their political activities especially significant; as they graduated, they formed new revolutionary cells among all arms of the far-flung Ottoman military establishment.

Although the political activities of students from the newly Westernized schools and students from the theological schools were generally at cross-purposes, the conditions that encouraged their involvement seem to have been similar. Both types of students felt the lack of a strong, confident Ottoman leadership that could meet the innumerable crises facing the Empire and restore the dignity and glory their predecessors had known. In a society in which education traditionally entitled one to entrance into the elite, the political decay threatened the students' futures. The challenge that Western reforms posed to the Islamic foundations of Turkish society directly affected the job opportunities open to the theological students. Similarly, students in the Westernized schools saw a daily deterioration in the Ottoman military situation, and if total disaster was to be avoided, change had to be brought about.

The more permissive attitude toward political discussion that evolved during this period encouraged both groups of students to voice their dissatisfactions with the *status quo*. Official policy varied from sultan to sultan, but with the rise of the literary-journalistic movement in the 1850's, new ideas were being discussed and debated. The once-accepted solutions to problems had been challenged, and students were eager to involve themselves in this debate.

From a cross-national perspective, it is interesting briefly to compare the role of students in the disintegrating Ottoman Empire with the role played by students in China under similar political conditions. In both countries the students had a historical sense of national grandeur that was frustrated under weak, inept traditional regimes. By 1900, this frustration was aggravated by the introduction of a more modern university system. Moreover, Chinese students abroad absorbed radical new philosophies and were shamed by the realization of the backwardness of their own country. The great allure which Sun Yat-sen's ideas had for Chinese students was comparable to the adulation accorded such Young Ottoman writers as Namik Kemal. But, in Turkey at the critical historical period, the main revolutionary stimulus was found in the military schools, and the military provided an organization through which revolutionary efforts could be effectively channeled. In Turkey, no rival to this organization developed, while in China lack of respect for the military was coupled with the existence of both the Communist and the Kuomintang alternatives.

Under the brilliant leadership of Atatürk, the Turkish army was successful in driving out the foreigners, and subsequently the traditional antipathy of the Turks toward the Russians made Communist ideology less of a threat to nationalism than was the case in China. In Turkey as in China, "a century of national humiliation and a succession of thwarted reforms imparted an irresistible allure to radical solutions," but the radical solution adopted by the Turks was very different from the course upon which the Chinese eventually embarked.

Students and the Republic's Single-Party Period (1923–1945)

Between the founding of the Turkish Republic in the early 1920's and the beginning of the multiparty period in the mid-1940's, student politics appears to have entered a quiescent state. The government, dominated by Atatürk's Republican People's Party, apparently met very little open opposition from university students. Their lack of activity is the more striking when contrasted with the opposition expressed by other groups in society during this period. A number of journalists, intellectuals, and politicians, along with certain religious and tribal elements were opposed to many aspects of the People's Party government, and they vented their opposition in various ways. For example, when in the 1930's there was a brief unsuccessful attempt to introduce a second political party, each of the above groups was quick to come to the new party's support. A comprehensive discussion of this period makes, however, no mention of any student participation in this effort. In order to understand the supportive role that students appear to have played during the first years of the Republic, it is necessary to examine Atatürk's unique position as a revolutionary leader. In the short course of five years (between 1922 and 1927), he legislated the political and social order of the Ottoman Empire out of existence. This was no simple task, and frequently he stood alone against the vested interest of enemies and the more cautious counsel of friends. Although the reforms were not uniformly adopted throughout Turkish society, Atatürk was extremely successful in his onslaught upon the values of the elite. Such was the main aim of his program—the transformation of society from the top down.

An analysis of students and politics in other developing areas suggests that "dynamism" is one of the most important qualities that students look for in their leaders. According to any such criteria, Atatürk was extraordinarily dynamic, and each of his reforms was justified in terms of making Turkey a truly modern society. More important for our purposes, Atatürk completely destroyed that part of the educational system (the theological schools) which would have provided opposition to his actions. At the same time, he placed great stress on the rapid expansion of secular education. Through these new schools he planned both to modernize Turkish values and to convince his countrymen that the path he had chosen for them was the correct one. Atatürk was eminently successful in this task.

If one were to compare the conditions that tended to dampen student political activity in the single-party period with those that had encouraged such activity during the previous century, a number of generalizations might be made. The most important difference was the changed political situation. While the Ottoman students operated in an unstable political environment, not knowing who would be successful in the next coup or counter-coup, the early Republican students looked to a vigorous leadership that successfully met every challenge. Similarly, Ottoman students were anxious about their personal futures, while students in the Republic anticipated promising careers in government, in politics, and in an expanding industrial sector. Finally, while the rebellious spirit of the Ottoman era encouraged opposition from journalists, the political situation during the early decades of the Republic did not. Atatürk's reforms had been too drastic and too unpopular to allow any criticism of them to be voiced. The only basis for political discussion of any kind was a fundamental acceptance of these reforms, and deviation was strongly discouraged.

Students and the Multiparty Politics Period (1946–Present)

The thesis that students were inactive during the single-party period because they were unified behind Atatürk and the dynamic modernization program upon which he embarked is supported by the events that followed the termination of single-party dominance. The 1946 decision by the Republican People's Party leadership to allow another party to compete for the support of the rural masses meant an inevitable relaxation of some of Atatürk's most unpopular religious reforms. The call to prayer could once again be recited in Arabic (rather than Turkish) and a Faculty of Theology was re-established. Many of the nationalistic youths interpreted such actions as a grave threat to the entire Kemalist revolution. An analysis of the Turkish press indicates that such concern stimulated students to political protest at the beginning of the multiparty period. Thus, in 1946 students denounced the fanatical religious behavior evident during the funeral of Marshal Çakmak (a former military figure with conservative support) and the activities of a sect that demolished statues of Atatürk.

Turkish student politics are largely confined to national issues. The

above-mentioned content analysis of student political concerns between 1950 and 1964 gives the following breakdown: 7 per cent
of the statements were on student affairs, 15 per cent on ideological
issues (mainly protests against the actions of Turkish Communists),
41 per cent on domestic affairs, 17 per cent on international affairs
(the Cyprus conflict), 17 per cent on the protection of Atatürk's reforms, and 3 per cent miscellaneous. These domestic concerns of
Turkish students set them off sharply from such student movements
as the Nigerian and the Scandinavian, which tend to take stands
on the problems of other countries.

One of the few overt protests of official governmental activity in
the pre-1960 period followed the dismissal of Political Science Faculty
Dean, Turhan Feyzioğlu. He had bitterly denounced the government's refusal to promote a faculty member who was critical of government policy. Approximately three hundred students walked out of
their classes at the Faculty in protest over the government's action.

This protest was mild, however, compared with the involvement
of university students in the 1960 coup ousting the Menderes government. Menderes had led his Democratic Party to an overwhelming victory in the first free election in 1950, and he was supported
by an apparently unbeatable combination of peasants, businessmen,
and members of the free professions. His unco-ordinated free-spend-
ing policies precipitated a spiraling inflation which especially hurt
such salaried groups as the bureaucrats and military men. Their
alienation was particularly intolerable because the Democratic Party
was accused of winning the support of the rural peasantry by sac-
rificing many of Atatürk's religious reforms. Since bureaucrats and
military men had long formed the backbone of the Republic's elite,
their frustration was understandable.

Menderes' repression of political opposition had grown increasingly strict and onerous during the late 1950's, while tension in the
major cities continued to rise. In 1960 he granted sweeping powers
to an investigating committee that would have acted to destroy all
open opposition, whether from other parties, newspapers, or other
organizations. This act touched off a general student protest. Students gathered at the Law Faculty in Istanbul and at the Political
Science Faculty in Ankara. When police were sent to break up the

demonstrations, serious clashes occurred in which one student was killed. Following these clashes, the universities were closed for a month, but almost every night students helped to incite riots on the main boulevard of Ankara. While these riots were not major affairs, the students continued to provide the major overt opposition to the Menderes regime. This was dramatically underlined by the spontaneous march of a thousand Military College cadets on the presidential residence. They were dissuaded from completing the march by their commanders, but the Turkish student had proved himself to be heroic in his battle against a repressive political regime.

It is important to remember that while the student demonstrations aroused public opinion against the regime and created an intolerably tense political atmosphere, they were not directly related to the May 27 coup that toppled the regime just one month later. Most accounts indicate that the coup was the result of long planning and deliberation by a group of military men. If anything, the student demonstrations were unwelcomed by the coup planners, since they served to warn Menderes and persuaded him to take counter-measures that he might not otherwise have taken. But the coup was successful, and the students' interpretation of their own role gave them a heady sense of power and righteousness. This experience appears to have altered the pattern of student political participation.

Before the coup, most student statements were meant only to be informative, but after the coup they became "much more dynamic, requesting quick action, containing warnings and sometimes even threats." Student actions immediately after the coup also demonstrated this new-found power. In 1960–61 they walked out to protest unpopular teachers, shortages of books, and poor food in university canteens. In almost every case (even when it was a protest over defining acceptable academic performance), the students prevailed. Explicitly political demonstrations were held by students in 1962 when they wrecked two newspaper offices in Istanbul and the Justice Party headquarters. (This Party is the most direct successor to Menderes' outlawed Democratic Party.) In 1963, about fifteen hundred students demonstrated in Istanbul against the release of ex-President Bayar for medical treatment.

A period of normalization seems to have set in after the burst of student political activism in the early 1960's. Student views are now expressed largely through press statements, various meetings, and occasional demonstrations. The main vehicles for the expression of their opinion are the large student organizations that recruit from various universities. Since 1960, the two major organizations—the National Turkish Students' Federation (TMTF) and the National Turkish Students' Union (MTTB)—have been supported by funds from the national budget. Both are legally obligated to remain politically neutral, although TMTF has long sympathized with the leftist parties—first with the People's Party and increasingly with the outspokenly Marxist Turkish Labor Party. MTTB has recently taken a much more pro-government position, roundly criticizing its rivals for dabbling in politics.

There appears to be some relationship between the level of student involvement and other significant dimensions of the political environment. The political atmosphere in Turkey was extremely tense and uncertain both before and immediately after the 1960 coup. Journalists were jailed, elections were thought to be rigged, and the two chief Parties were almost incapable of civil communication. Although the political climate was generally considered intolerable, no clear solution was in sight. Students, by openly demonstrating their protest, had an obvious impact on so fluid a situation. As in the earlier Ottoman period, students were encouraged to take matters into their own hands because none of the acknowledged political leaders was able to provide the direction that could assure them about their own personal future and about the future of the nation.

The political climate changed, however, when the Justice Party was elected to office with a large majority in 1965. Prime Minister Süleyman Demirel won a personal triumph over the reactionary extremist elements within his own Justice Party and thus gained the support of many moderates of various political sympathies. He has neutralized the potential opposition of the military by choosing the former General Chief of Staff (another acceptable moderate) to serve as President, and has also proved to be suprisingly successful in the economic field. The capable leadership provided by Prime

Minister Demirel has tended to reduce the political impact of students. They have not, however, been silenced, and the open climate for political discussion encourages them to make their voices heard.

The continuation of relatively restrained behavior on the part of the students is by no means certain. The leaders of Turkish student political organizations tend to be considerably more leftist than the student body, and thus may be motivated to lead other students toward more radical activism. The success of such efforts and the future role of students in Turkish politics are likely to be linked to political developments within the system as a whole.

Political Socialization in the Turkish Educational System

Any attempt to understand the role of students in Turkish politics since the founding of the Republic in 1922 must deal with the Kemalist legacy. Atatürk explicitly created the secular-nationalist system of education to win support for his ideological revolution, and his political successors have continued to use the schools as a means for inculcating a national identification into the traditionally privatistic rural populace. All political parties have made this a central goal of education. Atatürk's bust occupies a prominent place in every school, while history courses emphasize both Republican accomplishments and the achievements of the Turkish "race."

The effectiveness of such an educational system is clearly shown in the answers to a question asked on a 1963 national sample survey, "Who is the person in all the world, living or dead, whom you admire most—and why?" With each increase in the level of education, the respondents were more likely to identify Atatürk as the person they most admired and less inclined to choose a religious figure. Only 15 per cent of the respondents who had never attended school named Atatürk as the person most admired, while 53 per cent of those with a university education chose him. The proportion of those saying they most admired a religious figure declined from 16 per cent of those with no education to 1 per cent of the respondents with a university education. Similarly, with almost every increment of education, people tended increasingly to admire a specific person because of his "usefulness to the nation," rather than his religious beliefs.

The data also support the idea that nationalistic values are instilled early in the educational process. The proportion of the people choosing Atatürk as the person they most admired rose 33 per cent between those with no schooling (15 per cent mentioned Atatürk) and those with a middle-school education (48 per cent chose Atatürk). After middle school (middle school consists of three years following five years of primary education) the increase was slight, with only 5 per cent more respondents with some university education mentioning Atatürk than did people with some middle school. Additional evidence supporting the hypothesis that Turkish students acquire national allegiance during the first eight years of education, before they reach the *lycée*-level schools, is provided in a study by Frederick Frey. He compares the attitudes of students in their first year of *lycée* study with those in their last year and finds that no consistent changes in the politically relevant items can be observed. Such a finding indicates that relatively little political socialization takes place after a student enters the *lycée*.

Since political socialization in Turkey occurs at such an early educational level, all students seem to acquire similar political loyalties no matter what type of secondary education they receive. This is important, since an individual proceeds from middle school into one of the various secondary schools, which train their students for very different career paths. Although one might expect students in the less privileged schools to be less committed to the values that define the modern Turkish elite, this is apparently not the case. Students in different types of secondary schools are equally likely to say they would be willing to make a great personal sacrifice for national goals, that children must be taught loyalty to the nation, and that one should definitely vote in national elections.

Although attitudes toward the political system differ little among students in the various kinds of secondary schools, students in the elite regular *lycées* are more inclined to take an active role in politics. They are likely to feel that "participation in activities directed toward national improvement" would afford them more satisfaction in the future than their career or family life; they expect to be most interested in national affairs; and the subject they most frequently discuss with their families is national problems. Additionally, the political tendencies of *lycée*-level students might be expected to influence their choice of faculties. Since much of the research on students and politics has found that students in humanities and the social sciences tend to be both more participant and more radical than students in commerce, the natural sciences, and technical fields, different sorts of *lycée* students might be recruited to the various faculties. These generalizations are relevant to Turkey, since the Law and Political Science Faculties have furnished the greatest number of politically active students.

The differential recruitment of political activists does not, however, seem to be responsible for these inter-faculty differences. There are no obvious differences between the political attitudes and behavior of those students attracted to the politically activist faculties (Law and Political Science) and those attracted to other faculties. The *lycée* students who plan to attend the Law and Political Science Faculties are no more interested in national affairs, political careers, or political discussion than are students planning to enter other faculties.

Political Socialization at the University

By the time a *lycée* student has entered a Turkish university, he has been socialized to a high degree of national identification. While this nationalism remains very strong and might even increase during his first year at the university, there seems to be some value reorientation during the following years. Privatism increases, as does an emphasis on international rather than strictly national interests, while political activity decreases. The longer students remain at the university, the more likely they are to assume the role of a political spectator—interested in politics, but taking no active part.

An extreme sense of nationalistic zeal and a dedication to national service would seem to accompany the first-year students' awareness of their elite status. The first-year class may also be under less academic pressure than are students in the later classes. Under the Turkish educational system, at the end of each academic year students are examined in various fields to determine whether they will be allowed to pass on to the next year. While the yearly exam can be repeated, there is a rigorous selection process. Those who survive this process may develop a more professional orientation and feel it necessary to decide between devoting their time to political activities or to studies.

Additionally, the Turkish students' feelings about religion are profoundly affected by their university education. The longer a student remains in the university, the less likely he is to feel the need for religion in order to achieve a full philosophy of life. None of the *lycée* students planning to enter the Political Science Faculty felt they could do without religion. Twelve per cent of the freshmen at the Faculty felt they had no need for religion, but by the time they were ready to leave the Faculty, fully one fourth of the students had renounced the need for religion. Another study conducted in 1966 using a different sample confirmed this secularizing tendency in the Turkish university system. When asked "How important is religion in your life?" the proportion of each class giving one of the negative responses "of little importance" or "not at all" was as follows: 20 per cent of the freshmen, 35 per cent of the sophomores, 42 per cent of the juniors, and 49 per cent of the seniors.

The political relevance of the Turkish students' attitudes on religion should be particularly stressed, since the role of religion has been one of the main issues of Turkish politics during the multiparty era. The Parties which have won the popular support of the country (first the Democrats and now the Justice Party) have the reputation for liberalizing the stringent religious reforms introduced by Atatürk. As the table below records, a student's attitude toward religion predicts fairly well his feelings about other important aspects of politics in Turkey. Secular students are more likely to be interested in politics, to be "leftist," and to support an elitist view of the governmental process.

Additional insight into the role of Turkish students in politics can be had by comparing students at different types of university-level institutions—at, for example, the Political Science Faculty

TABLE 1:   THE RELATIONSHIP BETWEEN STUDENTS' ATTITUDES
TOWARD RELIGION AND VARIOUS POLITICALLY RELEVANT
ATTITUDES

	Importance of Religion		
	High	Moderate	Low
"Very much interested in politics"	18%	16%	29%
Describing selves as leftists or moderate leftists	36%	51%	80%
Defining government as government for the people	38%	42%	55%
Number of Respondents	269	184	214

and Robert College, a private institution founded under American auspices about one hundred years ago. Political Science Faculty students have traditionally entered high-level political and governmental positions, while the Robert College students, going to a foreign school located in a suburb of Istanbul, come from a more cosmopolitan background and are more likely to make their careers in the private sector. The Political Science Faculty students were more likely to have had fathers in governmental or military positions, and less likely to have had fathers in commercial occupations or in the professions.

The values of students at the two institutions are also quite different. The Robert College students demonstrate a higher commitment to internationalism as opposed to nationalism, than do the Political Science Faculty students. These differences appear to be reflected in the type of political activities in which the two schools have been involved. At the height of political tension just preceding the 1960 coup, there were bloody student riots at the Political Science Faculty. A few days later, the government closed Robert College after one hundred and fifty students took part in an orderly and peaceful demonstration.

Other differences among faculties have important implications for political behavior. It is generally agreed that students at the Ankara Law Faculty and particularly the Political Science Faculty were by far the most politically active during the disturbances leading up to the 1960 military coup. These differences in political involvement are reflected in a 1959 survey contrasting the leisure-time activities of students at these two Faculties with those of students in the Administrative Sciences division of Middle East Technical University. Middle East Technical University, a new institution founded with United Nations aid, is characterized by its modern curriculum, smaller classes, and emphasis on technical subjects, as well as by the fact that English, rather than Turkish, is the language of instruction.

There were regular differences in political interest among the three groups of students. Generally speaking, Political Science Faculty students, followed by students at the Law Faculty and Middle East Technical University, were the most interested in political news. Another difference among the Faculties, and one which has important political implications, concerns the students who spend their free time strolling on the streets. Such students are a common sight in downtown Ankara and can be readily mobilized for political demonstrations. Here again the 1959 survey showed the same rank order among Faculties as was discussed above. Sixty-one per cent of the Political Science students said they spent some of their free time strolling; the corresponding figures for the Law Faculty and Middle East Technical University students were 47 and 30 per cent respectively.

An elite status, as defined by social background, is also associated with a set of attitudes and behavior supportive of political activity. Having a relative in politics or government provides one indicator of "eliteness," although it is probably also a measure of political contact. Law students with relatives in politics or government are more likely to be activists than are those who do not have similarly placed relatives (44 per cent of those with relatives in official positions are categorized as activists as compared with 34 per cent of the other law students). Analysis of the Law School data on social-class origin (as defined by father's occupation) indicates that the proportion of activists increases with social class, while the proportion of apolitical individuals decreases.

Since the beginning of the multiparty period, Turkish students have become an active force in the political life of the Republic. Their most dramatic involvement was an important stimulus to the 1960 revolution, and Atatürk's proclamation that youth is "the owner and guardian of the revolution" is taken very seriously by many elements in the student population. Nevertheless, while the students are important as an efficacious pressure group and as self-conscious members of the educated elite, it is very difficult to say how politically "active" they are in comparison to other student populations. An impressionistic observation would be that Turkish student political activity (during normal times) takes place within the general bounds of the legitimized political system and uses both what E. W. Bakke calls "conservative measures" and mass demonstrations. Student groups make their positions known through press conferences, letters, declarations, and by direct involvement in such activities as labor disputes. Their organizations are supported by government funds, and there appears to be a relatively low level of antisystem activity.

While Turkish students are undoubtedly more politically active and efficacious than their American counterparts, they would also seem to be less involved and less revolutionary than students in some of the other developing countries. Although completely adequate data are lacking, several features in Turkish society and the Turkish educational system might be expected to dampen student political activism. Two of these are the persistent elitist bias in the educational system and the low level of unemployment among the educated classes.

It is necessary to clarify what is meant when the term *elitist* is applied to the Turkish educational system. For example, Frederick Frey suggests that there has been an elitist dynamic to the Turkish educational system during the Republic because there has been a more rapid expansion of the upper levels of the system (particularly *lycée* and university education) than of the lower, primary levels.

Such an educational investment policy results in a higher number of university graduates compared with developing countries that choose to invest their money differently. This aspect of the educational system would, however, not make it elitist according to one aspect of Seymour Martin Lipset's classification system. Lipset suggests that a distinction be drawn between elitist systems where admission to the universities is difficult and mass systems where "almost anyone who wants to enter a university may do so." He goes on to say that as a result of such mass admissions policies in Egypt, Japan, and India, attendance at the university has "skyrocketed" and far surpasses the rise in suitable job opportunities. In order to see how Turkey ranks relative to the other systems which Lipset has termed "mass" or "elitist," comparative figures on the size of various countries' higher educational systems are presented below.

If one considers Turkey's position relative to that of other developing countries, on this indicator it would seem to rank closer to the mass systems of India and Egypt than to the elitist systems of Nigeria and Sierra Leone. Turkey nevertheless possesses many other

TABLE 2:   CLASSIFICATION OF COUNTRIES ACCORDING TO PROPOR-
TION OF STUDENTS ENROLLED IN HIGHER EDUCATION

	Higher Education Enrollment per 100,000
Mass Education Systems	
United States	1983
Puerto Rico	1192
Philippines	976
Argentina	827
Japan	750
Egypt	399
Turkey	225
India	220
Elitist Education Systems	
Britain	460
Sierra Leone	19
Nigeria	4

attributes common to elitist educational systems. A relatively high degree of selectivity through examinations ensures that only a small proportion of the populace gains access to the university preparatory *lycées*. Only 3 per cent of all students entering primary school can hope to enter one of these *lycées,* although once this hurdle has been overcome, approximately 55 per cent will go on to the university. About 40 per cent of Turkish students entering the university eventually graduate. This compares favorably with the records of many developed countries. For example, in Sweden 32 per cent of those entering get degrees, in France 38 per cent, in the United States 45 per cent, and in Britain 65 per cent. Comparable data from developing countries are generally lacking, but Philip Altbach notes that "well over half of those who enter college in India do not finish their degree programs."

Perhaps a more important indicator of the relatively healthy nature of the Turkish university system is the low level of unemployment among its graduates, and the satisfaction that its graduates find in their work. According to the 1960 census, only 157 of Turkey's more than 47,000 university graduates reported that they were unemployed. Moreover, Turkish university graduates also seem to be relatively happy in the jobs they find. A recent survey reported that 65 per cent of the people who had graduated from the Political Science Faculty between 1946 and 1961 were satisfied with their jobs.

The role of the student in Turkish politics is perhaps no more complex than the role of students in the politics of any other state, and the Turkish student's level of political involvement has fluctuated widely over the last century. During periods of uncertain leadership, students have been much more likely to take political initiative into their own hands. Regardless of the time period concerned, however, the correspondence between student attitudes and those of the national leadership seems to have had an important effect upon student activity.

IV

Student Communities
in Asia
and Africa

Here is an example of a student movement, according to the author's interpretation, developing logically from historical conditions within a country, in this case, the most populous in the world. That movement became a major force in China's national politics.

11

Reflections on the Modern Chinese Student Movement

John Israel

The students of the Sung dynasty (960–1279) would scarcely recognize their modern descendants. The former were seasoned scholars whose erudition secured their place in society. Through mastery of the prescribed classics, they aspired to the highest rungs of officialdom. Even degree-holders who failed to gain governmental positions became members of the "gentry" elite, entitled to special privileges and charged with numerous social responsibilities. Intellectuals were also expected to criticize officials—even emperors—who failed to live up to the standards of the Confucian ethos. For two thousand years, the scholar-official elite served the Chinese state well.

By the time of the Opium War (1839–42), however, the traditional scholar had become an anachronism. The classics failed to prepare China for the multifaceted challenge of the modern West. Beginning in the 1860's, the Manchu (Ch'ing) dynasty sought reinvigoration through a series of reforms, but none were equal to the need. By the end of the nineteenth century, the combination of external pressure and internal decay had proved too much for the rulers of the sprawling empire. In 1911 the dynasty collapsed, and a republic was established. Republican aspirations were quickly

From John Israel, "Reflections on the Modern Chinese Student Movement," *Daedalus*, 97, no. 1 (Winter 1968), 229–250. Reprinted by permission from *Daedalus*, Journal of the American Academy of Arts and Sciences, Boston, Mass.

crushed, however, under the despotism of Yüan Shih-k'ai. From 1916 to 1949, national reunification eluded warlord rulers, the Kuomintang (KMT) government, and the Japanese. Throughout these years, reformers in various parts of the Chinese subcontinent followed in the footsteps of their Ch'ing forebears. In retrospect, even their boldest efforts were but preludes to the measures of Mao Tse-tung.

Youth and Revolution: 1895–1949

The Chinese student movement was both conditioned by and a condition of this historical transformation. Bridging traditional and modern movements was the Memorial of the Examination Candidates at the close of the First Sino-Japanese War (1894–95). More than twelve hundred scholars, who assembled in Peking for the triennial examinations, demanded a protracted war against Japan. In so doing, they played the historic role of heirs to their twelfth-century predecessors and forerunners of their twentieth-century successors. A truly modern student movement could, however, develop only with modern educational institutions. The first Western-style missionary college (St. John's) was founded in Shanghai in 1879, and the first modern public university (later to be called National Peking University, or "Peita") was officially established in Peking in 1898. But a certain ambivalence clouded educational reform: How could modern colleges prepare candidates for the traditional examinations? The contradiction was resolved in 1905, when the desperate dynasty abolished the thirteen-hundred-year-old examination system.

Thereafter no careerist incentive remained for memorizing the classics, nor was there assurance that alternative courses of study would bring success. The modern student thus felt an unprecedented degree of insecurity. His personal dilemmas were compounded by a pervasive sense of national shame stemming from China's backwardness and helplessness vis-à-vis the imperialist powers. Many resolved these problems by going abroad for study, hoping to return with the prestige of a foreign degree and a technological or philosophical understanding of the modern world. The Manchu dynasty, in its declining years, encouraged students to follow this path, assuming they would come home both skillful and grateful. By September, 1906, fifteen thousand Chinese were studying in Japan. From the government's point of view, the reform was a disaster; uprooted youths, free of Chinese controls and exposed to inflammatory ideas, provided an educated following for such radical reformers as Liang Ch'i-ch'ao and rebels like Sun Yat-sen. Students from all over China came together in Tokyo and returned to foment revolution. Recipients of government scholarships helped bring down the Manchus in 1911.

Deriving its energy from the unstable combination of China's historic grandeur and modern humiliation, the student movement developed an explosive potential. Its targets were oppression from abroad as well as inept government at home. It seemed increasingly obvious to young patriots that both would have to be eradicated if China were to become a strong modern state. The new education reinforced these sentiments. Reformers prescribed a stridently nationalistic course of study, conveyed to the younger generation through chauvinistic textbooks taught by patriotic teachers. Hence, the anti-imperialist theme of 1895 resounded with growing intensity in the twentieth century. In 1905 students joined merchants in an anti-U. S. boycott protesting discriminatory American immigration policies. When Japan presented Yüan Shih-k'ai with the infamous 21 Demands in 1915, Chinese students in Japan returned home by the thousands to join demonstrations against this threat to their nation's sovereignty.

The 1915 movement was a prologue to the Peking demonstration of May 4, 1919, which marked the emergence of students as a major force in national politics. The impetus for this historic demonstration was another manifestation of foreign imperialism, but its full significance can be understood only in the context of China's accelerating social and intellectual revolution. In the cities of China's eastern seaboard, where foreign-style institutions flourished under the protection of the unequal treaties, new social classes were emerging: bilingual merchants, financiers, and industrialists; an urban proletariat; a foreign-educated intelligentsia; and modern students. In the homes of the latter, a "family revolution" ensued as the experience, teachings, and institutions of the older generation became increasingly irrelevant to the needs and aspirations of the young. Revolutionary ideas were nationally disseminated through a multitude of popular magazines, newspapers, and political societies. The effects of these changes were felt both in cosmopolitan Shanghai, hub of economic modernization and refuge for China's political and intellectual rebels, and in Peking, which remained the nation's cultural capital.

On December 26, 1916, National Peking University acquired a new chancellor, Ts'ai Yüan-p'ei. This remarkable man, who has been called "the moral leader of the new intelligentsia and one of the greatest educators and liberals in modern China," promoted that startling idea that a university should be a forum for the free development of diverse views. To the horror of traditionalists, he brought to the Peita faculty such men as Hu Shih, who advocated replacing the time-honored literary language with the vernacular, and Li Ta-chao, who shortly later eulogized the Bolshevik Revolution and helped found the Chinese Communist Party (CCP). Ts'ai's Dean of the School of Letters was Ch'en Tu-hsiu, later the CCP's first secretary-general, but even in 1917 a cultural radical who supported the slogan "Down with Confucius and sons!" and recommended science and democracy as panaceas for China's ills.

The iconoclastic doctrines of these teachers found a receptive audience. Peita's students had ample reason to feel rebellious: Their personal futures were uncertain; the republican revolution had ended in chaos; the country was at the mercy of corrupt militarists and foreign aggressors; and their own parents persisted in preaching obsolete notions of virtue and filial piety. The halls of Peita resounded with a cacophony of names and isms: Dostoevski and Kropotkin, Russell and Dewey, Shaw and Ibsen, Wilson and Lenin; democracy, equality, science, socialism, individualism, self-determination, nationalism, internationalism, and Bolshevism.

China's young rebels contrasted China's dreary present with a hopeful future. As war ended in 1918, they heard Woodrow Wilson promise equality to nations and dignity for mankind. They felt certain that the Versailles Conference would recognize the claims of their country, which had sent two hundred thousand coolies to aid the allies on the Western front. Principles of justice demanded that China regain her sovereign rights to the province of Shantung (birthplace of Confucius), seized by Japan in 1915. But youthful hopes proved illusory. By the end of January, 1919, reports reached Peking that Great Britain, France, and Italy had signed secret treaties agreeing to support Japan's claims to Shantung. On the heels of these tidings came even more foreboding news: The Japanese had used the $74 Nishihara "loans" to bribe China's warlord government into acquiescence. Outraged by these events, representatives of various student groups gathered at Peita and planned an orderly protest demonstration for May 4. The demonstration began peacefully, but ended in violence when a group stormed the home of a pro-Japanese official, beat alleged traitors discovered within, ransacked the house and set it afire. News of May 4 reached China's new social classes via her modern communications. Students demonstrated in Tientsin, Shanghai, Nanking, Wuhan, and other cities. Workers staged sympathy strikes. Merchants joined an anti-Japanese boycott. Professors demanded the release of arrested agitators. Local student groups proliferated, and on June 16, 1919, delegates gathered in Shanghai and formed the National Student Association.

The organization of a national body was a formidable accomplishment, for the unifying influence of a common written language and shared nationalistic sentiments were counterbalanced by powerful centrifugal forces: mutually incomprehensible dialects, regional loyalties, and the country's size. Considering these obstacles and in view of China's lack of experience with representative democracy, it is not surprising that the national body came to function in a highly elitist manner. City and provincial congresses were composed of delegates popularly elected at constituent schools, and these groups in turn sent delegates to meetings of the national union. The structure operated, however, in a Leninist fashion, more centralist than democratic. Even at the local level, professional and amateur agitators skilled in propaganda, oratory, and controlling mass meetings were generally able to dominate the majority of less interested and less adept schoolmates. The absence of democracy notwithstanding, the

National Student Association had become by the mid-twenties one of the most influential voices of public opinion in China. It was less effective, however, as an organ of control, and even during nation-wide movements, the nature and intensity of student political activity continued to vary according to local educational, political, geograph-ical, and cultural conditions.

The May 4 Movement was the turning point in China's cultural upheaval. Just as the revolution of 1911 had constituted a definitive break with efforts at monarchial reform, the New Thought of the late teens marked a radical departure from attempts at halfway modernization in the world of ideas. For the first time, eminent teachers and men of letters advocated wholesale Westernization and total abandonment of China's Confucian heritage. The reaction of educated youth was highly favorable; henceforth, the more novel and shocking an idea, the more likely it was to win a receptive audi-ence. The demonstration of May 4 also ushered in a decade of radical anti-imperialism. Vehement protests against the unequal treaties alarmed China's foreign community, and an anti-Christian movement jolted missionary schools. Disenchanted with the fruit-less promises of Wilsonian liberalism and wooed by Soviet envoys, alienated intellectuals and students formed the Chinese Communist Party. Among them was Mao Tse-tung, a twenty-seven-year-old former Peita library assistant who had received his political bap-tism as a high-school student leader.

Sun Yat-sen, too, was carried along by the radical post-May 4 tide. Frustrated by twenty years of political failure, he welcomed the counsel of Comintern agents; he agreed to accept Russian aid, revamp the KMT along Leninist lines, form a united front with the Chinese Communists, and establish the apparatus for mass mobiliza-tion, including a Youth Bureau. During the mid-twenties, students under both KMT and CCP leadership organized workers and peas-ants for political action. In Canton, the KMT's newly-founded Whampoa Military Academy set out to mold an indoctrinated mili-tary elite under Commandant Chiang Kai-shek. Students from all over China flocked to this mecca on the Pearl River.

As Chiang consolidated his forces, a series of atrocities by warlords and foreigners stimulated student nationalism and boosted the fortunes of the KMT-CCP alliance. An incident on May 30, 1925, was the most famous of these. Like the May 4 demonstration, the immediate cause was an imperialist outrage: A Japanese foreman in a Japanese-owned Shanghai factory had shot and killed a Chinese worker. Protesting students in the foreign-controlled International Settlement had been jailed. When a crowd gathered in front of a police station to demand their release, a British officer impulsively ordered his men to fire. The slaughter of unarmed students by foreign police on Chinese soil evoked a nationwide storm of protest. Twenty-four days later, indignation reached a new peak when British and French machine-gunners mowed down Whampoa cadets and other youthful paraders in Canton. On March 16, 1926, more anti-imperialist student demonstrators were massacred by troops of the Peking warlord, Chang Tso-lin. When Chiang Kai-shek launched the Northern Expedition on July 9, 1926, China's educated elite responded with enthusiasm to the slogan, "Down with the Warlords and the Imperialists!"

Beneath the façade of unity, both KMT and CCP maneuvered for the inevitable showdown. Chiang struck first. On April 12, 1927, he began the Party Purification Movement. This anti-Communist campaign began in Shanghai and spread throughout the country. It resulted in the summary execution of many student radicals. The purge, rupturing as it did the bond between the KMT and a significant element of the younger generation, neutralized much of the enthusiasm that had been created by the success of the Northern Expedition and the establishment of a national government in Nanking. A further blow to student activists was the ruling party's decision to discontinue mass movements. Student unions were to be replaced by apolitical self-governing associations, and youngsters were to stick to their books.

Youth lost fervor for a government that wasted precious resources in fighting warlords and Communist remnants at the expense of social reforms, but they also recognized the Nanking regime as China's only hope. Indeed, they might well have set their sights on bureaucratic, technocratic careers had not Japan invaded Manchuria in September, 1931. The Chinese government's failure to resist prompted young war hawks to flock to Nanking. For three months in the fall of 1931, thousands of student zealots descended upon the capital, often lying on railway tracks to halt traffic until free transportation was provided. Foreign Minister Wang Cheng-t'ing (a former YMCA student leader) was nearly beaten to death by a student mob on September 28. But the protest was relatively peaceful until December, when a radical minority from Peiping steered the movement in a revolutionary direction. Violent demonstrators manhandled KMT officials and wrecked the offices of the party newspaper, thereby forcing the government to adopt suppressive measures.

Once leftists had been jailed or driven underground, youthful nationalism was dampened by increasing political, social, and economic stability and by a hiatus in Japanese aggression. Official exhortations to "save the nation by study" apparently were making an impression. New moves by the invader, however, brought students once more to the streets in December, 1935. The Japanese were demanding an "autonomous region" in North China, and Peiping students were alarmed by Chiang's ambivalent response: "We shall not forsake peace until there is no hope for peace; we shall not talk lightly of sacrifice until the last extremity." They feared they would become subjects of a North China Manchukuo.

Organized protest began at American-influenced Yenching and Tsinghua Universities rather than at National Peking University, the traditional center of student politics. Yenching was a liberal missionary institution, and Tsinghua had originally been established with American Boxer indemnity funds as a preparatory school for Chinese students planning to study in the United States. Yenching was partly protected by extraterritoriality, and both schools were located five miles outside the city walls, which gave them some freedom from Peiping police controls. Large demonstrations on December 9 and 16 provoked a nationwide response among students and intellectuals reminiscent of May 4 and spawned a National Salvation Movement, which pushed Chiang toward a united front with the Communists and resistance to Japan. In May, 1936, the pro-Communist National Student Association was founded. The contrast between this and the troublesome but still loyal NSA dissolved seven years earlier by the Ministry of Training symbolizes the leftward trend among student activists during a decade of KMT rule.

The majority of the student generation of the 1930's committed themselves to no political party. They offered their allegiance to whoever would lead the country against Japan. Because they realized that only Nanking had the power to fill this role, they applauded Mao Tse-tung's call for a national united front, but reserved their most enthusiastic support for Chiang Kai-shek when he indicated willingness to lead the nation into war. Though thousands of idealistic youth joined the Communists in the hills of Shensi between 1936 and 1939, tens of thousands retreated to the Nationalists' refuge in the southwest.

To the casual observer, the eight-year period of war witnessed an unprecedented unity of Chinese youth under the leadership of Chiang. Between the summer of 1938 and December, 1945, there was practically no discernible student movement—not even a solitary protest against their wretched diet and rat-infested dormitories. Indeed, during the early war years, as the government fought, students rallied to China's defense and risked their lives to aid her hard-pressed armies. But by November, 1938, a military stalemate had developed, and after December 8, 1941, it became apparent that the war would be won elsewhere than in China. Morale deteriorated behind the lines as the government diverted men and supplies to blockade the Communists, while inflation and black marketeering sapped China's economic and psychological reserves. In the colleges of Chungking, Chengtu, and Kunming, students pawned books and clothes to supplement meager government subsidies, prepared their lessons by kerosene lamps, suffered from malnutrition, and frequently contracted tuberculosis. Official policy dictated that these youths remain at their desks. Hoarded like the precious national resources they unquestionably were, the educated elite found no adequate outlet for their patriotic idealism. By late 1943, when students were finally encouraged to enlist in the army, cynicism had already begun to erode the foundations of academia.

The contrast with the Communist zones was striking. There students were trained and indoctrinated in special schools and sent to the countryside to mobilize the population for guerrilla warfare. The

Communists emerged from the war with sufficient numbers of trained, dedicated young cadres to govern an area of a hundred million people. The nationalists had increased the number of students in institutions of higher learning from 41,609 in 1936, to 78,909 in 1945, and 155,036 in 1947. Aside from a loyal following in the Three People's Principles Youth Corps, however, these students were apathetic, if not hostile, toward the ruling party.

In the cities of East China that had been liberated from Japanese rule, the war's end reunited two groups—refugees returning from exile in the interior and residents who had collaborated, actively or passively, with the Japanese and their Chinese puppets. For both of these groups, the psychological effect of eight years of war had been disruptive. The refugees nursed sentiments of self-pity and resentment. They viewed themselves as unsung heroes who had endured nearly a decade of unrequited suffering for the nation. Further sacrifice seemed unjust, especially since those who had remained behind seemed to have prospered by co-operating with the invader. Many of the latter, on the other hand, felt a need to atone for the compromises they had made.

Sensitive youth from these two groups crowded onto postwar campuses and provided the material for a series of student rebellions that reached a crescendo in the antihunger, anti-civil-war movement of May, 1947. In the emporium atmosphere of Shanghai and other cities, wartime restraints had given way to an *enrichissez-vous* atmosphere. An inflationary economy hungry for consumer goods favored importers, speculators, and influential officials. But in the schools, shortages and inflation meant further sacrifices for teachers and students. To returning refugees, the ramshackle housing, substandard diets, shortages of books and laboratory equipment, and restraints on freedom that had been endured as necessary during the struggle against Japan now seemed not merely unnecessary, but intolerable. Students who had spent the war years in occupied China were inclined to sympathize with the Communists on practical and psychological grounds. Many felt that they had no future under the Kuomintang, which discriminated in favor of youngsters who had shared the bitterness of wartime "exile." The CCP, in contrast, presented itself as a forward-looking organization dedicated to universal ideals of youth. By enlisting in this noble cause, they might expiate feelings of guilt over the past and open up new possibilities for the future. In a contest that seemed to pit young idealists opposed to war and oppression against the old cynics responsible for these plagues, such students unhesitatingly cast their lots with the former.

Caught in a downward spiral typical of governments in the final stage of revolutionary overthrow, Chiang's regime vacillated between reform and force. Eleventh-hour moves to establish institutions of representative government failed to placate American and domestic critics and did nothing to halt political polarization, stem the devastating inflation, or prevent civil war. In this milieu, the Communists channeled youthful frustrations into demonstrations against civil war, malnutrition, American military misconduct, and Chinese police brutality. The government's response was "counterproductive"; bully boys beat demonstrators, and gunmen assassinated opponents, while official propagandists asserted that the highest priority of postwar reconstruction was the extermination of Communist rebels. Increasingly, the government became convinced that force was the answer in the cities as well as the rural areas. Police arrested thousands of students and intellectuals suspected of Communist sympathies and muzzled the left-wing press. Such action lent credence to Communist charges of Fascism and won additional recruits for the widening ranks of Mao's supporters. As the People's Liberation Army swept southward, student reaction ranged from stoic acceptance to jubilation.

This historical survey must conclude on a cautionary note. While Chinese students, individually and collectively, were important in their country's modern transformation and an essential ingredient in the victory of Chinese Communism, the student movement was not a sufficient cause for this victory. Mao's contribution to Communist practice was not his utilization of students (a universal phenomenon among Communist Parties), but his use of peasants in a political-military context. Students contributed heavily to the CCP's leadership and were a source of harassment to the KMT, but mass movements of urban intellectuals remained ancillary to the struggle in the villages and on the battlefield.

Students in Chinese Society

To understand the Chinese student movement, one must take a closer look at its participants. Who were the Chinese students? From what social strata did they come? Which of them played an active role in the events we have described? Unfortunately statistics are limited, and it is impossible to conduct thorough field studies. The answers to these questions must, therefore, be more in the nature of gross generalizations than of scientific findings.

China's students have always been members of an elite. The traditional scholar-gentry was, however, not primarily an economic class. The key to advancement was neither wealth nor social position, but education. Commoners often achieved gentry status, and gentry families lost their social standing over the course of several generations. Everything depended upon success in examinations that were open to poor and rich alike. Of course, the wealthy enjoyed obvious advantages: They could afford to give their sons years of leisure for education and to send them to school or to hire tutors. They could rear them in a world of scholars, a universe remote from the life of the poor peasant. Furthermore, the wealthy landowner or merchant might buy his son a degree, a procedure that supplemented the regular examination system. Hence, in pre-modern China, social mobility existed both in theory and in practice, though never to the extent suggested by the Chinese Horatio Alger tradition.

During the twentieth century, when college and even high-school attendance has involved living away from home, educational expenses have increased. Moreover, the prestige of a foreign degree made costly study abroad desirable for those aspiring to high government office. Hence, China's students were a highly urbanized, upper-middle- and upper-class group during the first half of the twentieth century. Available data do not answer the question: "Which elements of this elite were political activists?" As I have observed elsewhere, "disproportionate numbers of student radicals came from the lowest groups that could afford a post-grammar-school education—landlords and 'wealthy' peasants." But how many of these radical thinkers expressed themselves in terms of political action is unclear. Communist recruitment in the schools was not necessarily from the most impoverished groups, nor were needy students averse to advancement via the KMT.

Regardless of which student sector may have been most active in politics, *all* students were members of a privileged elite. The cream of this elite were those who studied abroad, and it is noteworthy that these youths played a major role in the Chinese student movement from approximately 1905 to 1925. Personal confrontation with the modern world had a jarring effect on these students, as it so often does on young people from underdeveloped areas. Radical ideas and organizations in Japan, France, and (after 1917) the Soviet Union helped to turn these students toward revolutionary movements.

By the mid-twenties, the importance of overseas student leadership had declined due to the increasing self-sufficiency and radicalization of the indigenous student movement, and the emergence of a KMT government supported by and largely staffed by returned students. Moreover, more and more students were going abroad for personal rather than patriotic reasons. The gap between returned and native students widened during the Japanese invasion of the 1930's, when many Anglo-American-educated academicians (as well as those trained in Japan) supported the government, sought help from the League of Nations, opposed the radical nationalism of the younger generation, and rejected student arguments that the national emergency made it imperative to interrupt normal education. In the middle- and late-forties, when war had fused the academic community, foreign-trained professors became increasingly impoverished, disillusioned, and inclined to sympathize with student protests. A striking example of this metamorphosis was the American-educated poet, Wen I-to, whose criticism of the government and support of student radicalism led to his assassination in July, 1946.

Both the economic position and the social outlook of China's students changed during the war. Previously, the average student was insulated from the stark reality of daily life among the four hundred million Chinese, even though groups of activists spread propaganda in factories and villages. Arduous journeys from occupied areas to Free China, however, made a lasting impression on these young people. Others gained still more unvarnished views of society after joining the regular army, guerrilla groups, or auxiliary military service organizations. After 1937, even the sons and daughters of the wealthy, cut off from their families, often found themselves living on the margin of starvation. To provide for these youths, the government introduced a system of scholarships, which soon supported tens of thousands of students. But wartime and postwar inflation virtually wiped out the Chinese middle class and lowered to a proletarian level the standard of living for scholarship holders, as well as teachers and other salaried officials. Though school food strikes had been common during the twenties and thirties, the "antihunger, anti-civil-war" movement of 1947 was the first nationwide student movement directed against substandard diets.

Sources of Youthful Rebellion

The postwar student movement marked a victory for Communist propagandists who, after three decades of experience, had reached a high level of sophistication in wielding weapons of mass persuasion. But to assert that Chinese youth were duped by astute propagandists explains nothing. The question is *why* Communist slogans had such a wide appeal, *why* Leninism made so much sense to an educated elite, *why* Chiang Kai-shek was so easily cast in the villain's role, and *why* students helped to overthrow a lesser tyranny only to accept a greater one.

In the eyes of many observers, Chinese college students seem to have been driven to Communism by their relentless hostility to legitimate authority. The diversity of targets of school strikes and nationwide movements—England, Japan, and the United States, Manchus, warlords, and KMT, capitalists and landlords, principals and teachers, family and state—certainly suggests that there was an underlying impatience with established power. This, too, requires an explanation. Richard Walker has written that China's students and intellectuals were victims of "the mystique of 'the Revolution'" which "assumed an almost mystical and sacred quality in the language of the new literati." As Walker observed, Kuomintang as well as Communist propagandists encouraged this semantic confusion. The students' profound commitment to the mystique was, however, based upon much more than confused semantics, as Robert A. Scalapino indicated in his trenchant analysis of Chinese students in Japan during the first decade of this century:

> Many of the students, no doubt, became revolutionaries after a process of soul-searching and reflection that involved a consideration of alternatives, and used their intellectual facilities in reaching their decision. It cannot be denied, however, that the espousal of revolution was the most logical method of achieving an emotional release, a method with which reformism could not easily compete. To students discouraged and impatient, the commitment to revolution represented a concrete, dramatic personal act by which they could dedicate themselves to the cause wholeheartedly, unselfishly, and with finality. It did not involve them in any of the intricate compromises and potential corruption that reform efforts would inevitably evoke. It was a heroic, simplistic act so in tune with the psychological needs of the time.

This statement is remarkably applicable to students of subsequent periods—especially 1923–27 and 1946–49. There was evidently nothing mysterious about the popularity of the revolutionary mystique, nor was the mystique ubiquitous. During the most dramatic periods of the movement, student activists chose the most radical of mentors, but this by no means implies that all students at all times were willing to sacrifice short-range goals of national unity, social order, and educational development to take the path of revolution.

The history of the modern Chinese student movement also demonstrates that rebellion against established authority did not necessarily imply rejection of all discipline. Anarchism did enjoy a vogue among Chinese students during the first two decades of the twentieth century, but its influence waned under the competition of Communism and nationalism in the early twenties. A similar fate befell romantic and liberal individualism. Students' submission to Leninist leadership in the CCP and KMT suggests that they welcomed discipline in the name of nationalistic and revolutionary causes. Furthermore, every generation of students has upheld forces of unity and order when these appeared to be viable possibilities. Even in

1949 few students accepted the Communist revolution without reservations. Given a unified nation, unthreatened by enemies, many of them would have preferred the ideas of Hu Shih to those of either Chiang or Mao. Indeed, Hu's advocacy of literary reform, intellectual tolerance, political experimentalism, and the application of the scientific method to academic and social problems won a sympathetic hearing from students of the May 4 era and continued thereafter to find a sizable audience among nonactivists. Under conditions of imperialistic aggression and civil war, however, Hu's cosmopolitanism was unable to compete with strident nationalism. The rapid disintegration of the old social order called for something stronger than his prescription of "bit-by-bit, drop-by-drop" change.

The difficulties of the liberals were compounded by the social and mental chasm that separated Anglo-American-trained intellectuals from the realities of rural China. These men, who filled the majority of college positions, failed to win the support of socially-conscious students. Their analyses seemed shallow, their solutions inadequate, their frames of reference irrelevant. More enduring was the alliance between student radicals and liberal and leftist writers whose years abroad had been spent in Japan, rather than England or the United States. From the 1920's on, the writings of Lu Hsün, Kuo Mo-jo, and others profoundly influenced the younger generation, but these men were victims of political polarization and became identified with the Communist camp.

China failed to develop a social democratic tradition, in part because her introduction to foreign ideologies was telescoped—the ideas of Marx and Lenin following close on the heels of liberal constitutionalism. Moreover, her cliques of progressive, democratic intellectuals were poorly organized and unarmed. The National Salvation Association, formed in 1936 as an offshoot of the December 9 Movement, provided some organizational cohesiveness for student patriots and their nonpartisan allies, and the Democratic League had its student following in the forties. Flanked by the armed, highly organized KMT on the right and CCP on the left, however, the third forces were doomed. By 1949, the only choices left to the splinter parties and their student followers were to seek exile in Hong Kong or abroad, or to serve as window dressing on the mainland or in Taiwan.

For most students, the cause of China seemed best served by remaining on the mainland and working with the new rulers.

Students and the Ruling Parties: KMT and CCP

Perennial student dissatisfaction with the *status quo* has created problems for both KMT and CCP rulers. By evaluating their divergent responses under varying conditions, one may consider whether the modernization process in China has made student rebellion inevitable.

The Kuomintang suffered from internal weaknesses as it entered the political-ideological arena. In retrospect, it seems clear that this ruling Party, badly divided as it was, had slim hopes of satisfying China's college students. Filled with the high expectations common among youth in modernizing societies, these radicals were inevitably disappointed when mortal men failed to solve unsolvable problems. In industrialized countries, such as the United States and postwar Japan, young idealists may be expected to mature into integrated units of the "establishment." Yet this is impossible unless the established order offers well-defined rewards—social, economic, and psychological. Considering the series of convulsions that have shaken Chinese society since the mid-nineteenth century, it is not surprising that many of the young intelligentsia eventually were drawn into the Communist camp. Nor is it surprising that the temporary loosening of authoritarian controls in 1957 produced a student rebellion and that the staging of a massive revolutionary movement under official auspices was necessary to forestall another outburst a decade later.

But the CCP, for all its blunders, has controlled the student movement far more skillfully than its rival had. The Kuomintang's short-lived success with the younger generation ended when the Party came to power, and the abolition of extramural student organizations betrayed the KMT's lack of confidence in its own ability to compete with the Communists and other dissidents. Moreover, this negative policy failed to gain support from two key factions—the Ch'en Brothers' "Organization Clique" or "CC Clique" and the Whampoa Clique in the military. During the early- and mid-thirties, these groups competed, more or less clandestinely, with Communist organizers in the schools. After the outbreak of the Second Sino-Japanese War, the Party reversed its negative policy by establishing the Three People's Principles Youth Corps under Whampoa leadership. The Corps' achievements, facilitated by wartime patriotism, were nullified after V-J Day. Under attack from jealous Party regulars, the Corps was amalgamated with the Party in 1947.

In recent years, the Communists have been plagued by competition between civilian and military factions in their Party for control of the youth movement. Since the failure of the Great Leap Forward, militant Maoists have criticized the CCP and its adjunct, the Youth League, for their policies of retrenchment. These ideological purists, led by Lin Piao and his adherents in the People's Liberation Army, circumvented the League and organized the Red Guards in the summer of 1966. The Guards' countrywide crusade was made possible by the army's organizational and logistic support.

The generation gap, which perplexes Communist leaders today, is accentuated by a cult of youth that has provided opportunities and problems for adult politicians ever since the May 4 Movement. Students led both KMT and CCP through their formative years, but both the KMT (which had been in existence for more than two decades before 1927) and the CCP (which had operated for nearly three decades prior to 1949) inevitably lost touch with the younger generation. The KMT, as we have seen, responded negatively to the challenge. During the early fifties, the CCP promoted student political action in a series of mass movements controlled by the Party and the Youth League. But from the mid-fifties to the mid-sixties, functions of mass organizations were appropriated by the Party-League apparatus, League leadership became the preserve of middle-aged men, and its membership grew older. The generational crisis is not likely to be resolved by the Red Guards' attempt to reaffirm the values of the youth cult by glorifying a seventy-three-year-old patriarch.

The Red Guard imbroglio reminds us that the CCP's relationship with the students has not been free of contradictions. Since the twenties, the Party has realized the value of students in organizing workers, peasants, and intellectuals. By defining the class nature of students as wholly or partly *petit-bourgeois,* the Party has been able to use them both as allies in united fronts and as scapegoats for the Party's failures. Communist ideologists have, however, found reliance upon such a privileged elite embarrassing to the Party of the proletariat. Thus, students have been expected to lose their sense of separate identity and to become one with the masses. Party ideologues repeatedly quote Mao Tse-tung's dictum:

> The ultimate line of demarcation between the revolutionary intellectuals, on the one hand, and nonrevolutionary and counter-revolutionary intellectuals, on the other, lies in whether they are willing to, and actually do, become one with the masses of workers and peasants.

Practical as well as ideological problems have compounded the Party's dilemma. By the Yenan period, the CCP was no longer a clique of intellectuals, but a rural-based political-military movement. This made it difficult for CCP to absorb the urban-intellectual youths who streamed in from Peiping, Tientsin, and other cities. From the viewpoint of the veterans of the Kiangsi Soviet and the Long March, these recruits were bookish and undisciplined. Thought reform was the Maoist cure for such ailments. The wartime movement labeled *cheng-feng* ("to correct unorthodox tendencies") was the first in a continuing series of attempts to remold students and intellectuals.

Tensions underlying student-Party relations since the mid-1920's still exist. Students remain largely bourgeois in family origin, hence untrustworthy, though their skills are needed as much as ever. CCP leaders fear that nearly half a century of revolution may be negated by residual habits of traditional careerism and modern professionalism among the young. The very structure of Chinese education contains built-in contradictions. The Communists inherited a university system modeled on the West's, manned by a Western-trained faculty, and designed to produce graduates dedicated to the disinterested pursuit of truth via "scientific" disciplines. With their newly acquired skills, these youths have sought to enter careers that would both further their own interests and modernize their fatherland. The Communists regard such attitudes as unfortunate hangovers from China's feudal and semicolonial eras. The pursuit of individual self-interest is thought to be incompatible with the development of the state, and the disinterested quest for scientific truth is considered secondary to the development of a "correct" Maoist *Weltanschauung*. The attempt to reconcile the contradictory purposes of education is formulated in the slogan, "Both Red and Expert." Changes in emphasis between these two desiderata have produced a series of crises, the most recent of which is the Great Proletarian Cultural Revolution with its offshoot, the Red Guards.

Red Guard membership initially was granted only to politically active students of proletarian origin. Youngsters with these qualifications had been accepted in institutions of middle and higher education during the Great Leap Forward, when it was more important to be Red than expert. It was they who suffered when the pendulum swung back, and academic performance became more important than ideological orthodoxy. Hence, in the spring and summer of 1966 they became enthusiastic recruits in campaigns to expel "bourgeois" chancellors, to revamp the system of entrance examinations, and to close the schools so that students could devote all their time to politics. These youth have but one hope for advancement in the highly competitive educational and economic systems—that political activism will replace academic achievement as the principal criterion of success. If the Communist leadership fails to satisfy their expectations, its quest for a generation of revolutionary successors will be doomed to failure. On the other hand, if it ceases to reward academic and technological achievement, its vision of a modern industrialized China will be shattered, and the country will be forced to fall back on its overcrowded rural hinterland.

Thus the CCP, like the KMT, has been trapped by its own ideology, by its failure to satisfy the expectations of youth who have taken the Party's teachings too literally. The Nationalists lost their student following by not acting sufficiently nationalistic; the Communists are now threatened by rebellious youth who demand that they practice Communism. The challenge posed by the Red Guards is likely to plague the Party long after the current leadership struggle is concluded.

The course of the Chinese student movement follows logically from China's history. The nation entered the twentieth century stumbling in the shadow of her past brilliance. Unlike Russia, where centralized despotism made anarchism attractive, China was weak, divided, and exploited. Hence, the goals of the student movement were state-oriented, those of internal unity, solidarity against foreign foes, national power through modernization and national identity through social revolution. Nationalism was equally important in helping students retain their personal identity as Chinese even while they were discarding their traditional heritage in favor of foreign innovations.

The nationalism of the 1905–1911 movement was both racialistic and modern. Its assumption was that China would grow strong if the alien Manchus were dethroned and traditional governmental forms were replaced with republican institutions. Nationalism in the garb of anti-imperialism and anti-Christianity developed rapidly after the 21 Demands and reached its peak after the May 30 incident. Like anti-Manchu nationalism, it blamed foreigners for China's woes, and this enhanced its appeal. Students supported the goal of the Northern Expedition—national unification via military conquest—but failed to appreciate Chiang's continued obsession with this program during the Japanese invasion of the thirties. Civil war had less nationalistic appeal than anti-imperialistic war. Between 1937 and 1945, KMT and CCP vied for popular support, each arguing that it embodied the principle of national solidarity against the Japanese.

After the war, the KMT contended that its struggle against Communist rebels carried on the task of national unification begun in the fight against the Manchus and continued in the Northern Expedition and the anti-Japanese crusade. But instead of a decadent dynasty, venal warlords, or imperialistic Japanese, the KMT faced a resurgent Communist movement. Mao, who had also established his patriotic credentials during eight years of resistance, offered a "new democratic" China as an alternative to the discredited government of the postwar Kuomintang. Convinced that the KMT was the main obstacle to internal harmony and that continued attempts to extirpate the Communists could lead only to interminable civil war, the students became Chiang's harshest critics during this crucial period.

Even though successive generations of Chinese students may be characterized as nationalistic, this does not imply an absence of change. Political circumstances altered the quality of that nationalism from decade to decade. The most influential force for change was the intrusion of partisan politics into every sphere of student activity: hence, the enormous difference between the nonpartisan May 4 Movement of 1919 and the highly politicized May 30 Movement six years later, to say nothing of events in 1935 and 1947. This intrusion reached its logical conclusion after 1949, when the student movement became a tool of Party control. Partisan politics have similarly engulfed other areas of Chinese life—most notably in literature where the social consciousness of the twenties evolved into the revolutionary polemics of the thirties, the patriotic homilies of the war years, and then state indoctrination after 1949.

Student politics have also varied greatly in intensity. Movements have flourished in modern China when governments appeared weak and inept. Only those able to control the nation's territory, manage its educational system effectively, and carry out energetic programs in domestic and foreign policy have generally succeeded in avoiding massive student protest: hence, the frequency of student disorder during the late Ch'ing and warlord periods. The promise of unity and reform gave the Nanking government relative immunity from 1928 to September, 1931, and from 1932 to December, 1935. The December 9 Movement erupted in the least-controlled university (Yenching) of an insecure area (North China), endangered by vacillation in foreign policy. National resistance to Japan and tight KMT control of Southwest China's campuses dampened student protest during the war, but governmental weaknesses encouraged its reemergence in 1945.

There has been a tension in Chinese student thought between the desire for personal liberty and the quest for a strong state, but by and large liberty has been a secondary issue. When the government has been strong, students have grumbled about suppression of civil liberties, but they have not rebelled. Only weak governments have had to answer for repressive policies. No rulers allowed greater academic freedom than the warlords who were more concerned with fighting battles than with running schools, but none elicited more bitter student opposition. KMT thought control failed because it was conceptually and operationally deficient, not because students valued freedom of thought above all else. CCP means of coercion have been more oppressive and more effective. The Communists mastered techniques of internal social control; the Kuomintang always seemed to approach students from the outside. Internal discipline, whether in a Peiping school or a Yenan thought-reform center, was more acceptable than external control by school administrators or military police. Pro-Kuomintang students were easily detected, labeled "running dogs," and isolated. Pro-CCP students were admired as self-sacrificing idealists.

Aside from its technical proficiency, the CCP was fortunate to arrive on the scene just in time to collect the fruits of revolutionary harvest. A century of national humiliation and a succession of thwarted reforms had imparted an irresistible allure to radical solutions. In the politics and literature of the students, as of the nation at large, unsuccessful fathers bequeathed a profounder radicalism to their sons. The generation of monarchial reform symbolized by K'ang Yu-wei (born 1858) was followed by one of republicanism epitomized by Sun Yat-sen (born 1866) and finally by the Communism of Mao Tse-tung (born 1893). In this context, the neo-Confucianism of Chiang Kai-shek (born 1888), modeled as it was upon the conservative reformer Tseng Kuo-fan (born 1811), seemed strangely out of place.

The intellectual, psychological, and moral vacuum left by the breakdown of the universal Confucian order was too vast to be filled by the relativistic pragmatism of John Dewey and Hu Shih. A new and totalistic world view was necessary—one that would explain China's failures without undermining national pride. Hence, the appeal evoked by a theory that blamed imperialists and reactionaries, but exculpated the Chinese people. Leninism did this. It analyzed a perplexing and oppressive environment in simple terms and plotted a corrective course of action. In its united-front version (incorporated into Mao's New Democracy), Leninist doctrine reserved an important role for the *petit-bourgeois* intellectuals. This was essential to an intellectual elite whose consciousness of its own political pre-eminence had survived the demise of Confucianism.

Mao offered China's students an attractive blend of the modern and the traditional, a combination by no means unique to Chinese Communism. Superficially, Chinese Communism appeared to be anything but modern. Under Mao's hegemony, life in the regions was technologically primitive compared with the urbanized sector under Chiang. In terms of social mobilization, however, Mao's efforts to bring the masses into politics were most modern even though they drew upon an indigenous tradition of peasant rebellions. Mao adopted a radically modern ideology, but he *adapted* it to Chinese conditions by finding the source of absolute virtue in the downtrodden rural masses. In the Communist countryside, students found assurance that they could be both pure and progressive, radical reformers and 100 per cent Chinese. On the other hand, Chiang's attempt to foster Confucian values in a foreignized urban environment seemed to combine the least appealing features of past and present.

Similarities between the recent Red Guard phenomenon and student movements of the past can be found only at a high level of historical abstraction. For example, frustrated careerism and betrayed idealism continue to unsettle China's youths. Students still view themselves as incorruptible social critics, and the purity of their protests is, as before, compromised by adult intrigue. One can isolate features of the Red Guards reminiscent of the traditional censorate, the Boxer uprising, and the post-May 4 student movements, to say nothing of Hitler Youth.

The historian, however, is more impressed by the discontinuities. The most striking of these is the change in scale. In December, 1931, the capital city of Nanking was deluged with an unprecedented 16,600 demonstrators. In the late months of 1966, Peking received eleven million. This is indicative of a second fundamental change: The present government is the first in modern Chinese history capable of disciplining and mobilizing students on all levels throughout the country. Even the Red Guards, a product of internal struggle, testify most eloquently to this development. Unlike pre-Communist student movements, they represent an induced rebellion of part of the system against the whole, not a more or less spontaneous attack by an extralegal revolutionary force. Finally, the nationalistic component of the Red Guards is relatively weaker than it was in pre-1949 student movements. To some extent, this is a tribute to the Communists' success in removing the two principal targets of student protest: internal disunity and foreign exploitation. But chaos, for which the Red Guards are partially responsible, has shattered national unity and invited outside interference. Thus, there is no reason to suppose that adulation of the Maoist cult has permanently superseded the tradition of nationalistic student protest.

The world-famous *Zengakuren* of Japan is analyzed in its social context. Three types of student movements are distinguished: in-campus, co-campus, and extra-campus. The first are concerned only with an individual institution and are run by its students. The issues are directly relevant to their campus life. These movements occur spontaneously and attract a majority of the enrollment on the campus involved. When, however, issues directly relevant to student life cannot be solved within a particular institution, students of many colleges cooperate with each other, thus running a co-campus movement. Formal organizations like *Zengakuren* are founded in this way. When political disputes of a broader-than-educational significance become the central concern of students, cooperation with non-student organizations like political parties and labor unions is necessary. Movements of this kind are named extra-campus. In post-war Japan, these three types of student movements can be seen in the periods from 1945–47, 1948–50, and 1951 to date, respectively.

Gradual radicalization, federation, and bureaucratization are found in both pre- and post-war student movements. But the pre-war movements were run by underground, cohesive minorities, whereas the post-war movements have mobilized the majority of Japanese university students. The latter are open, legal, heterogeneous, and not very cohesive mass movements.

12

Comparison between Pre- and Post-War Student Movements in Japan

Michiya Shimbori

History of Zengakuren

Since June, 1960, the word *"Zengakuren"* has been added to the vocabulary of other languages than Japanese, from which it originated.

Zengakuren is an abridgement of *Zen*-Nihon-*Gakusei*-Jichikai-So-*Rengo*, which means literally "All Japan Federation of College Student Governments." Although the association was formally organized on September 18, 1948, political movements among Japanese college

From Michiya Shimbori, "Comparison Between Pre- and Post-War Student Movements in Japan," *Sociology of Education*, 37 (Fall 1963), 59–70. Reprinted by permission of the American Sociological Association.

students can be traced back to much earlier times. While most writers recognize that the student political movement began hand in hand with the spreading labor movement after the First World War, a few contemporary writers say that this movement is as old as Japanese higher institutions, starting its history in 1876. Anyway, it is certain that Japanese students did not begin their movement against the political regime all of a sudden, but that they had a fairly long tradition along the same lines.

Although the students had a political movement prior to the formal organization of *Zengakuren,* it is proper for us to pay attention first to the *post-war* development of student movements. In the first few years after the Second World War, when there was scarcely an elite of substantial power except the occupying forces, there was no student political movement. This period is characterized by the uprooting of the war leaders, the anarchy of the political and ideological orders, and by the disastrous destruction of the economy. The main concern of the people was to survive each day. The evacuated, the jobless, and the returned soldiers crowded into the destroyed cities. The whole value system and the class which had ruled the country were regarded with disgust. Nevertheless this economic, political, and ideological anarchy did not necessarily lead to utter despair in the people's minds. It may be said that, in a sense, there had been no period when the Japanese were more idealistic or more oriented to their future than this. The pre-war value system was dominated by an authoritarian, semi-feudalistic, ultra-nationalistic ideology, and this fact was favorable to keeping the Japanese from desperate pessimism at the defeat, since they had been accustomed to following and internalizing the value system given from above. The occupying forces imposed a thorough reform in the name of "democracy." This newly-introduced value system was easily accepted and appreciated because of its universal applicability. The people were convinced that it could be realized in a country which had lost everything and which, therefore, was like virgin soil. "Government of the people, by the people, for the people," "Switzerland in Asia," "equality of human rights," "abolition of all armed forces" were phrases given by the occupying Americans and accepted by the Japanese people.

Thus, in this period, when the only power elite was the occupying forces which could not be criticized or attacked, and when the people consumed their whole energy in maintaining a mere existence, there could not be a student movement of a political kind. In the educational world, democratic reform—including the introduction of a one-track system and of coeducation; the abolition of nationally unified textbooks; the purge of militaristic curricula and teachers; and the callback of previously-fired democratic, liberal, or communist professors—was imposed by General Headquarters and enforced by the Japanese government. The survivals of the pre-war order were easily removed. The occupying forces, the government, and the students implemented the democratic reform in education.

Student movements in this period focused on "democratization" of the campus. Their efforts were devoted to purging the militaristic professors; just distribution of rations or of the products of the school farm; reorganization of the student government; and more voice for the students in school administration. We define this kind of student movement as an "in-campus movement," because it is confined to the students of a particular institution and its activities take place on a particular campus. The years which immediately followed the war saw frequent "in-campus" movements. For instance, two months after the end of the war, in the Ueno Girls' Middle School, Tokyo, students won a victory over the school authorities in their claim for democratization of the administration by going on a strike.

These in-campus movements developed spontaneously and fought separately. There were no common targets for attack among students in various schools, but there was a general slogan of "democratization of the campus." Gradually, however, the movements came to be organized beyond the limits of each individual campus. This happened mainly because of three political events: the governmental policies of 1) increased fees (1947); 2) decentralization of national universities (1948); and 3) the "red-purge" (1949). These policies were ordered by General Headquarters and were to be enforced by the Japanese government. They were taken to be real and vital threats to their welfare by the academic world of Japan.

In October 1947, the Ministry of Education showed its intention to raise the fees of the national university students by 300%. Historically, the leading higher institutions of Japan were established and given various privileges by the government. One of the privileges is low fees, which attract a great many bright students of humble origin. The students, who were suffering from miserable economic conditions after the war, were indignant at the news, thinking it a challenge to equality of educational opportunities. In December, 1947, CIE published a plan which recommended reorganization of national universities into local ones, supported by prefectural governments instead of the central government, after the model of the American state universities. This plan met ardent opposition on the part of academic men. Many felt that the financially and academically poor local authorities could not ensure a high standard for universities; that the nationally-founded universities had enjoyed a precious freedom from lay control or from control by narrow local interests; and that the higher institutions were distributed—as they should be—according to nationwide considerations and not local ones. Not only the so-called progressive professors and students, but also the governmental Committee on Educational Reform, and the Association of Accredited Universities showed strong opposition to this plan.

Facing this opposition, the CIE and the Ministry of Education, in March 1948, substituted a plan to establish boards of trustees, again after the model of American state universities. The idea of lay control of higher institutions along with the proposed strengthening of the supervising power of the Ministry, was again seen as a threat to academic freedom. The National Association of University Professors, the Committee on Educational Reform, the Japan Academy of Higher Learning, and some university presidents expressed opposition to this plan, and at last the government withdrew this "University Bill" in May 1949.

These conditions stimulated a different kind of student movement from the previous ones, since the problems were national in nature and could not be effectively attacked by the students of a particular college. The students resisted the governmental plans. The raising of fees and the proposed bill on university administration, as distinct from "democratization" of a particular campus, were issues common to all campuses. Faced with these new problems, the students united.

The government plans to raise fees and to reorganize university administration mobilized the students' energy easily, and the leaders of various organizations made quick use of the fact.

Thus, the *Zengakuren* was organized on September 8, 1948, with 168 national, 31 municipal, and 61 private universities as its members. The membership of *Zengakuren* consists of student *governments* on various campuses, *not* of individual students. And student governments, as a rule, have all the students as their members automatically. It is reported that student governments in 76.5% of the national universities held membership in the *Zengakuren* in 1959, so that more than half of the students in the national universities have at least nominally a relation with the *Zengakuren*.

However, student governments differ in their aims. While it is commonly held by neutral researchers that the Communists took a decisive role in organizing the *Zengakuren,* and while it may be argued that its movements have been always the outcome of agitation by Communist leaders—the majority being always indifferent—the crucial point is that the *Zengakuren* has developed along a line different from the intention of its originators. It has really mobilized the majority of the students throughout the country *under certain circumstances.*

Following the struggle against the proposed University Bill, the so-called "Red-purge *Toso*" (struggle against the Red-purge) stirred the students into action. On July 19, 1950, Dr. Eels, consultant for the CIE, publicized the intention of the occupying forces to dismiss "Red" professors. This announcement had a most profound impact upon academic circles. The following two years saw a great many resistance movements by the students. Eels was scheduled to give speeches on "Academic Freedom," "Academic Freedom and Communism," and the like on several university campuses to propagate the policy. He met a strong protest on the part of the students and he stood helplessly on the stage. The struggle against the Red purge culminated in the general strikes on June 3 and October 5, 1950, as well as in the fight between students and policemen in the Students' Assembly at the Waseda University on October 19, and at the Kyoto University on November 25, 1950. Faced with this violent resistance, the government and the administration authorities could not implement their initial intention, except in a few private universities. These are examples of the second stage of the student movements.

Thus, gradually, the student movements passed from the first stage with spasmodic demonstrations, isolated organizations, and "campus" concerns through the second stage with nationwide, permanent, co-campus organizations but still with concerns related to academic life, to the third stage with the same organizations as in the second stage but with "extra-campus," political concerns not directly related to education.

In the third stage, purely national political matters stimulated the student movements. Some of the issues were: whether Japan should conclude a peace treaty with the western nations as early as possible or with all nations, including the Communist camps, even if this could come only later; whether or not Japan should protect her safety by means of a U.S.-Japan Security Pact; whether or not Japan should revise the Constitution for rearmament; whether or not Japan should agree to a universal nuclear test ban. All of these were controversies in which students were involved as citizens rather than as students. Their movements were characterized at this stage by cooperation with non-student organizations. Therefore, they can be named "extra-campus" movements in contrast to the second stage when the movements were still run mainly by students themselves. Roughly speaking, the first stage covers the period from 1945–47, the second 1948–50, and the third 1951 to date. (Nineteen fifty-one is the year of conclusion of the Peace Treaty at San Francisco.)

Pre-War Student Movements

As said before, student movements can be traced back to much earlier times; they are not exclusively phenomena of the post-war period. The pre-war period had two cycles. The first ran roughly from 1874 to 1917, from the period of the *Jiyu-minken Undo* (a movement which struggled for civil liberties) to the period of the Russian Revolution. The second proceeded from 1918 to 1944: from the period of *Taisho* Democracy, a democratic movement during and after the First World War which struggled for universal suffrage, to the end of the Second World War.

The ideology in both cycles began with democracy and developed into socialism, syndicalism, anarchism or communism. However, the pre-war student movements were concerned from the beginning with non-academic, political matters as well as issues affecting the campus.

In-campus movements in the pre-war period, apart from various kinds of school revolts, were usually in defense of academic freedom. The pre-war movements were a result of governmental efforts to purge progressive and critical professors. Another important pre-war movement was against introducing military training into the college curriculum. After the First World War, the government tried to employ surplus army officers in the schools, and the military authorities propagated the necessity of military training in school. In 1923, a dramatic event occurred at Waseda University where a pro-military student organization called The Study Group on Military Matters was to be founded. The opening assembly was attended by leading generals as well as the President and some professors. They were barracked and could not complete their address. In the student assembly after a couple of days, some five thousand students, half of all the enrollment, participated in attacking militarism in education and the Study Group, as a result, could not be formed. Starting with this episode, both in- and extra-campus movements against military training were seen elsewhere and mobilized a great many students. A co-campus organization, named the National Student Union against Military Training, was organized, sponsored by the Student Federation of Social Science, which was an offspring of the Federation of Students.

Distinct from the in-campus movements, co- and extra-campus ones did not occur spontaneously, but were organized deliberately by leaders. They were not stimulated by a particular affair as were the in-campus movements, but affected by a more or less general atmosphere of the time. The difference between the pre-war and post-war movements consists in the fact that in the pre-war period a sharp line could not be drawn between co- and extra-campus movements. Co-campus, federated organizations were, from the beginning, political and non-campus oriented. In the post-war movements, as seen before, co-campus organizations developed from in-campus into extra-campus ones by an evolutionary process.

Another important difference lies in the fact that the pre-war co-campus organizations afforded membership to individual persons, not to the whole body of students in an institution, as in the post-war ones. This means that the pre-war organizations were more or less closed, "underground societies" in time of oppression, while in the post-war period any student is a potential member of the organization and thus can participate in any action he considers urgent. Thus the pre-war, co-campus organizations were formed and led by non-students, participated in by a minority of member-students, and fused with non-campus organizations.

Many influential organizations were born in 1918, the year of the end of the First World War when the ideology of democracy and socialism poured into Japan, the Russian and the German Revolutions had a strong impact upon intellectuals and laborers, and the class conflict grew keener owing to the rapid development of capitalism, industrialism, and urbanism during the War. *Rogaku-kai* (Association of Laborers and Students) around Tokyo and Kyoto Universities, *Shinjin-kai* (Society of New Men) in Tokyo University, *Minjin-domei* (Union of Common Men) in Waseda University, *Gyomin-kai* (Society of Pioneers) around Waseda University, *Kensetsusha-domei* (Union of Builders) around Waseda, *Fushin-kai* (Society of Common Faith) in Hosei University, *Shakai-shiso-kenkyu-kai* (Society for the Study of Social Thoughts) in the First High School were founded mostly in that year. Although most of them were organized within the campus, they cannot properly be called "in-campus" organizations because membership was not restricted to the students of a single university. Cooperation was sought with the students of other universities, with laborers, and with intellectuals. Progressive professors and alumni helped in organizing and acted as consultants. For example, *Shinjin-kai*, the most famous and influential organization of the time, was formed in 1918 by a group of progressive students who had gathered around Professor Sakuzo Yoshino, the intellectual leader of *Taisho* democracy. They published a journal entitled *Democracy* and ran lectures by sympathizing intellectuals. Laborers joined the Society. Thus the Society was from the beginning an extra-campus as well as in-campus organization, and so also with other associations.

In 1922, *Gakusei-Rengo-kai* (Federation of Students) was formed to unify those who had already cooperated in the "campaign to rescue hungry Russians" in the preceding two years. Likewise in 1923, *Koto-gakko-Remmei* (High School League) was founded by representatives of several high schools in order to propagate Communism among students. These were typical co-campus organizations. Since all forms of socialism, to say nothing of communism, were tabooed legally, and organizations with the slightest inclination toward socialism were at once suppressed, many of them were underground organizations with a few militant devotees. For instance, the High School League, in spite of its grand name, was founded in secret by some ten members who had been endeavoring to establish a society for the study of ideological matters, and it did not last long.

As the action movements with a revolutionary orientation were suppressed, the students who had been concerned with non-campus matters moved in safer and more socially acceptable directions. One was the formation of study groups, and the other, formation of *non-militant* action organizations. The *Shakai Kagaku Kenkyu-kai* (Society for the Study of Social Science) and *Gakusei* Settlement (Students' Settlement Working) movements were initiated and spread in 1924.

The students' efforts to find a safer channel for their movements in the form of study groups can be traced in the following way. The movement for universal suffrage in 1923 and 1924 had not won substantial victory, but on the contrary, the legal basis for suppressing social movements was laid in 1925 under the name of the notorious *Chian Iji Ho* (Law to Maintain Order). Terrorism at the hands of militarists and chauvinists became a common experience for progressives. The disorder following the Great Earthquake in Tokyo in 1923 gave the government an excuse for forceful suppression of radicals. Moreover, the Communist Party of the time was thrown into confusion by the opinion that it should be liberalized and enter into "the mass" before undertaking a communist revolution.

All this had a profound effect upon student movements around

1924. Formerly the members were urged to take an active part in revolutionary movements but now this emphasis on "practice" was replaced by "theory." It was claimed that a theoretical study of revolutionary doctrine had to procede practical activity.

In 1924, the assembly of *Gakusei Rengo-kai* discussed whether theoretical study or practical movements should come first, and a conclusion was reached in favor of the former. The organization changed its name to *Gakusei Shakai Kagaku Rengo-kai* (Student Federation of Social Science). The Federation, although it resumed the initial practical orientation now and then, and met with continuous suppression, attracted a relatively larger number of students, and lasted until 1929; then it was reorganized into the Student Group of Communist Youth. Already on March 15, 1928, the government arrested Communist leaders, including students, and shortly after, the administrative authorities of all schools forbade student organizations with a political orientation. Thus the Federation became an underground organization.

The Student Settlement movement, on the contrary, had a much more fortunate fate, because its activities were humanitarian and peaceful. Professors and students built a settlement in a slum area which served as a university extension for laborers, a nursery school for their children, and a medical clinic for them. The students entered into the proletariat and helped them with their knowledge and skills. This moderate type of student movement, although it became a refuge for revolutionary students, survived until the outbreak of the Second World War. This was also the case with the student cooperative movement. This movement, which was initiated by the members of the Society for the Study of Social Problems at the Waseda University in 1926, ran a cooperative store at many universities.

Similarities

Reviewing the history of student movements in pre- and post-war Japan, we can generalize their similarities in the following way:

1. Student movements were likely to appear first in times of social emancipation. If we begin the history of pre-war student movements

with 1874, the time was known as *Jiyu Minken Undo* (Movement for Civil Liberties and Human Rights), or if we begin with 1918, it was the time of *Taisho* democracy and the Russian Revolution. In both periods, the demand for democracy was quite popular, and the government itself was inclined to inaugurate a new regime along this line. The post-war movement began in 1945, when the old regime was overthrown, and the people were emancipated under the occupation policy. In short, the emergence of student movements in an overt form is possible in a more or less democratic social climate or when the oppressive power of a reactionary political elite is weakening.

2. In-campus movements appeared naturally and spasmodically. They were concerned with matters related directly to student life on the campus of their own institution, for instance, raising the fee, firing a favorite professor, imposing military training, appointing an autocratic principal. They were stimulated by particular events. They could usually mobilize many students and succeed in realizing their initial aim, but the organization was usually loose and short-lived. Academic freedom was the commonest ideology of movements of this kind.

3. Extra-campus movements tended to develop stimulated by more general social movements, e.g., the campaigns for universal suffrage and trade unionism before the war; and movements against *Hakai Katsudo Boshi Ho* (The Law Prohibiting Destructive Actions), *Anzenhosho Jyoyaku* (The U.S.-Japan Security Pact), United States military bases and nuclear testing after the war. These were all nationwide controversies of the period. Movements of this kind cooperated closely with outside organizations, and had a more or less solid and continuing organization of their own. They usually met with attempts at suppression on the part of the elite in power, and the probability of success was lower than for in-campus movements.

4. Some of the in-campus movements were necessarily organized into co-campus ones. For example, introducing military training, purging Red professors, or raising the fees in governmental universities were proposed or enforced by the government, so that they could not be fought solely within a single campus. Intercollegiate cooperation became necessary. Since Japanese higher education has been built and controlled by the government, and the most active leaders

of the student movements have been in the national universities, not the private ones, the transformation from in-campus into co-campus movements was natural. When this transformation occurred, the organization of the movement grew clearer.

It is also common to the pre- and post-war movements that most of the co-campus as well as the extra-campus movements took form in metropolitan areas, where most of the students gather and where most of the leading universities are located; where the target of attack—the government—is also located; where organizations such as labor unions are powerful; and where social problems are highly visible.

5. The ideology and tactics of the movements were likely to become more radical as time passed and as movements went from in-campus through co-campus to extra-campus form. The moderate claim for democracy or liberalism developed into a demand for socialism and still further to communism. Tactics, too, proceeded from the moderate and peaceful type, such as lectures and student assemblies, to more violent types, such as general strikes and mass demonstrations.

The reasons for this last are several. The more organized the movement, the more necessary are radical professional leaders. The more suppression there is, the more violent the counteractions. The more political the movement, the more influential are non-student revolutionary organizations. The more idealistic the students, the more thoroughgoing and clear-cut is their ideology. A circular process can be noticed. The more radical the movement, the greater the suppression and the less the possibility of success, thus the still more radical the movement. The result is professionalization of leadership and greater distance between leaders and followers. Also, professors who had been consultants or sympathetic guides of student organizations could not continue to be associated with the radical students.

Differences

1. While before the Second World War political movements could mobilize only relatively few students and non-political movements mobilized more, the post-war political movements mobilized

a general majority of the students. The political organizations of the pre-war period were mostly underground and had a radical revolutionary ideology, while those after the war were open. The former were composed of members who were keenly class-conscious and revolutionary, and recruited only those who had been converted to a definite ideology. Their members had a high degree of solidarity, loyalty, sense of mission, and heroism. Between the members and the rest of the students there was a strong barrier, psychological as well as organizational. After the war, all students were potential members of all student organizations, and they could participate in any action if they wished.

Thus the post-war student organizations were less cohesive, and less continuous, and the number of mobilized members was in flux. The psychology of the participants in the post-war movements was also characterized by less loyalty to the organization, more diverse attitudes toward the ideology, less feeling of grandeur or mission, and less sense of guilt. The movements themselves lost the dark complexion of underground, unlawful associations, and were taken for granted. They grew from monopolization by half-professional leaders, to a phenomenon of the masses of ordinary students.

2. The more diverse attitudes toward ideology; the greater number of participants; the heterogeneity of the members; the ease of being either active or passive in organizations—all these contributed to a growing autonomy of the students in post-war extra-campus movements. In the pre-war extra-campus movements, the students were eager to assimilate themselves to non-student members, especially laborers. To accomplish this, for example, they put off their college uniform and cap, which symbolized the status of a student. The movements were often led by organizations other than those of the students.

On the other hand, in the post-war extra-campus movements, the students gained more hegemony and autonomy. Sometimes they became far more radical than the former sponsoring agency, so that they were dismissed from membership in the extra-campus organization.

3. It follows that the post-war organizations were more likely to be split into many opposing factions.

4. Co-campus organizations or federations became more popular after the war. Before the war, such federation, if any, was nominal and regional. After the war, federation was built on a nationwide scale. Thus the student movements could no longer be monopolized by the active students in the metropolitan areas. This was partly due to the rapid development of mass communication and transportation facilities, and also to the decentralization of higher education.

5. There were fewer *counter*-movements, i.e., movements *defending* the elite in power after the war than before. The pre-war period saw a great many conservative student organizations which were against progressive students. Ultra-nationalistic, chauvinistic, militaristic, Emperor-centric, or shintoistic ideologies which opposed all kinds of civil state regimes whether democratic, socialistic, or communistic, were their leading principles. The students with these ideologies, led by conservative professors, were organized as soon as the progressive movements began. When the leftist organizations were forced underground, these rightist organizations became the only lawful ones. But their members were limited in number and could not get much sympathy among the majority of the students. After the war, this kind of counter-movement scarcely existed. All the members of the progressive student movement enjoyed freedom of expression, without any forceful or legal opposition on the part of the government or rightist organizations.

Here we have an example of a student movement that was at
one time deeply involved in the nationalist agitation that lead to
India's independence. Since that time student activism has been
limited in scope, and its causes have become rooted more in educational and economic problems than in politics.

13

The Transformation of the Indian
Student Movement

Philip G. Altbach

Students constitute a key element in the economic and political development in many of the new states of Asia, Africa, and Latin America. In some nations they have toppled governments, in others they
have played a significant role in nationalist struggles. In almost all of
the developing nations, the student community constitutes a primary
source of technologically trained manpower, and an important impetus to the process of modernization. The elites which will have a
major responsibility for shaping the affairs of the emerging nations
are, to a large degree, recruited from the student community.

In many nations, the student movement—that segment of the student community which has organized itself for political or social action—has made significant contributions to political development. In
several of the new states, student movements have been involved in
revolutionary political struggles, in educational and cultural reforms,
and in a range of political and social concerns. Students have gained
valuable training in political methods and ideology through the
student movement. In many instances, the student political movements have been instrumental in shaping political and social attitudes
of the emerging (and occasionally the incumbent) elites in the developing nations. These student organizations, often the largest Western-
oriented groups in the nation, have proved to be a spiritual and ideo-

From Philip G. Altbach, "The Transformation of the Indian Student Movement," *Asian Survey*, 6, no. 8 (August 1966), 448–460. Reprinted by permission of the University of California Press.

logical "home" for those individuals who seek to engender Western values and methods.

Student organizations have often provided an important adjunct to the formal education which emerging elites receive in schools and colleges. The extra-curricular role of the student movement, as well as the views of this movement on educational issues can provide a valuable source of information on educational policy and development in the new nations. It is a fact that much of the student "discontent" so much discussed by educators and politicians has its roots in grievances directly related to education.

India offers a particularly interesting model for examining the role of the student movement. Its long tradition of Western education has built up a sizeable Westernized class. It has seen indigenous organized political activity at least since the founding of the Indian National Congress in 1885. The long struggle for independence from the British, which went through a number of significant stages and ended in the non-violent mass movement led by Gandhi, also provided a training ground for political activists and forced the Westernized middle classes to build a broad based movement. Almost two decades of independence has allowed indigenous political institutions to develop and problems of economic development, educational reform, and political stabilization to reveal themselves.

The Indian student movement has been intimately concerned with most of these developments, and was deeply involved in and committed to the nationalist movement. It can be divided into two distinct phases which mirror some of the important changes which have taken place in Indian society. Prior to Independence in 1947, the students took an active part in the political life of the nation, and were organized into a number of powerful movements. Political groups were quite influential in the student community and provided strong support to the nationalist movement. Since Independence, the student movement in India has all but collapsed. Most of the organizations which exercised so strong an influence on the students have disappeared, and the spirit of nationalism and sacrifice has left the campus. Indian students exhibit something of an ambivalence about the society in which they must take their place, and there is a notable lack of enthusiasm for the vital tasks of nation building.

The Student Movement and the Independence Struggle

Prior to 1920, the small Indian student community had little experience with politics, and concerned itself primarily with its academic program and with cultural affairs. But as the nationalist movement grew and was gradually transformed under Gandhi's leadership from a middle class "debating society" into a militant mass movement, the students took an increasingly active role in politics. The impact of nationalism was combined with Western intellectual influences— particularly the ideas of the British Fabian socialists and later the Russian Communists. During the 1920's, many student groups were formed which took an interest in politics. The nascent Indian Communist movement, as well as the left-wing of the Congress, were active on the campuses, and discussion groups devoted to politics were popular. The right-wing Rashtriya Swayamsevak Sangh (RSS), which emphasized Hindu nationalism and cultural regeneration was also born during this period and had a strong element of student support.

Gandhi's Non-Cooperation movement of 1920 was the first political struggle in which students were involved on a substantial scale. The call for students to quit their colleges and support Congress-sponsored "national colleges" received substantial backing. Although the national colleges were short-lived, the traditional educational structure was temporarily thrown into confusion. Students helped with Congress campaigns and meetings, and when Congress leaders were arrested, students assumed the leadership of the movement.

The 1920 movement provided the students with valuable political experience and established the student movement as a part of campus life in India. The organizations formed in the course of the struggle continued to exist, and politically minded students involved themselves in "constructive" social service projects and in study circles. Youth Leagues were formed in major educational centers with the help of leftist Congress leaders, and the first annual All India Student Conference was held in 1920 to provide coordination to the growing student political movement. The dominant trend among the politically minded students was radical, and Gandhian traditionalism and non-violence had much less influence than socialist ideologies. The annual student conferences, which normally attracted more than 3,000 student delegates from all parts of India, provided left-wing Congressmen with a platform and with support for their views.

While only a minority of the Indian student community was politically active during the 1920's, it was during this period that the movement established itself and gained both organizational experience and some degree of ideological sophistication. Student cultural associations also came into their own and became an important part of campus life. Organizations devoted to debating, drama, literature and other subjects blossomed at many colleges, often with the support of the college authorities. For the first time, students were involved in large numbers in the planning and administration of extracurricular activities. While unrelated to politics, such activities gave students a sense of confidence as well as training in organizational matters.

The 1930's brought an intensification of the political struggle in India and along with it a growth in the student movement. Gandhi's militant Civil Disobedience movement of 1930 involved students on an unprecedented scale, and many of the activities calculated to impair British administration in India were carried out by students. Colleges were closed, agitations launched, and illegal publications distributed. Hundreds of students were dismissed from their colleges or were sent to jail. While the struggle died down after almost a year, the student movement continued its activity, and the All India Students' Federation was organized in 1936 to provide a unified voice for the student movement. From the beginning, the AISF was strongly nationalist and radical in its political views. Communists, socialists, and Gandhians worked harmoniously within the AISF and provincial affiliates were organized in all parts of India. The annual AISF conferences, held at the same time as the sessions of the Indian National Congress, attracted upwards of 3,000 delegates and the top Congress leaders addressed the students.

In this period, the newly-formed Congress Socialist Party had a strong influence on politically minded students, as did the small but articulate Communist Party. Study groups trained cadres in ideology as well as in organizational tactics. Many committed student leaders became active in the growing trade union movement or in the cultural organizations sponsored by the leftist political groups.

In addition to the "mainstream" nationalist student movement, a number of other important trends existed within the student movement. Many Muslim students, previously apathetic or pro-Congress, were influenced by Mohammad Ali Jinnah's call for a separate Muslim state in India and joined the Muslim League's All India Muslim Students' Federation. This organization did not participate in the independence movement, but instead pressed for Muslim rights and defended Muslims when they were attacked. Muslim student organizations also shaped the political ideologies of a whole generation of Muslim leaders, and were particularly important because of the relative backwardness of the Muslim community in India.

The Hindu right-wing also gained strength. The RSS appealed to militant Hindu nationalism and to anti-Muslim and anti-Christian sentiments among the Hindus. By upholding traditional Hindu values, then under attack from Westernized elements in India, the RSS was able to attract many students, particularly in smaller colleges. Its para-military program which emphasized physical training and discipline, appealed to many students. The Hindu Students' Federation was similar in ideology to the RSS, although its approach was somewhat more sophisticated. As a counter to the RSS, secular-minded leftists organized the Rashtra Seva Dal (RSD), which also sponsored a para-military program in addition to other cultural and social activities. The RSD was devoted to secular values and did much to overcome the communalism of both Hindu and Muslim extremists. Its strength was mainly in Maharashtra, while the RSS drew most of its support from the Hindi-speaking areas of north India.

By 1938, the Indian colleges were highly politicized. While the "mainstream" leftist student groups had a dominant position, they were by no means unchallenged. As the nationalist movement gained strength and militancy, students took a more active part in the struggle, and many voluntarily left the colleges to work in the labor movement or with Gandhian constructive programs. The increasing ideological sophistication of the student movement also created problems, and the factional infighting which has become characteristic of Indian politics grew rapidly.

The split in the All India Students' Federation in 1940 was indicative of this trend. The differences between the Communists on one side and the socialists and Gandhians on the other came into the open in 1940. The Communist faction was able to impose its support for the Soviet Union and its strong criticism of the Congress on the AISF. The socialists led a walk-out, and two separate student organizations were formed as a result. The bitterness engendered and the energy wasted during these disputes weakened the student movement, sowing the seeds of further factional problems later.

During the 1942 "Quit India" movement, the students played a key role; the nationalist student movement (the Communists at this time were actively supporting the British war effort) succeeded in closing most of India's colleges for extended periods, and involved masses of students in the struggle. Students who had not previously been involved in politics worked for the Congress and participated in almost daily demonstrations. Committed student cadres took part in sabotage campaigns and tried, with some success, to disrupt British administration. When the adult Congress leadership was arrested, the students took over much of the leadership of the struggle and acted as a liaison between underground leaders and the movement. Student groups published illegal newspapers, and even operated a clandestine radio station.

The 1942 struggle was the apex of the student movement in India, involving for the first time a majority of the students. Thousands were jailed, and many thousands were dismissed from their colleges. The militancy of the 1942 movement was retained, if on a reduced scale, until the end of the Independence struggle. The nationalist student movement had achieved substantial influence on the campus, and many of the best students participated in the struggle.

By 1946, however, the student movement had lost much of its impetus. While the Students' Congress (the nationalist wing of the movement and successor to the non-Communist wing of the AISF) remained a large and active organization, its emphasis returned to campus issues or the Gandhian constructive program. Many radical student leaders were disillusioned by the compromises which the Congress leadership found it necessary to make in order to achieve Independence without further bloodshed. The 1946 mutiny of the Indian Navy was a further shock to them, since the Congress ordered the militant sailors to surrender to the British in the interest of a compromise. Many active student leaders participated in the movement, and this event marked the end of the politically significant phase of the student movement in India.

A number of important factors had contributed to the growth of a militant student movement in pre-1947 India. The student community itself was fairly small and homogeneous. Most students came from upper middle or upper class and caste backgrounds, and the educational emphasis was strongly on the liberal arts. Higher education usually insured a fairly high status job after graduation, and most students did not have to worry about financial problems while studying. The colleges themselves were relatively compact, and communication between colleges was not too difficult. From the beginning, many of the best students were involved in the student political movement, particularly in the left-wing groups, and this helped to make the movement more "respectable."

In the 1930's and 1940's, India was a highly politicized nation, particularly in the cities and towns, where most of the colleges were located and from which the vast majority of the students were recruited. The heady revolutionary atmosphere had its effect on the students, and it was not difficult to create interest in the student movement. Western political ideologies had a powerful influence on the students and stimulated much thought and discussion. Thus, the immediacy of the nationalist struggle was combined with an ideological ferment, thereby creating a politically conscious student movement.

The Student Movement since 1947

By 1947 the student movement had lost much of its momentum, and many of the key student organizations had all but collapsed. With a few isolated exceptions, the student movement was never able to regain its militancy and has been steadily weakened. The causes for this decline are complex; it is only possible to mention some of them briefly here.

Perhaps the most important factor was the end of the independence struggle. Prior to 1947, political issues were clear and dramatic—the British had to be driven from the subcontinent. Respected nationalist leaders, such as Nehru and Jayaprakash Narayan, encouraged students to take an active part in the political struggle. Following Independence, the Congress leaders reversed themselves and urged students to stay out of politics. Furthermore, students learned that compromise was a necessary ingredient of practical politics; the issues were no longer obvious. The spirit of self-sacrifice which had marked the independence struggle almost disappeared, and many political leaders and others were more concerned with their own careers than with ideology or national development.

As the student movement lost its main *raison d'être,* the attitude of government and educational authorities changed drastically. The powerful Congress and Socialist student organizations were abandoned by the adult leaders and ignored by most of the students. The Communists retained their interest in the student movement, but embarked on a disastrous program of violence against the government, thereby losing most of its support.

The student community and the educational system were also undergoing substantial changes during this period. Between 1950 and 1960, the number of arts and science colleges in India grew from 498 to 1,039, and the enrollment doubled, from 310,000 to 691,000 students. Higher education became available to young people from rural or lower middle class backgrounds, and unemployment of graduates, always a problem in India, assumed substantial proportions. The quality of instruction declined as the number of students increased. The homogeneity of the student community was shattered by this influx of students. Thus, the physical and sociological composition of the student community made the creation of a movement much more difficult. Higher education was no longer a preserve of the elite, but became a necessity for many middle level government or private jobs.

As a result of these and other pressures, the student movement has substantially changed its role and function since 1947. The mass political organizations of the pre-Independence period have either collapsed or have become debating societies of modest proportions. The most active student groups on the Indian campus today are the local organizations devoted to cultural or social concerns, most of which are sponsored by the college or university. The various elected college unions, again under official sponsorship and supervision, are often able to coordinate the various extracurricular activities. The interest of the student community has shifted from the political realm to cultural and social activities.

Among the most popular organizations on the Indian campus are the various linguistic associations, organized as separate groups. A typical college in Bombay will have a Marathi Literary Society, a Hindi Mandal, a Gujarati Dramatic group, an English Literary Society, and others. While these groups probably tend to limit the social contacts of the students to members of their own linguistic community, they do provide an outlet for student energy and are valuable in an educational system conducted in a language which is only imperfectly understood by many of the students.

Religious and communal student groups also continue to exist, although they are less important than the linguistic associations. Christian, Sikh, Muslim, Parsi, and other minority religious communities have organized their own student groups, which have some following on the campus. Most of these groups have no political interests and are intended to provide a social center for the students involved. Debating clubs, film societies, and discussion groups are popular at most colleges, and an attempt has been made to provide an adequate athletic program for the students.

A number of the all-India student organizations still exist, and retain some degree of influence. The largest of the pre-Independence student movements, the Students' Congress was disbanded in 1948. Congress leaders expressed interest in the formation of a non-political student organization, and the socialists agreed to unite with them in the formation of the National Union of Students. Founded at a large congress in Bombay at which Nehru and the socialist leader Jayaprakash Narayan spoke, the NUS proved unable to rid itself of the heritage of outside political manipulation and soon floundered. The National Union of Students remained fairly active for several years after its formation, but eventually, political infighting together with a negative attitude by most educators destroyed the organization. An attempt was made to make the organization representative, but when less than half of the universities in India joined, financial problems made NUS operations precarious. After an initial burst of enthusiasm, the NUS found itself virtually leaderless and forced to rely on students more interested in their own personal advancement than in building a student movement. Factional disputes caused a split, and by 1958 the NUS was, for all practical purposes, dead.

Another group, the National Council of University Students of India (NCUSI), was formed subsequently to fill the vacuum created by the disappearance of the NUS. But this new group has faced many of the same problems as its predecessor—opposition from educators and political leaders, student apathy, and careerism among its own leaders. The Cold War has brought the problem of foreign subsidies, for both the East and the West are interested in gaining as much influence among the Indian students as possible and have been willing to support student organizations. The Russians have traditionally supported the Communist-sponsored All-India Students' Federation, while the NCUSI has reportedly received funds from Western sources, further removing it from the campus. It seems quite unlikely that the NCUSI will be able to build a representative student association in India even though it has generally stayed out of partisan Indian politics. At present the organization has branches in less than one-third of the universities, with a few ongoing programs to prove its usefulness to the student community.

The political parties in India have had a rather ambivalent attitude toward the students in recent years. The Congress Party, for instance, has sponsored its own youth affiliate; moreover, it has vacillated between encouraging student participation in politics and warning against such participation. The Youth Congress was formed in 1949. Despite its claims to be the largest youth organization in India, it has not succeeded in making any impact on the campus and has served mainly as a "front group" for aspiring Congress politicians. Its few social service projects have attracted some interest; yet, the Youth Congress had almost no active chapters in India before its recent dissolution because of internal political conflicts. The organization took part in Congress election campaigns and saw a short burst of activity during the Chinese invasion of 1962, when it was responsible for obtaining support for the government from the youth and students.

The oldest student organization in India still in existence is the AISF, founded in 1936. Under Communist control since 1940, the AISF claims to be the largest representative student group in India. In fact, however, it is almost non-existent outside of the major centers of Communist strength in India—Bengal and Kerala. Furthermore, the recent split in the Indian Communist Party has aligned many sections of the AISF with the "left" Communists, thereby arousing the opposition of the "right" faction. The AISF does continue to have major influence in the colleges of Calcutta, although much of its activity has been more in the cultural and social area than directly concerned with politics. The AISF has also failed to attract the kind of dedicated and able leadership that it did in the past years, and the organization faces both political and organizational crises. It is doubtful if it has more than 1,000 active members in India (compared to more than 50,000 two decades ago) and probably boasts less than twenty-five affiliates, out of a total of more than one thousand colleges.

The Samajwadi Yuvak Sabha (Socialist Student Organization) was founded in 1953 by the Socialist Party when the NUS experiment failed. The SYS has been adversely affected by the various splits within the Indian socialist movement in the past decade. Never intended as a militant movement, the SYS has acted as an educational arm of the socialist groups in some areas, although it has only a small number of affiliates limited mostly to northern India. The strength of the SYS has declined along with the viability of the socialist parties; it can probably boast of less than 500 active members. Its discussion groups have provided some of the few forums for serious political debate among students, but even these have been too limited to make any real impact on the campus.

One of the most important of the student organizations in India today is the Akhil Bharatiya Vidyarthi Parishad (All-India Students' Organization). This group, usually called the Vidyarthi Parishad, has maintained that it is non-political, but there is strong evidence to suggest that it is the youth wing of the rightist Hindu communalist parties. The Vidyarthi Parishad concentrates on a culturally oriented program and scrupulously avoids broader political issues. The association claims that teachers, students, and administrators should cooperate and not oppose one another. Professors serve with students on various governing bodies of the Parishad.

The Vidyarthi Parishad was founded in 1955 by students and teachers who had been involved in the militant right-wing RSS. The organization, under competent and dedicated leadership, has grown steadily and now has strong roots in the Hindi speaking areas of northern India. With a sprinkling of members in other parts of India, the Vidyarthi Parishad comes close to being an all-India organization. The organization has strongly stressed patriotism, but has also engaged in a good deal of social service work such as textbook libraries for needy students and a limited scholarship program. Its program, which has emphasized cooperation with college administrators, has succeeded in gaining the sympathy of many principals. The political composition and emphasis of the Parishad is, however, quite clear. A large proportion of its members were formerly in the RSS, including a majority of the National Council. The communalist views of many of its members are evident, even though the Parishad has refrained from making inflammatory statements.

The reasons for the limited success achieved by the Vidyarthi Parishad are simple. Competent leaders have provided an active program which has relevance to the student community. Social service and cultural activity has been combined with occasional demonstrations for student rights. Although the Vidyarthi Parishad claims 50,000 members, it is unlikely it has more than five thousand active supporters, and it is certainly true that the association lacks broad campus support. That it is probably the most active student organization in India is more an indication of the general weakness of the student movement than of the strength of the Vidyarthi Parishad.

These are the main national student organizations. There are other groups, such as national associations of religious groups like the National Council of Catholic College Students, but these generally make little impact on the student community. The government has made several attempts to foster constructive work among students.

The Bharat Sevak Samaj (Indian Service Association), a semi-official group, has sponsored social service projects in various parts of India and has succeeded in involving students in its work. The scope of this work has, however, been limited and student potential for service has not been adequately tapped. The Congress Party as well as local colleges have also sponsored service projects and students have enthusiastically responded when asked to participate in village uplift work and other projects.

Student Indiscipline—the Bogey of Indian Higher Education

While the problem of student "indiscipline" in India has received much attention in recent years, its seriousness has probably been exaggerated by educators and other officials. "Indiscipline" has been variously defined; the term is often used to describe any student action which does not meet with the approval of the government or of educational officials. Actions ranging from violent demonstrations protesting an examination or a fee increase to peaceful meetings or petitioning have been labelled "indiscipline." If one takes into account the poor conditions of a large proportion of the student community, the attitude of many administrators toward student grievances, and the falling standards in much of Indian higher education, it is surprising that there has not been more indiscipline. For, in fact, student indiscipline has been limited to a relatively small number of educational institutions and is not characteristic of the student community.

Among the most famous examples of student indiscipline are Banaras Hindu University and Aligarh Muslim University, two of India's most venerable institutions. At both of these schools, faculty politics had succeeded in lowering the standards of the institution and the morale of both teachers and students. The Banaras incidents, which caused the university to be closed temporarily, were investigated by a Government commission which found evidence of mismanagement and favoritism.

Other examples of indiscipline which give some indication of its scope and impact were the linguistic rioting in Madras state in 1965, in which students took a leading role in agitating against the imposition of Hindi as a national language, and the 1964 student demonstrations in Orissa which led to the resignation of the chief minister on charges of corruption. Calcutta has traditionally been politically volatile and is one of the few places in India where the student political movement has continued almost unabated. Student protests against stiff examinations, bad instructors, or other real or imagined injustices related to university administration have been widespread. Students in Bombay have demonstrated recently against a college principal who allegedly kicked his students, against increases in university fees, and against poor living conditions.

Thus, student indiscipline is more often than not directed against a specific administrative policy rather than at broader educational issues or matters of political importance, although politics has provided an important undercurrent to post-Independence student agitation. Another characteristic of student indiscipline is its generally spontaneous nature, for most student agitations are not planned by politically motivated student agitators or by non-students, but are the result of spontaneous student action. Lack of organization is a hallmark, and there have been many instances when self-appointed student leaders have prepared lists of demands only after the agitation had been launched. While political parties have tried to exploit student demonstrations, and sometimes with success, they have rarely initiated them.

The causes for student unrest in India are not difficult to perceive. The educational system is characterized by poor standards of instruction, especially in the liberal arts (where most of the indiscipline seems to originate), by inadequate facilities such as libraries and laboratories, by an outmoded curriculum, and by poorly trained teachers. Students have few outlets for their energy, and demonstrations are perhaps such an outlet. Many students begin their collegiate careers at the age of fifteen or sixteen and lack the maturity that a few extra years would give. Furthermore, students living in hostels and away from their families for the first time are probably affected by their freedom, particularly in view of India's strict family system. The generational problem, present in almost every society, lies somewhat below the surface in India, although it probably influences the students. Finally, the economic uncertainty of many Indian students is clearly a cause for ambivalence and indiscipline. Many students must hold part time jobs, and a survey of students in Calcutta pointed out that a substantial number were undernourished. It is difficult for graduates, especially in the liberal arts, to obtain suitable employment, adding a further factor of uncertainty to the plans of many students. The amount of "wastage" (the number of students who do not finish their college educations) in India is quite high, and many of these former students remain at the universities.

Despite these factors and the everyday frustrations to which the student in India is subjected, amount of indiscipline is surprisingly small. Most of India's 1,500 colleges have never witnessed any agitation. And while many institutions have been subjected to an occasional isolated demonstration, such actions are the exception rather than the rule. The centers of student unrest in India which have received so much attention in recent years—Aligarh, Lucknow, Calcutta, Banaras—offer interesting case studies, but are by no means typical of educational institutions in India.

The Future of the Student Community

The age of the student movement in India seems to have ended, and ideological politics play a very small part among the students. Almost all of the national student organizations are bureaucratic structures rather than functioning movements. No one, the government, politicians and educators included, have been able to arouse the students. In essence, the Indian student community is without direction and without ideology. Life remains difficult on the subcontinent, and students are much involved in the day-to-day struggle for existence and future employment.

But political or educational interest among students is not dead. On the contrary, strong movements can be launched when the students feel involved with a particular issue. The Orissa agitations and the Madras riots are indications of this fact. Fee increases or arbitrary administrative action can mobilize the students into a well organized campaign. But these are *ad hoc* and essentially directionless movements—aimed at a specific goal. When the aim has been achieved (or soundly defeated) the students retreat into their apathy and no ongoing movement is created. It is almost certain that students will continue to play a sporadic although occasionally significant political role in India. The creation of a movement similar to that which characterized the student community during the Independence struggle is very unlikely.

It is impossible to predict when or where student unrest will occur in India. Students in Madras, for example, have a tradition of serious scholarship and a notable lack of unrest, yet they participated in one of the most volatile student agitations in post-Independence India. There are, however, some parts of India which have retained a tradition of student activism, notably Calcutta, Delhi, and some of the northern cities in which indiscipline is more likely to occur. It is also possible to state with some degree of accuracy, that student unrest is more likely to occur in the arts colleges, and hardly even constitutes a problem in the technological institutions. Missionary administered colleges have had less trouble than other institutions, perhaps because there is often a more satisfactory teacher-student relationship at these institutions. Some pattern does exist—traditions of student activism, poor educational opportunities, or a particularly important political event can trigger a student movement. What is lacking is any ideological or organizational base in the Indian student community.

The Indian experience may have some relevance to other developing nations. India has been independent for almost two decades, and has had a chance to develop stable institutions and patterns during that time. In India, the small "modern" segment of the society moved from a high awareness of politics and participation in an all encompassing mass movement to the more mundane and difficult tasks of building a modern nation. The tension and commitment of the Independence struggle has not been maintained. The idealism of the independence period has also been muted by the responsibilities of family and the awareness of caste and linguistic particularism. Corruption in government and private enterprise has become widespread. The students have been affected by these changes. They have high expectations of the society, and when utopia seems very far off, they often give up the fight. Furthermore, the educational system itself has changed. While during the pre-1947 period, college students constituted something of a presumptive elite, this is no longer true.

The future of the student community in India is uncertain. It is likely that the current trend toward a-politicization and a lack of social concern will continue along with increasing problems for both the educational system and the individual student. The harnessing of the student community remains a challenge to the government and the educational authorities.

> Even though Korean students overturned the strongarm rule of
> Syngman Rhee, they have not organized themselves effectively
> enough to become a significant force in national politics. This
> essay, by an American scholar who spent three years teaching in
> Korean universities, explains why.

14

Korean Students and Politics

William A. Douglas

In most underdeveloped countries, students play a large role in the
national political life. During the years that Syngman Rhee ruled
Korea, however, it appeared that Korean students were an exception
to the rule. Their activities had no influence upon the course of
national politics. Rather, any student activity that went on was a
result of political events, since the students docilely marched in the
hundreds of demonstrations sponsored by Rhee to give the appearance of support for his policies. Any other form of political activity
was forbidden to the students who were regimented by the Student
Defense Corps set up by Rhee's Liberal Party.

The political inertness of the Korean students was puzzling, since
they appeared to be subject to the same influences as the highly political students of Latin America, the Near East, and Southeast Asia.
Though still young, they formed a sizeable portion of the nation's
supply of persons with modern education, and thus were in a position
to swing more weight in society than students can hope to do in a
Western country where a large part of the population is educated.
They also were subject to the forces of cultural and social change.
In the process of Westernization, the old Confucian philosophy had
become discredited, family ties and local loyalties had been weakened, and ways of life had changed as technical innovations and
urbanization took effect. In other developing nations, the loss of a

From William A. Douglas, "Korean Students and Politics," *Asian Survey*, 3,
no. 12 (December 1963), 584–595. Reprinted by permission of the author and
the University of California Press.

philosophy to which the students can commit themselves, together with the absence of a community to which modern loyalties can be attached, has led to the growth of nationalism to fill both gaps. When students must study under adverse economic conditions, when they face only unemployment upon graduation, and when their expectations are unrealistically raised by exposure to foreign films and books, the resulting nationalism also becomes intensely emotional and often produces violence as the students release their frustrations. All of these factors existed in Korea, yet the students during the Rhee era appeared to be politically inert.

In April 1960, the students made dramatically clear that their political interest had merely been repressed by the Liberal Party's controls. Enraged by the rigging of the elections the previous month, they surged into the streets, putting to good use the training the Liberals had given them in how to conduct demonstrations. In Seoul on April 19th, political indignation changed into mass hysteria which produced a truly remarkable revolution. It was completely the students' show, for the adults merely stood on the sidewalks and applauded. The students surged down the streets, burning police stations, invading the homes of rich Liberals, and converging on government buildings. The next day the army refused to move against the students, and within a few days Rhee resigned and the Liberal Party gave way to a transition cabinet.

This remarkable event seemed to shift the students from political insignificance to a position as the determining factor in Korean politics. The ideas which had motivated the students in their violent leap to political prominence were rather obscure. The slogans they shouted favored democracy and free elections as replacements for Rhee's dictatorship. However, commitment to democracy could not have been the real reason for the revolt, since polls show that the students actually favored autocratic leadership and thought democracy "unsuitable" for Korea. Neither was anti-Americanism the cause of the revolt. Students who participated are unanimous in stating that their outburst was against Rhee's domestic policies, not his relationship with the U.S. Certainly the student revolution had no class content, for the students came from the same social strata, mostly middle class and above, as the Liberal Party politicians they over-threw.

In part, the revolt was an outburst of anger at the repression of the students by Rhee's Student Defense Corps and of disappointment that the unpopular Liberals had grabbed four more years of power through illegal means. The main factor in the revolution, however, was not what the Liberals did do, but what they failed to accomplish. Under Rhee, Korea was marking time. The economic growth rate was declining, the modernization of rural areas was at a standstill, and the nation's political structure was anachronistic and corrupt.

The students constituted one of the most modernized groups in Korean society, for they grew up after independence and during the period of the massive American military and diplomatic presence. The older people's attitudes had been formed during the Yi Dynasty and under Japanese colonial rule. Thus the students were more quick than the general public to feel, perhaps only vaguely and uncon-sciously, that the process of modernization was at a standstill. They also had a less fatalistic attitude towards the abuse of power by the government. To their more modern minds, Rhee's maneuvers during the election seemed like anachronistic "absurdities," as they put it, whereas to the adults they appeared as merely the most recent mani-festations of age-old and inevitable phenomena. The adults suffered more directly from Rhee's repressions than did the students, who had no family or economic responsibilities, yet it was the students who acted, not the wage-earners or the professional class. The extra factor at work among the students was their frustration, conscious or un-conscious, at the failure of the Liberal Party to provide the leader-ship which Korea needed to get through the period of modernization. The April Revolution was mainly an outburst caused by this frus-tration.

For six months after the revolution the students continued to de-termine the direction of Korean politics. Though they lacked any basic political philosophy, they were all agreed on the immediate policies which should be adopted. They wanted emphasis on eco-nomic growth in all government policies. They wanted the govern-ment to force austerity, and the students themselves set up committees to tell citizens to stop smoking foreign cigarettes and to shift from foreign to domestic hair oil. They also wanted punishment for the Liberals who had rigged the March election.

The students forced their demands on the politicians by means of continuing demonstrations. After the students had shown their power so forcefully on April 19th, no politician could afford to ignore their desires. Both the interim government during the summer and the newly-elected government of John M. Chang in the fall followed the policies advocated by the college students. For six months Korea experienced "government by demonstration." As long as the students were still excited enough that they would take to the streets spontaneously to shout their demands, they dominated Korean politics.

Gradually, however, the revolutionary ardor cooled and spontaneous demonstrations became less numerous. The last demonstration which really influenced government policy came on October 11, 1960, when students invaded the parliament and shouted from the rostrum that action should be speeded on bills to penalize the Liberals guilty of corruption and election-rigging. This was the last spontaneous outburst and it marked the temporary end of effective student influence on Korean political life.

Once spontaneous student political activity ended, the only way in which the students could continue to influence national politics was by creating permanent organizations through which to express their demands in a regularized, continuing fashion. For maximum influence they would have required a national student federation such as those which exist in Japan and many Latin American countries and play such important roles in the politics of their countries. However, in Korea after the revolution, no effective student organizations appeared, even on the local campus level, and all attempts to build a national student federation failed. As a result, student opinion could not be translated into effective political pressure, and therefore the students were not a major factor in post-revolutionary Korean politics after October 1960.

The failure to form effective student organizations stemmed from three basic weaknesses among the potential student leaders: factionalism, corruption, and careerism. The tendency towards factionalism was a result of the nature of social relationships between Korean students. Student life in Korea, both political and recreational, is based on small cliques composed of one strong personality and five or ten subordinate personalities. These cliques serve to build up the egos of the clique leaders, who bask in the admiration of their supporters, and who are usually very jealous of each other. The cliques also give a feeling of security to the subordinate members, often country boys who would otherwise be lonely and confused in the big city universities. Frequently the personal cliques are hold-overs from middle-school days, and such early ties may be extremely important even in adult life in Korea. The appeal of the middle-school tie stems from the fact that after middle-school a student's contacts with others become increasingly more impersonal.

This pattern of social life based on small, highly personalized cliques, together with a tradition of factionalism left to Korea by the squabbling aristocrats of the Yi Dynasty, leads Korean students to regard public life solely as a struggle among personalities and their supporters. In the mind of a Korean student, organizations have no abstract existence apart from the particular personalities who compose them. Despite the Westernized names of the student groups, after the April Revolution no "organizations" in the Western sense were formed—only personal cliques which were thought of by the students as "Kim's group" or "Pak's group." The groups were correctly viewed as vehicles for the personal ambitions of their leaders. Given these attitudes, the size of a unified student group was limited to the number of students a single leader could personally contact and dominate.

Large student organizations in Korea can thus be built only by combining a number of factions. After the April Revolution, however, the students never succeeded in doing this, and no national federation appeared. In every attempt, when an election was held to determine the prospective organization's leadership, those factions whose candidates lost simply seceded from the proposed organization. They knew that the leader of the winning faction would convert the entire organization into his personal fief by giving positions only to members of his own faction. Thus for the losers to remain in what the Western mind would call the "organization" would actually be to remain inside someone else's group, which would be a useless exercise. This chronic factionalism resulted in the creation of a large number of student organizations, none of which was powerful enough to have any significant political influence. It was estimated in late 1960 that there were 67 private student organizations in Seoul.

Corruption among student leaders was also a factor preventing the creation of sound student organizations and thus it impeded the development of any real student influence in politics after the end of the spontaneous mass demonstrations. The desire for graft is frequently the primary motivation for the activities of student leaders. The mass of the students are well aware of this fact, and therefore they have little respect for their leaders. Periodically, reform candidates compete in student elections, but usually they soon become corrupted themselves in the process of winning office and holding it.

To be elected to a post in a student government, for example, a candidate needs support from the most powerful of the high school alumni associations within his college. The candidates expend large sums on wining and dining the leaders of the small personal cliques within the high school alumni associations, for the latter can manipulate their friends from middle-school days and thus influence which way a particular high school association will jump. This system of election politics forces a would-be reform candidate to acquire a sizeable campaign fund, and those who contribute naturally expect to get their money back with interest after their candidate is elected, and they usually do. A reform candidate who remains "pure" can hardly hope to be elected.

Careerism in 1960 supplemented the debilitating effects of factionalism and corruption. Even those student leaders who were financially honest, or tried to be, regarded participation in student politics as a way to advance their personal prestige and influence, and to get "connections" which might be beneficial to them in their careers after graduation. Since each student group usually existed only to promote its leader's personal fortunes, there was no basis for cooperation between student groups, and a merciless competition resulted which kept the Korean student movement divided. Careerism, like corruption, discredited the student leaders in the eyes of the mass of students, and left the leaders with no actual support. They thus had no base from which to operate on the national political scene.

The discouraging picture of Korean student organizations should not lead the observer to infer that all the students are as corrupt as their leaders, for the forces of corruption and careerism have led to a divorce between the "clean" majority of students and the leaders of their organizations. The latter, having no support, are in no position to influence student opinion. The views of the students are formed in informal gatherings presided over by respected students, usually those with high marks, who hold no formal positions. These responsible opinion leaders, who remain in the background, are actually more powerful than the public student leaders whose corruption attracted so much disapproval in Korea in 1960.

From time to time, some of these respected students try to become reform candidates in the student elections, with the unfortunate results described above. They also then lose their informal positions of influence, for upon announcing their candidacy, they are immediately suspected of being opportunists, even if their motives are actually pure. Thus a student must choose between influence or position, as these two are incompatible in the Korean student community. Similar splits between influential "pure" individuals and discredited activists in the formal positions exist in many other segments of Korean society.

There is one type of student group in which a congruence of influence and position is possible. In each college department, the students usually form an academic association to study problems within their major field. These associations are primarily academic in purpose and are divorced from the factional mainstream of student politics. Therefore the "pure" student can and does often hold a position in such an association without losing the respect of his fellow students. These associations and their leaders are thus of key importance in the formation of student opinion, but of course any direct and permanent entry into the fields of campus or national politics would make them subject to the same weakening forces that hamper the other student organizations. Therefore they are inhibited from taking any direct action to represent the students on the national scene.

Along with these academic associations, the average Korean campus contains many other kinds of groups such as sporting clubs, religious organizations (primarily Christian), and English-study clubs.

These groups generally perform their functions well and are led by responsible students. However, they retain their integrity by remaining aloof from national politics and from the mainstream of the campus power struggle.

After the April Revolution there were primarily two types of student organizations which sought to play political roles: the student governments and private student political groups. The officers of the student governments are chosen in free elections, but as shown above, these contests are characterized by factional struggles and vote-buying. At some universities it is not unknown for the candidates to spend several thousand dollars during campaigns to become student-body president. Another abuse within student governments is for the candidates to employ other students as thugs to beat up opposition candidates and intimidate the student voters.

The need to pay off election debts compels the winners to embezzle student government money. This is sometimes accomplished through over-valuation of purchases made by the student government, with the officers pocketing the difference between the real and the recorded price. Another device is for the officers to receive kick-backs from firms competing for contracts with the student government for printing or for providing supplies. Some student government officers profit from bribes given by ambitious faculty members who desire expressions of student support for their efforts to become college deans or university presidents.

With practices of this type going on, it is understandable that in most schools the student government leaders are distrusted and disliked by the average student. The officers may have received a majority in the free election, but it does not necessarily follow that they have majority support, for they may have won through vote-buying or have been chosen as the least undesirable of a generally unattractive group of candidates. This situation is not without its parallels in Korean national politics.

After the April Revolution, the student government leaders had so little support and were so involved in their own factional maneuvers that the campus governments were unable to represent the students effectively in national politics, even though government leaders did give weight to opinions of individual student officers for a few months, until the weakness of the student governments became evident to all.

The private student political organizations also proved unable to serve as the real voices of the students. As mentioned above, they were weak and disunited due to factionalism and careerism. With no treasuries, such as the student governments possessed, corruption within the private groups took a different form. Funds were accepted from adult politicians in return for public expressions of "student support" by the group for the ambitions of the political leaders. Businessmen also paid the private student groups to lobby for less severe laws against profiteering. The sums received by student groups from politicians and businessmen sometimes amounted to thousands of dollars. However, the rank-and-file students were contemptuous of these corrupted private organizations, and as their lack of support became obvious, the groups lost their subsidies from the politicians, who realized that they had been wasting their money.

The only exception to the general ineffectiveness of post-revolutionary student organizations was the National Unification League, a group composed of anti-American, socialist students. Formed in November 1960, it was aimed at eliminating foreign influence throughout Korea and at national unification achieved through North-South Korean talks, among other means. Most of the League's members were anti-American, but were also strongly anti-Communist. They were attracted to the League by its nationalistic position and its blaming of South Korea's economic difficulties on "imperialist" scapegoats. The organization's leaders, however, were widely rumored to have Communist sympathies and, possibly, Communist support.

These leaders of the League were motivated by the desire for eventual political power, rather than for immediate financial gain or "connections." Though their methods were no more pleasant than those of other student groups, the League's leaders were not divided by rivalry for immediate benefits. Nationàlism was also a unifying factor in the League. The possession of an ideology gave its leaders a goal greater than their own personal interests. Thus there was less petty profiteering in the League than in other student groups which had nothing for which to work except profits and prestige for their leaders. The League remained unified even though its leadership contained three or four strong personalities who normally would have formed divisive factions. Without an ideology to cement them together this unity would have been impossible.

The League sponsored demonstrations, issued literature in both English and Korean, and held discussion meetings for students. Through these activities it represented on the national scene the opinions of the large portion of Korean students, whether League members or not, who were intensely nationalistic and who resented the necessity for South Korea's dependence upon the U.S. The League also represented the views of a tiny minority of pro-Communist students, though the mass of nationalistic students opposed this leftist portion of the League's propaganda. Just prior to the military coup d'etat, the conservative students were beginning to coalesce in opposition to the League. The general public, which in South Korea is strongly anti-Communist, was concerned by the League's activities, and this concern was one factor which created an environment allowing the military to seize power without any public opposition.

Though the League thus had some influence on national politics and did have some importance as an outlet for the student's nationalism, its membership remained minute, due to its unpopular leftist line. Therefore it was unable to really represent the majority of the students on the national scene, any more than the student governments or the other private student groups were able to do. Thus between October 1960, and the military revolt in May 1961, students did not play a large role in Korean politics.

When the military junta seized power in 1961, it immediately banned all social organizations, and this included all private student groups. Student governments continued to exist as before, but were forbidden to take any kind of political action. The military government's policy was that students should study and should play no role in politics, and the government enforced this policy fairly successfully throughout the twenty months that political activities were banned in Korea.

To make the ban stick, the military government arrested a number of the leaders of the former private student groups shortly after the junta seized power. The conservative leaders were soon released, but the officers of the former National Unification League were tried and sentenced to long prison terms. The arrests of students lost the junta much of the good will with which the students had greeted the coup, and this was true even among students who had never supported the groups whose leaders were jailed.

A few months after the coup, some private groups, such as the Student-Association for the United Nations, were allowed to revive, but were forbidden any political activity. The vast majority of the numerous former organizations remained dissolved until political activities began again in early 1963. The ban on student political activity did not extend to international student contacts, and in 1961 and 1962 Korea sent delegations to international meetings sponsored by the International Student Conference and by the International Student Movement for the United Nations. In both years, Korean grantees also participated in the Foreign Student Leadership Project sponsored by the U.S. National Student Association.

In the fall of 1961 the military government began a move which appeared directed at creating some positive controls over the students to supplement the purely negative ban on student political action. All student governments were ordered to associate themselves with the government-sponsored National Reconstruction Movement. The students were opposed to this directive, since they feared it was a move towards government regimentation such as had existed under Rhee. Most student governments merely added the word "Reconstruction" to their titles, but continued to remain independent in fact. At Seoul National University, however, which is the most influential educational institution in the nation, the student government refused even to change its name. The government was angered, but allowed the matter to drop.

Some tension was created between the government and the students in April 1962, when the junta banned a street parade which the students had sought to stage in commemoration of the 1960 revolution. It was not until the summer, however, that the students actually defied the political ban to the point of engaging in public political activity. In June, a Korean suspected of burglary was beaten by American army officers, and Korean nationalists were outraged. At two Seoul universities the students staged rallies and street demonstrations, in spite of a police ban, demanding the conclusion of a Status of Forces Agreement with the U.S. so as to discourage such incidents. These demonstrations made clear that the students' political interest, especially on nationalistic issues, had been only suppressed, not eliminated, by the military government. However, with private groups banned and the student governments restricted by the government, the students, just as in 1960, could exert real political pressure only when they were sufficiently aroused to stage spontaneous demonstrations.

At the beginning of 1963, political activities were again allowed in Korea, and the political situation became very confused as the military junta dissolved into openly squabbling factions. On March 16th, General Park Chung Hi announced a plan to extend military rule for four years. The U.S. government soon issued a statement opposing Park's plan, and this aroused the students' nationalistic sentiments. On March 29th, about 300 students at Seoul National University staged an illegal rally at which they denounced U.S. interference, opposed Park's plan for extended junta rule, and for good measure criticized the factionalism which was already rampant within the reviving civilian political parties. On April 9th, Park in effect retracted his proposal, and student opposition was possibly a minor factor in prompting his decision. On the anniversary of the April 19th Revolution, the Seoul National University students again demonstrated against any extension of military rule, and a number of students refused to accept from a dictatorial government some medals intended to honor them for their actions during the revolt against Syngman Rhee. The April events demonstrated again that when the students' emotions are aroused, by nationalism or by the memory of the truly heroic April Revolution, they can then overcome their disunity and organizational weakness sufficiently to take important political actions. This fact raises the question of the future role of Korean students in politics.

Spontaneous student action, through petitions, demonstrations, and protest meetings, will undoubtedly continue to occur sporadically, whenever student emotion on some issue rises to the point where action does not require prior organization. These issues will be primarily nationalistic ones, producing demands for the conclusion of a Status of Forces Agreement with the U.S., complaints against political strings on American aid, and protests against alleged or real American influence on the course of domestic Korean politics. No anti-government outburst comparable to the 1960 student revolution appears likely for some time to come, as it would take years of extreme misrule for discontent with any present or future Korean government to build up to the point required for such mass violence.

The outlook for continuous, organized student influence on Korean national politics appears dim, and many Korean students do not desire such regularized influence anyway. They feel that students should mix in politics only in extreme cases, at which times spontaneous action will always be possible. They argue that creation of a national union, for example, would simply make it easy for the government to regiment the students by seizing control of the union. Even those students who do feel that regularized student political participation is desirable will probably have little success in creating it in the near future.

The first difficulty is that student governments will continue to be distrusted, and thus can have influence only in situations where the formal positions of the officers necessarily put them in charge of things, such as during the annual celebrations of the April 19th student revolution. It is uncertain whether the student governments will succeed in forming a national federation. The outcome will depend upon whether nationalism can sufficiently unify representatives from the mutually jealous universities. Even if a national student federation does appear, it may well be no more truly representative of student opinion than are the present discredited student governments which would form its parts. Only nationalism could provide the officers of such a federation with a goal greater than their own personal interests.

As for private student groups, their future depends upon the nature of General Park's new form of rule beginning in December. If it is authoritarian, political activity by private student groups, especially of a radical nature, will be severely limited. If the new government provides a free political climate, then the pattern of late 1960 would reappear. Many small, disunited, and discredited organizations would spring up, and there would be one or two more effective groups capitalizing on nationalist emotions among the students. Such groups would probably be radical and irresponsible, like the former National Unification League.

In general, with both student governments and private groups, nationalism will be the only unifying force capable of making a student group effective on the national political scene. The danger in this is that nationalism among the students tends to be irresponsible and irrational. In this situation, there is a constructive role for such world student organizations as the International Student Conference, the International Union of Socialist Youth, the International Student Movement for the United Nations, and the American union's Foreign Student Leadership Project. They should encourage the growth of responsible nationalistic organizations capable of making actual contributions to the achievement of such legitimate goals as Korean unification, less economic dependence upon the United States, and greater freedom of action in foreign policy. If responsible groups are not built, the students will merely vent their frustration in noisy and disruptive demonstrations.

To summarize, Korean students are potentially just as politically active as the students of any other underdeveloped country, but they have been prevented from becoming a political force by such special factors as government repression and student corruption and disunity. The domination of Korean political life by the students in 1960 was an exceptional phenomenon, which is not likely to be repeated soon. Though spontaneous outbursts will continue periodically, only nationalism can enable continuous student influence on national politics, and the great question for the future is whether that nationalism will be responsible or destructive.

This essay analyzes the organization, orientation, and political significance of fifty-four student organizations in Africa. Note how student activism began in Europe, shifted to Africa, and how in some countries it became important in providing leadership for national development.

15

African Student Organizations:
The Politics of Discontent

Donald K. Emmerson

In the beginning, most African student organizations in European universities were informal clubs created to ease loneliness, share news from home, and provide mutual self-help in dealing with the immediate practical problems of living in a strange new environment. Often these groups were short-lived, lasting only so long as their leadership remained in Europe, but others developed into enduring bodies, active not only in promoting the welfare of their members, but in advocating political and economic reforms in Africa as well.

Early Beginnings in London

One such association was the West African Students' Union (WASU), founded in London in 1925 by a Nigerian student named Ladipo Solanke. From its outset, WASU was a political body. At the early meetings, held by a dozen West African students gathered in Solanke's room, discussions centered on whether Africans could regain their lost sovereignty by peaceful constitutional means. The students hoped that WASU, as a forum in which the young intellectuals of West Africa could gather to discuss the problems of na-

From Donald K. Emmerson, "African Student Organizations: The Politics of Discontent," *African Report*, 10 (May 1965), 6–12. Reprinted by permission.

tional development in their home territories, would grow to become a major training ground for future West African political leaders.

Subsequent events largely justified these hopes. The Union's founders, all of them law students, returned to West Africa to become prominent judges, lawyers, and politicians. As the years went by, WASU "alumni" achieved positions of responsibility throughout West Africa. Among those who met with Solanke in 1925 to establish the Union were J. B. Danquah of Ghana and W. Davidson Carrol of Gambia. In 1945, WASU's active members included Kwame Nkrumah, who had arrived that year in London fresh from his experience in the United States as president of the African Students' Association of America and Canada. Nkrumah was later elected WASU Vice President. Although an East African, Jomo Kenyatta was also a member prior to his return from England to Kenya in 1946.

In 1929–33, Solanke, on a trip through West Africa in search of funds for the fledgling WASU, set up a number of branches in Sierra Leone, Ghana, Nigeria, and even as far south as Leopoldville. For the first time, returning students could keep in touch with one another and communicate their thinking to audiences on African soil.

In London, the Union's policies grew increasingly militant after 1930 and began to touch upon events outside West Africa such as the Italian attack on Ethiopia in 1935. The British system of indirect colonial rule came under mounting criticism as WASU leaders argued that the interest of the traditional African rulers thus sustained tended increasingly to coincide with those of the British colonial authorities. WASU also began to develop close contacts with the Labor Party and other liberal political groupings in Britain.

The movement remained strong and active through World War II, advising Labor MPs on African matters and holding conferences and seminars on West African problems and world affairs. Developments in the Soviet Union were followed avidly by the membership as interest deepened in the adaptability of various socialist experiments to African needs.

In 1946, WASU took part in the formation of the Communist-led International Union of Students (IUS). Since then, the Union has sent delegations—with IUS-provided airplane tickets—to every major event organized by the IUS. As WASU representatives travelled to East Berlin, Prague, Moscow, and Peking, the Union's policies grew stridently anti-Western in tone and the concept of African nonalignment in the cold war became less and less appealing to many WASU members.

The late George Padmore, in his book *Pan-Africanism or Communism?* (New York, 1956) quoted Ademola Thomas, of WASU, as having said in a speech to the Conference of Commonwealth Communist Parties in London in 1954: "There can be no real advance in Nigeria's fight for national liberation until all genuine Marxist elements come together in a united party which will fulfill the role of Marxism and working-class leadership within the broadest national front and so advance the struggle against imperialism and its reactionary puppets."

This new emphasis was vociferously expressed in the slogans of the 1961 WASU Congress: "Cooperate more closely with our friends!" and "Fight our enemies!" One delegate to the Congress said there was no "middle way" for Africa and that if the Soviet system proved superior it should be adopted as a model for the African revolution. Another accused the United States of attempting to flood Africa with unemployed American workers. A third denounced Tshombe as an African version of Alexander Kerensky. The statements of WASU's most recent leaders have been somewhat less extreme.

Precise membership figures are difficult to determine, but WASU undoubtedly gained adherents as the West African student population in England expanded rapidly in the postwar period. In 1945, according to one source, the Union was 1,300 strong. Another placed membership in the same year at around 100. Whatever its formal numerical strength, the organization has continued to rely heavily on a small group of radical activists; many of these also belong to the Committee of African Organizations, which encompasses much of the African nationalist community in London. Since 1960, WASU has suffered from acute discontinuity of leadership and its cadre of active members has grown progressively weaker. At the opening of the 1961 Congress, only three of the 17 members of the Union's previous executive committee, elected in 1958, were still in office. At the close of the meeting only an estimated 75 delegates remained.

African Students in France

In France, where African students were much less numerous than in England, organized activity began much later. It was not until shortly after the liberation of Paris in 1945 that a group of students from sub-Saharan Africa formed the *Fédération des Etudiants d'Afrique Noire en France* (FEANF).

Between 1946 and 1950, FEANF looked to the major French African nationalist party of the time, the *Rassemblement Démocratique Africain* (RDA), for guidance and support. From its birth in 1946, the RDA developed what amounted to a parliamentary alliance with the French Communist Party in the legislative organs of the Fourth Republic; FEANF reflected this cooperation, adding its own insistent voice to the RDA's demands for self-determination in French Africa. But when the RDA severed ties with the Communists in 1950, FEANF and RDA parted ways. Since 1951, when its first Congress was finally convened, FEANF has been intransigently hostile to the more moderate African leaders such as Houphouet-Boigny.

Conflict with authority has long been characteristic of FEANF. The major decision of the 1951 Congress was to demand that the French Overseas Ministry allow African students in France to operate their hostels and foyers through administrative student committees elected by the students themselves. The Ministry refused. Since that time, FEANF supporters have had many clashes with the French Government, occasionally ending in the expulsion from France of those involved.

Like WASU, FEANF soon joined the IUS and expanded its activities to the international plane. At its annual congresses, in its own journal, *L'Etudiant de l'Afrique Noire,* in publications such as *Présence Africaine* and *La Voix de l'Afrique Noire,* through the travels of its leaders in Eastern Europe and Asia, and in the conversations of its members over cafe tables along the left-bank Boulevard St. Michel in Paris, FEANF kept up its verbal attack on two fronts: against the colonialism of the French Republic and the "neo-colonialism" of France's African "puppets" (*"les fantoches"*).

FEANF's vigorous attack on independent African governments extends even to those considered rather radical in the West. FEANF had urged all of French Africa to reject de Gaulle's proposed constitution in the referendum of September 1958. Sekou Touré therefore gained considerable prestige in FEANF's eyes when Guinea voted a resounding "no." But at the sixteenth FEANF Congress in 1963, the outgoing executive committee, perhaps remembering Sekou Touré's handling of the 1961 teachers' strike and the subsequent expulsion of the Soviet Ambassador in Conakry, wrote in its official report to the delegates: "The diplomatic orientation of the Guinean leaders is subject to the pleasure and the baton of American imperialism." FEANF was not solely concerned with African problems, however. The slogans of the thirteenth FEANF Congress in 1961— *"A bas l'imperialisme yanqui!"* and *"vive la révolution du peuple cubain!"*—were more explicit than the slogans of the WASU Congress held the same year.

In the light of this militancy and intransigence, it may seem ironic that a number of FEANF leaders returning to their home countries performed a complete *volte-face,* entering the bureaucracies of French-speaking Africa with quiet pledges of loyalty to the very same governments they had so recently denounced from Paris. In Senegal, Dahomey, Togo, Upper Volta, and other former French African colonies, FEANF "graduates" provided cadres from the ministerial level on down. Their options were very limited, however: to join the establishment or to become a subversive, illegal opposition. In most states, there was nothing in between.

WASU membership is on an individual basis, but national rivalry is high and delegates from the same country often vote as a bloc at WASU congresses to ensure the election of their compatriots. In the past few years, Union executive bodies have included a preponderance of Ghanaian students.

FEANF, as its name indicates, is a federation of territorial student associations from French-speaking sub-Saharan Africa. By the mid-1950s, FEANF had established its hegemony over nearly all these associations, which either affiliated to the parent body or were expressly created as FEANF sections. Like WASU, FEANF jealously guards the exclusive right to represent its constituency, both in negotiations with its host government and in relations with the IUS and its non-Communist counterpart, the International Student Conference (ISC).

Are WASU and FEANF Outmoded?

Both organizations are ardently pan-Africanist and vehemently opposed to what they term "neo-colonialism." Thus their conception of African unity differs sharply from that of the governmentally based Organization of African Unity (OAU). FEANF and WASU advocate unity through revolutionary *mass* action; many of their members believe the overthrow of all "neo-colonialist" regimes in Africa to be a necessary first step.

The deference and status accorded WASU and FEANF in recognition of their prestigious anti-colonialist past have inevitably been jeopardized by the proliferation of nationally-based student unions, and by the creation of an OAU committed to non-interference in the affairs of sister states. By the late 1950s, many student leaders in Africa, particularly in the English-speaking countries, were contending that the primacy of student movements headquartered in Africa and in close touch with events there should be clearly established within any pan-African student framework. Under this interpretation, FEANF and WASU would no longer be given equality of status with African-based organizations but would play only secondary supporting roles. These leaders also disagreed with WASU's and FEANF's radical policies.

FEANF's and WASU's defenders in Africa—largely among the French-speaking student unions—argued that the number of students in an African country often constituted only a handful compared to the number studying in Europe. Moreover, since WASU and FEANF had demonstrated beyond question their vigorous opposition to imperialism, colonialism, and neo-colonialism, they should be admitted with full rights into any pan-African student movement.

This issue was hotly discussed at the first Pan-African Student Conference (PASC) in Kampala in July 1958, resulted in the breakup of the second PASC in Tunis in August 1959, and generated considerable tension at the third PASC in Nairobi in August 1964.

Emergence of National Student Unions

The emergence of national student unions in the various African states may often be traced to the formation of student councils in individual institutions of higher learning. As the students tested their new-found syndical power by raising questions related to university life in talks with college deans, colonial administrators and, in the post-independence period, the national educational authorities, they began to see the value of linking their efforts with those of the student councils at whatever other embryonic universities and institutes might exist in the country. Thus, nationally based student associations were born with substantially greater numerical power to defend student interests.

In this manner, for example, the Students' Union at the University College of Ibadan sparked the formation of a National Union of Nigerian Students (NUNS) in 1956. NUNS now includes local student councils in Ife, Lagos, Zaria, and Nsukka as well as Ibadan. In Congo-Leopoldville, the student council at Lovanium University was instrumental in establishing the *Union Générale des Etudiants Congolais* (UGEC). In Kenya, the Students' Union of the University College (SUUC) is the kernel of the recently formed National Union of Kenya Students (NUKS).

Students at the senior institutions of higher education in a given country naturally tend to assume leadership in the national union and may seem somewhat condescending toward their newly-affiliated colleagues in less prestigious institutions; this occasionally causes tension and resentment. But whatever stresses the new association is subject to during its formative years, the logic of the move onto a nationwide base is soon apparent in the greater authority with which the union's leaders can speak.

This kind of organic growth from a local to a national entity is far from an absolute rule of development, however. In what is now Zambia, the National Union of Northern Rhodesia Students (NUNRS) was created despite the lack of a university in the territory; students from the University College in Salisbury, Southern Rhodesia, from Europe, and from various post-secondary and technical schools in Northern Rhodesia met in Lusaka in 1963 to form the new Union. In Algeria, the *Union Générale des Etudiants Musulmans Algériens* (UGEMA) began as the student wing of the Algerian independence movement. At that time, the student council at the University of Algiers was run by the sons of French *colons,* several of them later to become prominent in the *Organisation de l'Armée Secrète* (OAS) and the resistance to de Gaulle. Following still another pattern of development, student organizations from the Portuguese colonies were created in Morocco, France, and Switzerland in the absence of any universities in Portuguese-controlled Africa.

Structures Vary

The structure of African national student unions ranges from the simple to the extremely complex. Usually, the union is composed of one or more of three tiers: individual members, affiliated departmental councils, and affiliated university-wide councils. Individual membership alone occurs most commonly in organizations from countries without a university, as in the case of the exile associations from the Portuguese colonies. In other unions, individual membership and departmental council affiliation may be combined: those who hold membership are organized into local units according to their university departments and these units are attached to the national organization.

The *Union Nationale des Etudiants du Maroc* (UNEM), to cite one example, has organized *corporations* in each department of the University of Rabat which act as the focus for local student activity. The *corporations* are combined into one *section* for each university city. The *sections* send delegates to the annual congress in rough proportion to the total combined individual membership of their *corporations*. The *corporations* are generally concerned with the problems peculiar to their respective departments—the curriculum, laboratory facilities, and so on—whereas the *sections* deal with university-wide problems such as housing and welfare, in addition to transmitting directives from the executive officers to the departmental council leaders for implementation. The organization of individual UNEM members in their various university departments ensures that the Union will be able to mobilize its constituency rapidly and effectively for national action such as a strike (refusing to attend classes) or a demonstration.

In countries with several or more universities, the structurally highest tier—university-wide student council affiliation—may also be found. But to meet unique local conditions, such unions sometimes mix the different levels in a complicated amalgam. A good illustration of this complexity lies in South Africa, where the non-racial, anti-apartheid National Union of South African Students (NUSAS) is based on affiliated, university-wide student councils elected by the students.

In certain white South African universities, where conservative sentiment predominates, the student council may have withdrawn from NUSAS. At these universities, NUSAS has attempted—with varying success—to organize special affiliated committees, elected by individuals who are considered NUSAS members, with the hope of eventually bringing the student council back into the Union. Furthermore, several conservative white student groups, supporters of the Verwoerd regime, have encouraged students on NUSAS-affiliated campuses to "disaffiliate" from NUSAS. On such a campus, although a student belongs to NUSAS only through the student council, which has affiliated on his behalf, he may resign individually from the Union.

Still another variation occurs at the University College of Fort Hare, which in 1959 was converted into a government college exclusively for students of the Xhosa tribe. Today, the majority of students at Fort Hare, although they have no legally affiliated NUSAS council or committee and are expressly forbidden all contact with NUSAS, still consider themselves part of the Union. At other such "tribal colleges," where contact with the Union is also barred, support for NUSAS is of an informal character.

Several national student organizations representing French- and Portuguese-speaking Africans have overseas branches. In the United States, for example, UGEC (Congo-Leopoldville), the *Union Nationale des Etudiants Algériens* (UNEA, formerly UGEMA), the *Union Nationale des Etudiants Angolais* (UNEA, Angola), and the *Union Nationale des Etudiants de Mozambique* (UNEMO) have branches through which students from these countries studying in the US may keep in touch with their national union and developments at home. The Algerian branch in the US is worthy of particular note as a militant, well-run organization which helped to maintain a strong sense of national identity among its members and raised funds and material for Algerian refugees during the 1954–62 war for independence.

National student organizations with overseas branches are not only able to expand their membership, but have easier access to sources of aid: other national unions, the ISC, and the IUS. Among the dangers of establishing such branches is that they may become more assertive and less willing to submit to the authority of the home office. This may be one of the reasons why many French-speaking and all of the English-speaking African unions have avoided establishing overseas sections. Those in Sierra Leone, Ghana, and Nigeria, for example, have preferred to mandate individual "student diplomats" in Europe to attend various national and international events and generally promote the organization's interest abroad.

Financial and Leadership Problems

Financing the national union is a major problem. Membership dues can only provide a small amount. International student organizations, university administrations, political parties, and governments can provide more substantial aid, but the union's leaders may fear such ties will compromise their independence. In most cases, funds are obtained from a combination of these sources, but the amounts raised are generally insufficient to meet the administrative, travel, printing and other expenses incurred by the union's executive, to say nothing of the needs of the union's local units.

Discontinuity of leadership is a problem in nearly every African student union, as members leave the university in successive annual waves to enter adult society. At the national student congresses and assemblies which lay down fresh policies and elect new officers, successful majority coalitions can sometimes be built upon the "new broom" arguments of candidates running on reformist planks. In some cases, the actual leaders may be eager to withdraw from student politics to improve their academic performance; in others, criticism of the outgoing executive committee may trigger lengthy debate. Depending upon the intensity of such conflict, the congress may range in duration from a few days to as long as two weeks.

African student unions have attempted to solve the problem of leadership discontinuity in several ways. Some, such as the Liberian National Union of Students (LNUS), have tried to establish "alumni associations" to advise the newly elected officers, but such advice may be resented as interference. Other unions, as in East Africa, try to secure funds to maintain at least one full-time officer. Financial limitations and the reluctance of able leaders to lose a year of education have tended to impede such efforts. A more effective solution may lie in bringing prospective leaders into positions of lesser responsibility at an early date, so that when they accede to national office their experience will be deep and varied and their commitment to work for the organization beyond question. The problems of insufficient funds and irregular leadership not only inhibit the development of organizational potential, but in extreme cases may reduce the union to a personal possession of its officers.

An even more serious weakness of African student organizations lies in the divergent avenues of policy which open up before each new executive committee. Newly elected leaders must ask themselves certain questions, knowing that the answers they give may cause sharp dissension among their constituents.

Should the union be a political association or should its scope be limited to syndical matters, *i.e.*, issues of education and student welfare? In a revolutionary context, the answer is apparent. Algerian students clearly felt they had to devote their energies first and foremost to political and even military action to wrest their nation from French rule before problems relating to student housing and university administration could be usefully examined. In consequence, many members of UGEMA left their studies in France and elsewhere to join the *maquis*. Similarly, the student associations of Portuguese-dominated Africa today consider themselves closely related to their respective national revolutionary movements.

In independent countries, the choice is more difficult. In Morocco, to cite one acute case, UNEM has acted on both fronts, arguing that political and syndical action are inseparable in the struggle against King Hassan and for improved education.

In an organization like UNEM, which has publicly labelled its government "feudal," "reactionary," and "neo-colonialist," the more radical among its members may find a contradiction between such vividly critical terms and any concurrent attempts on the part of their leaders to solicit reforms from the Ministry of National Education. The more apolitical sectors of student opinion, on the other hand, may feel that priority should be given to immediate student problems such as housing, scholarships, and the quality of education.

The delicate balance between these two priorities may well have been shaken by recent government actions against UNEM. The Union's immediate past president was condemned to death in absentia under a charge of subversion. The current president, Mohammed Halaoui, was arrested on similar charges in September 1964, held until April 1965, and then released only "provisionally." Finally, the monarchy tried—and failed—to obtain a court order dissolving UNEM. These events, underscored by recent student rioting in Casablanca, may lead UNEM's officers to emphasize political action. At the same time, Union leaders are unlikely to forget that "bread and butter" welfare gains may be essential to keeping constituency satisfaction high.

Are Students Always "Left-of-Center"?

Casual observers have been prone to generalize about the "naturally" left-of-center orientation of students in the developing areas, but student opposition in Africa is found both to the "left" and "right" of governments. In fact, issues of *conscience,* which almost invariably have political implications, and matters of *practicality,* which tend to be limited to the realm of student welfare and university problems, may be more useful analytic rubrics here than the vaguer, value-laden categories of "left" and "right."

Issues of conscience have a special appeal for students. In Nigeria, for example, NUNS has vigorously opposed French nuclear tests in the Sahara, apartheid in South Africa, and what it considers corruption in its own government. It is frequently for this kind of protest that leaders can count on widest support from constituents. The less sensational practical welfare and educational problems, while of deep concern to individual students, may have little mass student appeal when compared to those "burning issues" which call for moral outrage rather than mundane technical solutions.

Even university problems are sometimes seen as broad moral issues, however. For example, the National Union of Ghana Students (NUGS) has in the past viewed the difficulties faced by the University of Ghana in securing a firm place in Ghanaian society as a case of the violation of a moral principle: academic freedom.

Yet there are obvious dangers facing a union which concentrates exclusively on broad, universal issues to the neglect of student welfare problems: some of its constituents may become disaffected, feeling that they are not deriving any concrete material benefit from membership.

The leaders must also ask themselves a related question: Should cooperation with the government or with adult opposition elements be sought at the risk of the union's becoming a partisan political group advocating party or governmental interests, or should the union maintain complete autonomy from all non-student forces and seek to represent only genuine student opinion?

Almost without exception, African student leaders publicly argue that the student should participate actively as a member of society in national development and, if necessary, national liberation from colonial or "neo-colonial" rule.

In some cases, *e.g.,* Tunisia and Tanzania, this desire for participation in the society may lead to fruitful cooperation with the government in concrete practical projects such as school construction and anti-illiteracy campaigns. But when the students' desire to play a role in society carries political overtones critical of the incumbent regime, severe conflict with the authorities may result, endangering the independence and security of the union.

The Loyal Splinter Groups

Fears that their students may be "getting out of hand" have driven several African governments, particularly in former French colonies such as Senegal and the Ivory Coast, to encourage, directly or indirectly, the formation of loyal splinter groups to weaken the existing associations.

In 1959, for example, Houphouet-Boigny declared the existing anti-government *Union Générale des Etudiants de Côte d'Ivoire* (UGECI) "dissolved," although it continued to operate in France and informally in Abidjan. He then stimulated the formation of a counter-organization, the *Union Nationale des Etudiants de Côte d'Ivoire* (UNECI). In November 1963, the Minister of National Education declared that UNECI's headquarters would thenceforth be located in Abidjan, that its Paris office would be closed, and that membership in the Union would be a necessary prerequisite for any student wishing to obtain state aid of any kind, including employment "within the public or private sector on state recommendation."

Despite or perhaps partially because of these moves, UNECI has had only limited success in gaining adherents. At a congress convened in the Ivory Coast in July 1964, its structure had to be revamped and its name altered specifically to include secondary school students, who may prove more amenable to government policy than their seniors in France have been.

In addition to encouraging the formation of counter-associations, African governments, as in Ghana, may try to indoctrinate the students before they enter the universities and thus weed out potential malcontents. This may be one explanation behind the recent decision of the Scholarship Secretariat in Accra that all students wishing to study at any university in Ghana must take a preparatory two-week "orientation course" at the Kwame Nkrumah Ideological Institute in Winneba.

The "unruly" politics of African student associations came up for discussion at the Addis Ababa Conference in May 1963, but as yet no unified approach has been taken to the problem. Several governments have simply co-opted their students into mandatory membership in the ruling party's youth wing, as in Guinea where technically all Guinean students must join the *Jeunesse du Rassemblement Démocratique Africain* (JRDA) and no student organizations outside the JRDA are tolerated. The Government of Mali has adopted a similar approach.

In countries where no national student union yet exists, as in Malawi, the government may quietly advise prospective young organizers that independent student activity would cause an unnecessary dispersion of national intellectual resources and will consequently not be permitted. Where such organizations already exist and tend to oppose the government, as has been true to varying degrees in Morocco, Ghana, Congo-Leopoldville, and South Africa, the national union leaders may be arrested and detained in an attempt either to destroy the association entirely or to warn the student leaders of the limits within which their criticism will be tolerated.

Cooperation or Disaffection?

Despite the intensity of organized political activity among African students, it would be false to assume that they are all or nearly all politically-oriented activists. In most cases, the national student union involves only a handful of students in its day-to-day work and the depth of its active support differs not only from country to country but fluctuates sharply over time in proportion to the degree of student interest in particular issues. Apathy toward politics is by no means unknown in African universities. Many students are apolitical, and most of the politically active have not developed any consistent ideological framework to sustain and rationalize their policies and protests. Where the colonial and immediate post-colonial experience of a given country has been marked by repression and authoritarian measures, however, politically minded students have tended to adhere more consistently to an ideology, whether Marxist-Leninist or pan-Africanist in character.

This ideological vacuum is rapidly being filled. Organizations such as the Nigerian Youth Congress (NYC) in Ibadan and the *Mouvement Etudiant du Parti Africain de l'Indépendence* (MEPAI) in Paris and Dakar offer the students not only a framework for partisan political action, but a set of underlying ideological assumptions as well. It now seems clear that the two sets of alternatives—politics vs. syndicalism, absorption vs. autonomy—will be answered not only by the various national union executives and their members, but indirectly by the governments, the youth wings, and the political parties. Embedded in the solution evolved over time in each particular case will lie the answer to the question which ultimately encompasses both dilemmas: cooperation or disaffection?

V

Latin America's
Student Power

This essay offers a general analysis of the most politically active students in the world, those in the Latin American universities. These students have frequently been among the staunchest fighters for political freedom but also ruinous in their impact on educational quality in the universities. The author explains why.

16

Students in Latin-American Politics

Francis Donahue

When newspapers headline "Terror Reign Closes University" or "Student Slain by Police," most American readers expect to find a Latin-American date line. At least they did until recently. And they were usually not mistaken, for in no other area of the world are students so deeply involved in politics as they are in the Hispanic countries of this hemisphere.

To judge Latin-American students by United States standards is to misread the student political movement in the Latin countries, and also a significant part of political life in the area. Latin students are bellwethers of political stability or instability in their countries. They are usually dissatisfied with their society and with means available to achieve both their personal and national objectives. They feel impelled to protest, often violently, against injustices in the national fabric. They are, generally speaking, more influenced by Marxist, Communist, and Socialist thinking than by French or Anglo-American political doctrines. Impatient with the slowness of social progress and with the growth of functional democracy, they strike out for quick solutions. Frequently the real or imagined opponent against whom they protest is the "rightist United States," which, in their minds, is closely associated with Latin-American dictatorships.

From Francis Donahue, "Students in Latin American Politics," *Antioch Review*, 26, no. 1 (Spring 1966), 91–106. Reprinted by permission of the editors.

The Political University

Latin students are considered repositories of the ideals of their nation and spokesmen for their people. As a result, the university in Latin America has generally evolved into a political university as contrasted with the professional university in the United States. This is not to say that the Latin university is simply a political instrument. Not all students participate actively and regularly in politics. Most attend the university for professional reasons. Yet a minority of student politicians, representing political groups or factions within the country, organize or pressure students into strikes, protest marches, and even armed opposition to the government.

Students do not conceive of their role as limited to the traditional cultural, professional, and scientific pursuits. To these they add the social element—which means they consider it their duty to put their knowledge, enthusiasm, organizing ability, and even their lives, at the service of their country. For them, the university has a peculiarly nationalistic and political function: it is to be used as an institutional base in the struggle to achieve economic advancement, social reform, and a more democratic society. They consider themselves leaders of the less vocal elements of the population: the workers and the agrarian masses. Particularly has this been the case in the last forty-eight years as an increasing number of students have come from the middle and lower strata of the population and therefore share the political, social, and economic aspirations of those strata.

Contributing to the political role of students is the fact that Latin Americans, throughout their national life, have always shown great respect for educated people. In a region where the average education of people over fifteen scarcely goes beyond the second grade, the university student belongs to an educated pressure group. It is a fact of national life that students, through strikes and protest demonstrations, have been able to exert strong influence designed to guide, change, or even overthrow national governments.

Latin populations are young. Life expectancy in the Hispanic countries does not compare with that of the United States or many European countries. Over 70 per cent of the Venezuelans are under thirty. It is not surprising that after a successful overturn of government, some new cabinet ministers are of university age.

Close scrutiny of Latin social and economic patterns reveals additional reasons why students are active in politics. In the Hispanic family the youngster is exposed to the adult world at an early age. His ideas and conversations mature early. At twelve or fourteen he often holds fixed political views and musters arguments to support those views. Since World War II, even high school students have participated in strikes and political manifestations.

Students are keenly aware of the great improvements their countries need. Through motion pictures, magazines, newspapers, trips abroad, and through propaganda from the more developed countries, they are exposed to more prosperous societies, to more equitable distribution of wealth, to wider participation by the people in national affairs.

While on campus, students are close to the problems of their countries. Most major universities are located in the downtown area. The University of San Marcos (Lima) fronts on a street where the heartbeat of the country is felt. The University of Chile faces busy Alameda O'Higgins. Also located downtown are the Universities of Buenos Aires, La Plata, Havana, Montevideo, Asuncion, Rosario, Cochabamba, and others.

Administrative control in the university, and even class schedules, encourage student participation in politics. In most institutions, students form part of the major governing body of the university. Since many collegians work full or part time, class schedules are arranged accordingly. Classes often begin early and let out at about 9:30 A.M., to be resumed in the late afternoon. Attendance is optional. On most campuses student advisers are unknown. Most professors are professional people who hold at least one more position and who, even if they wanted to, could not devote full time to teaching because salaries are too low. At the University of San Marcos during the 1958–61 period, only 138 of the 2,280 faculty members were employed full time. Beginning instructors at the University of Buenos Aires receive twenty dollars a month. In Argentina, part time instructors are dubbed *"profesores de taxi,"* because they often commute from office to classroom by cab.

Students are generally on their own from the day they matriculate to the day they graduate. They tend to organize among themselves, often on the basis of political affiliation. It is not uncommon for students to emerge from evening classes and move on to a sidewalk cafe to discuss political or labor problems, the administration of the university, or even the need to protest an increase in movie prices or streetcar fares.

Latin campuses spawn vigorous political leaders who spend much of their time developing a following and perfecting tactics designed to organize strikes and protest actions and to carry out political terrorism. Many remain on campus for several years, biding their time until they can make a swift transition to the national political arena. Such "professional students" usually register for one class, and neglect to take examinations, year after year. They are mature in years and political experience. Federico Muñoz, at thirty-one, headed the Venezuelan Student Federation. When Efren Capiz Villegas, at forty-five, led a revolt at the University of Morelia (Mexico), in 1963, he had been working for his degree for seventeen years.

From positions of leadership in student politics have stepped many of the future leaders of the Latin countries: Fidel Castro in Cuba, Raul Haya de la Torre in Peru, Baltasar Brum in Uruguay, Romulo Betancourt in Venezuela, to mention but a few.

In most countries student political organizations carry the banners of national parties. And they are often financially underwritten by these parties.

Political Aspirations

Although slogans and types of manifestations vary, Latin students, as politically oriented and organized into student federations, share certain long-range objectives for their countries. They favor political democratization, land reform, a diversified economy, and programs of economic nationalism often directed against the United States.

In the majority, they are opposed to what they term U.S. economic penetration of their countries. They score the U.S. State Department because it has allegedly supported and shored up dictators in the Hemisphere, due to U.S. concern for stable regimes and its desire to protect U.S. investments. U.S. recognition and presumed backing for Latin strongmen—the Dominican Republic's arch-dictator Rafael Trujillo, Nicaragua's Anastasio Somoza, Venezuela's Marcos Perez Jimenez, Manuel Odria in Peru, and Humberto Castello Branco in Brazil today—have been interpreted as Washington's preference for stability in Latin countries no matter what the cost in political growth or human rights.

Cayetano Rodriguez del Prado, leader of the Peking-line Communist Party in the Dominican Republic, told the press, in November, 1965, that he first encountered Communism while a student at the national university. He added that at eighteen he was imprisoned and tortured by dictator Rafael Trujillo, but he insisted that he considered his prime enemy not Trujillo but the United States, which, he said, helped Trujillo stay in power.

Latin students point to U.S. Ambassador Thomas Whelan's long and close friendship with General Anastasio Somoza, the ingratiating yet ruthless dictator of Nicaragua. When an assassin's bullet caught up with "Tacho" Somoza in 1956, a U.S. plane, at Whelan's suggestion, rushed the stricken dictator to Gorgas Hospital in Panama for treatment.

Venezuelans were galled in 1954 when President Dwight Eisenhower awarded their dictator-president, Marcos Perez Jimenez, a Legion of Merit medal. Four years later they reacted angrily to news that former U.S. Ambassador to Venezuela, Fletcher Warren, had written a letter wishing success to Venezuela's hated secret police chief, Pedro Estrada. The latter had reportedly been responsible for torturing or killing hundreds who opposed him and the Perez Jimenez regime.

U.S. aid to Cuban strongman Fulgencio Batista, in the form of continued relations and "hardware" under the Military Assistance Pact, was keenly resented by students, by Fidel Castro, and by a great majority of the Cuban people during the 1957–59 period.

On the positive side, Latin students generally espouse a number of shared, long-range aspirations for their individual countries. Aldo Arantes, President of the Brazilian Student Federation, has made a reasoned exposition of those aspirations in terms which, according

to Gerald Clark in *The Coming Revolution in Latin America,* mirror
the consensus of student opinion in several areas of Latin America:

> We have a low cultural and economic life because we have al-
> ways looked elsewhere, and for this reason the student mission today
> is more important than it would be, say, in Canada or the United
> States. The most important class is the student class because we
> are clean; other groups have interests that are dirty. Students have
> the responsibility to show the people of the country what are the
> real issues, the right ideals. First, there is something wrong when
> other countries are always trying to exploit us. These countries—
> yes, especially the U.S.—try to sell us clothing, Coca-Cola and cars.
> They spread the word through advertisements; and people think it
> is good to buy Coca-Cola, without considering whether it is good
> for the country. Sixty per cent of the pharmaceutical companies
> here are foreign. Foreign investors are against us developing our
> own steel industry because they wouldn't get immediate returns.
> They don't want Brazil to wake up. . . .
> The first fundamental is agrarian reform because Brazil is mainly
> an agricultural people. Most of the land is in the hands of rich men
> who don't do anything to help the nation as a whole. Banks don't
> lend money to poor people; they lend it to the rich, and the terrible
> thing is that much of the land in these few hands is not even being
> put to use. . . .
> We must also have a planned economy, and this means state
> ownership of the basic industries: transportation, steel, and so on.
> Foreign capital should be applied by the State, never by private
> industry, and this includes loans from international banks. . . .
> Half of our people are illiterate because they have been kept that
> way deliberately by men who feel that mass ignorance gives security
> to their rule, that once a person gets an education he begins to
> demand improvements in life. We really haven't a national con-
> science in Brazil; and so one of the first things is to educate the
> people. . . .
> The Cuban revolution was a good thing . . . it represented the
> beginning of freedom in Latin America. . . . the revolution is the
> fundamental thing. Fidel is incidental. Only by revolutionary proc-
> esses can our needs be reached.

Paths to the Political Present

Behind the contemporary Latin-American university stretch four
centuries in which the academic community with its peculiarly
political configuration was forged. This lengthy period was punc-
tuated, sharply, by a seminal movement dating from 1918.

Colonial universities, which ultimately totalled twenty-four, conferring 150,000 degrees from 1551 through 1825, were institutions
designed to train the sons of the ruling oligarchies. Instruction was
mainly classical and religious in orientation. Law, medicine, theology,
and civil engineering were the favored disciplines. The Viceroy and
the Archbishop participated on an equal footing with the Rector
in developing these institutions. During the entire colonial period—
and down to 1918—universities were aristocratic and exclusionist.
The lower classes were largely barred from the classrooms; the middle levels scarcely existed. Learning was regarded as a value in itself,
with relatively little concern for its functional content.

These medieval universities in America, patterned after the University of Salamanca, produced many of the leading figures in all
fields. Yet they did not serve as breeding grounds for political agitation. Instead, they constituted an integral part of the static social
pattern of life.

Following independence (1825), universities were oriented toward
the French model. Their goal was to produce professional men educated for specific careers, some of which were merely imported from
France and had little or no basis in Latin-American reality. Emerging from this was a type of disintegrated professionalism among the
educated classes.

In the nineteenth century, the university continued to turn
out many of the intellectual leaders. Several led the fight against
Caudillismo (dictatorship), the reigning political way of life after
the idealistic constitutions of the new republics proved unworkable.
Later, some intellectuals lost the esteem of their fellow countrymen
as they joined Porfirio Diaz in Mexico as his "Brain Trust," or supported Ecuadorian Gabriel Garcia Moreno or other dictators.

In 1918, when a group of students in Cordoba (Argentina)

drafted the University Reform Program, they set in motion the most far-reaching movement in the history of Latin-American education. The Reform was designed to assure greater student participation in the administration of the university. It was also designed to rectify the all-inclusive emphasis on professionalism inherited from the French tradition and to inaugurate a social and grass-roots orientation, one which had no counterpart anywhere in the world at the time.

The University was to be a republic of students. No longer were professors to be hand-picked by the aristocracy, but rather by open competition. They were to be appointed for a definite period, approximately seven years, with contracts renewed, if warranted, upon academic review of their work. Students were to participate in the academic review.

Students insisted on their right to attend only the lectures of their choice, to be graded only on the basis of examinations, and to repeat a course as often as they wished. They called for relaxed entrance requirements, student financial aid programs, and abolition of almost all tuition. They demanded student representation on the Governing Board of the institution.

Closely associated with these demands was the new guiding principle that students should work for the interest of the community, and particularly for those of the lower economic and social strata. In essence, they considered themselves major agents of change in their society.

Emphasis on the financial aspects, and on education as instrumental in effecting social change, underscore the fact that the student body was changing. Individuals from without the old oligarchies were pressing for access to the universities. This was triggered in part by the small but growing industrial development, creating a need for better-educated middle-level workers.

The Reform Movement spread rapidly. In 1919 it was proclaimed at the University of San Marcos, and at about the same time students in Santiago de Chile, Havana, Mèxico, Quito, and the Central American capitals espoused the new doctrine.

Until 1918, then, the Latin-American university had been basically an upperclass institution responsive to the oligarchic trend prevailing in social life. After 1918, students from the non-elite classes were starting to sit next to the sons of Creole aristocrats at the Universities of Mexico, San Marcos, La Plata, and others. It was they who sparked the Reform Movement.

Despite opposition on the part of conservative elements, the students generally succeeded in winning their demands. As they moved into governing positions in the universities, they began looking toward an even wider role in the governing of their nations. Conscious of their status as future leaders of the countries, they came to demand a national hearing, after 1918, even before they had left the classroom.

Fruits of the Reform

Out of the Reform Movement emerged two major principles and one phenomenon of Latin-American student life, all highly significant today. The principles are university autonomy and student participation in university administration (*Co-Gobierno*). The phenomenon is the student strike.

Since 1918 the struggle to ensure university autonomy has been arduous, but generally successful, in the Latin countries. Under this principle of autonomy, the university reserves the right to rule its own domain without government interference. It may appoint or dismiss university personnel and create or abolish departments, schools, or divisions. Since it assumes full responsibility for all internal administration, no government troops or police are allowed within the precincts of the university.

So important is this principle in Latin America that institutional autonomy is usually incorporated into the first articles of university statutes. In some cases, it is spelled out as a specific right in the national constitution.

Yet, over the years, this principle of academic extra-territoriality has often been violated. Latin governments have flouted university autonomy and closed down local universities to prevent student militants from inciting or continuing opposition to their regimes. During the 1955–59 period, Fulgencio Batista shut down the University of Havana for more than three years. Central University in Caracas was shuttered by dictator Marcos Perez Jimenez for two years during the same period. Many other institutions in Ecuador, Peru, Bolivia, Argentina, and other countries have suffered a similar fate at the hands of Latin strongmen.

On some occasions, national troops or police have contented themselves with sealing off students in their academic redoubt, without invading the sanctuary of the university. Students then settle down for an extended stay on campuses, in dormitories and classrooms, dramatizing their opposition to the government or its policies. One dormitory at Central University in Caracas has been dubbed "Stalingrad" because it is used as an armed camp to which student political activists flee to escape the police.

The second major principle is student participation in the administration of the Latin university (*Co-Gobierno*). Students, faculty, and alumni share in the formulation of policy and in decision-making on both scholastic and administrative matters. Student representation is established at from one-fourth to one-third of the total membership of the top Governing Board of the university, as well as on the Councils of the individual faculties. In Bolivia, students enjoy a representation equal to that of non-student members on university bodies, a fifty-fifty ratio unique in the Hemisphere.

The Governing Board, among its other duties, elects the Rector, usually for a two- to four-year term. But the Rector does not always complete his term. A student strike may well turn him out of office. Students are also very active and influential in the Faculty Councils which elect the Deans. The latter are equally insecure in their positions.

At the University of Uruguay (Montevideo), students are assured of 25 per cent of the Council seats in each Faculty. They control ten votes in the election of the Dean, who needs twenty-four votes to be elected. They cast twenty votes in the election of the Rector, who needs forty-six votes to take office.

During the elections, particularly those for the Rector, student groups frequently engage in vigorous campaigning, with rivalry often keyed to the political orientation of the candidates.

An extreme case of student control of the university is seen in

Bolivia where students clearly have the upper hand. They are better organized than non-student representatives and attend meetings of the Governing Board more regularly. They often exercise control over faculty appointments and tenure, over suspension and dismissal of instructors and administrative personnel, and even over course content. Recently, a Bolivian professor remarked that it was quite possible for an eighteen-year-old freshman to cast the deciding vote on a proposal to alter the content of an advanced course such as "Community Development."

When students deem it necessary to go beyond the Governing Board, or the university confines, in order to achieve their goals, they do not hesitate to resort to the strike.

In late 1964, student riots throughout Bolivia contributed significantly to the overthrow of the government of U.S.-backed Victor Paz Estenssoro. Venezuelan students played an active part in the 1958 toppling of Marcos Perez Jimenez. Actually, Venezuelan students have long been in the vanguard of the struggle to eradicate dictatorship from their country. For their efforts, they have earned the support and the affection of a majority of their fellow citizens.

It is Peru which offers the classic example of a student strike in action, sparked by the two major principles of university autonomy and *Co-Gobierno,* both threatened at the same time. In 1960, the Medical Faculty at the University of San Marcos ruled out *Co-Gobierno.* It claimed that its work was of such a complex nature that student participation, or "meddling," could not be permitted. The Faculty threatened to resign if the traditional one-third student representation on the Faculty Council were restored. Students bristled, and went out on strike. The walkout ultimately affected the entire student body of more than 10,000.

At about the same time, Peru's Superior Normal School, located near Lima, was the scene of another student strike. Touching off this manifestation was violation of university autonomy. The Peruvian Government had decided to remove the school from its previously autonomous status and convert it into a dependency of the Ministry of Education. When Government-appointed officials arrived at the school, students locked them out and then barricaded themselves in the school plant, remaining there until food ran out.

Next, they staged a seventeen-hour protest march to Lima, where they joined forces with fellow strikers from the University of San Marcos.

At stake, and sharply dramatized, was the violation of both autonomy and *Co-Gobierno*.

Students set up a common kitchen in Lima and accommodated themselves in make-shift lodgings in the gymnasium, settling down for a long stay. Campus loudspeakers demanded a special session of Congress to overturn recent decrees relative to the University and the Normal School. Seventy-five thousand Peruvians attended a mass meeting at which students demanded the resignation of the entire Presidential Cabinet. This they did not get, but they succeeded in bringing about the resignation of the Ministers of Education and Justice.

When the strike ended, two months later, the students had not yet attained their objectives. Subsequently, however, both autonomy and *Co-Gobierno* were restored to the two institutions.

The President of the San Marcos Student Federation, who had been on campus for fourteen years, later explained that the strike, besides protesting the publicized grievances, had pointed up unsatisfactory conditions at the University, due mainly to paltry Government support for higher education.

Opposition to the Political University

Since 1945, attempts at curbing student behavior in the politically-oriented university have received a cold reception. Latin Americans, long-time victims of right wing military dictatorships, generally insist that the government keep hands off the universities. Venezuela's "Law of Universities," enacted after the fall of Marcos Perez Jimenez, grants immunity from all government authority to anyone within the confines of the campus.

Striking evidence of a government's reluctance to provoke student wrath on campus was seen in November, 1964, when national authorities refused to dispatch police to the campus of the University of Chile (Santiago) to put down a club-wielding melee between

Christian Democratic students and a coalition of Communist and Socialist students. Cause of the fracas was the appearance on campus of Dr. Rafael Caldera, leader of Venezuela's Christian Democratic Party, who had been officially invited to deliver an address at the University. Dr. Caldera was pelted with eggs but escaped unharmed.

While the majority of Latin students are pro-Western, Communist and pro-Castro leaders have wielded considerable influence on campuses in recent years. Through their own efforts and through alliances with non-Communist collegians, the Reds have often succeeded in electing candidates to high administrative and academic positions in the universities. On several occasions, when national governments have moved to oust Communists from these posts, there have been outcries that university autonomy was being violated, coupled with student strikes in which non-Communists participated to defend university autonomy.

On the intellectual front, some minor opposition to the political university has appeared recently. It has not been aimed at eradicating political influence so much as it has focused on the need to improve the quality of academic training so the universities may turn out graduates who are the professional equals of the products of leading U.S. and European institutions. Its proponents are mainly Latin-American professors trained abroad, who are working for professional reform within their individual faculties.

While this opposition has no official organization, it does boast an eloquent spokesman in Arturo Uslar Pietri, perhaps Venezuela's leading intellectual, a man respected by all sectors of the population of his country, and by intellectuals and statesmen throughout the Hemisphere. Uslar Pietri notes that there is inadequate discipline at Central University (Caracas) and that student preparation and the level of instruction both leave much to be desired. He explains that many professors do not meet their classes regularly, and that students often fail to appear too. Under such circumstances, it is practically impossible for a university to fulfill its professional obligation to supply technically and professionally trained people to run a modern state like Venezuela.

For Uslar Pietri, adherence of Venezuelan students to the University Reform Movement changed Central University from an institution of professional, scientific, and intellectual formation into a bridgehead in the national political struggle. University goals were adulterated. Students looked to the example of Cordoba when they should have looked to Paris, Princeton, London, Gottingen, or Moscow Universities for inspiration and guidance.

This is not to say, adds Uslar Pietri, that there should not be politics at the university. Yet university politics, if it is to be the politics of the street, cannot help but prejudice the professional objectives of Central University.

As an antidote, the Venezuelan intellectual offers the following statement for regular meditation by students and professors alike: "A first-class country cannot be forged by a second-class university."

Recently, Venezuela has taken mincing steps toward imposing greater academic discipline and curbing political activities of students. The Governing Board of Central University has decreed that a student of any Faculty failing a course on two consecutive occasions is ineligible to continue in that Faculty for two years. This was aimed partly at student militants who fail courses regularly but stay on to continue their political careers. The first implementation of this regulation saw the Dean of Engineering drop some 260 students from his Faculty.

At various times students have virtually controlled the National University of Honduras (Tegucigalpa). Leftist political agitation has been particularly marked in the Schools of Law and Economics, whose courses lend themselves to the teaching of ideology. Since 1960, however, a university reform program has concentrated, not on denial of political activity to students, but rather on the introduction of new courses in areas which do not encourage the teaching of ideologies: biology, chemistry, and physics. In many cases these new studies have helped to lessen the drive toward political discussion on the part of students.

Bolivia has also adopted an indirect attack on student political agitation. In establishing a new Technological Institute at La Paz, the Government claimed the nation needed a school organized along technical lines related to the petroleum industry. A second and unstated reason was that the Government hopes the newly established institution may allow for a fresh start, keep the students educationally oriented, and reduce political pressure which builds up regularly on other campuses.

Heart of the Matter

At the heart of the problem of student political agitation lies the fact that influential Latin-American figures—intellectuals and political leaders alike—do not want to politically defuse the students of their countries. They recognize the salutary effect that student opposition may have as a deterrent to more extreme actions by a dictatorial regime. They acknowledge that students have often been the staunchest supporters of and fighters for freedom, justice, and democracy in their countries. At the same time, they recognize the destructive consequences, educationally speaking, of prolonged absences from the classroom due to student strikes. They are keenly aware of the politically charged atmosphere on campus caused by frequent student and faculty elections, and the use of university grounds as privileged sanctuary for student political activists and revolutionaries. In a word, they are concerned because the universities have frequently been obliged to postpone their specific educational missions because of political developments.

Professor Mario Bunge of the University of Buenos Aires, after admitting that Latin students may devote too much time to politics, asks:

> But who ruled that the politically indifferent, or the cynic, is the ideal citizen? Who ruled that politics are to be the monopoly of professional politicians? I am in favor of a politically neutral, purely scientific university, but I do not find it objectionable that, outside the university, those students who feel it their duty, engage in politics—especially if they are in favor of democracy and national independence, which are still the goals to be achieved in most Latin-American countries.

Peruvian intellectual Carlos Cueto Fernandini states the case in this fashion:

In the opinion of the most distinguished scholars of Peru, political partisan activities within the university should be stopped, and I quite agree with this. May I say however that this problem is not, strictly speaking, a university problem. It will become less acute when political parties develop, when democracy becomes stronger and better established, when the fear of dictatorship is vanquished. In the meantime, much effort will have to be expended in order to keep the university free from phenomena such as student strikes, assemblies degenerating into mob riots, and political harangues. This effort is indispensable nevertheless, because one of the capital responsibilities of the university, if it is to meet the demands of modern Peru, is to raise the quality of academic training.

The dilemma, as expressed or hinted at by these intellectuals, is simply this: how can we make the university more professional and less political while not blunting the actual or potential political thrust of the students who constitute a major force in national politics?

What is needed, then, are politically minded students off campus, working for the good of the nation. Also needed are professionally minded students—the same students—on campus, preparing themselves to assume administrative, technical, scientific, and professional roles in their developing countries.

A harbinger of a partial solution to the "politics vs. education issue" on Latin campuses—a solution which would allow for both politics and education—is seen in a recent suggestion by Jovito Villalba, leader of Venezuela's *Union Republicana Democratica* Party, himself a former student leader. Following a sharp debate on the question of university autonomy, occasioned by the entry of government secret service agents on the grounds of Central University, Mr. Villalba suggested that student residences and dormitories be moved off campus and removed from the protection of university autonomy. Reacting sharply to this suggestion, the students, through Communist Jose Rafael Zanoni, acting Student Federation President, proposed that Villalba be declared "persona non grata" at the University.

Villalba's proposal seems to point to a means whereby students can continue their political activities, as individuals, without the protection of university autonomy, while at the same time not period-ically hamstringing professional activities at the university.

Despite the merit which some Latin Americans may see in the Villalba solution, there is no clear indication today that the politically oriented, student-dominated university in Latin America is in danger of being replaced by any other type of institution.

VI

Student Rebellion
in the
United States

Even though this selection deals with only one minor episode, it gives the flavor of town-and-gown clashes in nineteenth-century America. It illustrates how a trivial incident could bring to the surface the latent antagonism, based on class tension, between elitist students and resentful working people of the town.

17

The Oxford-Cap War at Harvard

Kenneth Wiggins Porter

A town-and-gown disturbance between Harvard students and the Boston citizenry which local historians of that period seem to have overlooked was the "Oxford-Cap War" which raged irregularly from the fourteenth to about the twenty-fourth of May, 1842. The students' view of the campaign is set forth in a letter written from Cambridge by Francis Lowell Lee, Harvard junior, June 15, 1842, to his older brother Henry Lee, Jr., later known as Colonel Henry Lee, who was then traveling in Europe.

> This spring appeared pregnant with glorious events, first, in my mind is the celebrated and far spreading *Oxford-cap war,* an occurrence which both Cambridge and Boston will long remember. Details, On the third of May 1842. Exhibition day. the Cambridge students, Undergraduates according to previous arrangements, appeared in the full blooded Oxfords.

Concerning this headgear, Benjamin Robbins Curtis, Jr., discussing Harvard student-costume, remarks: "At one period, a mostrosity was introduced, in the shape of a high imitation of the Oxford cap; but the imitation was a bad one, and it did not last a great while." A Democratic daily in Boston was more descriptive, commenting, with good-humored irony: *"The Cambridge Boys* wear the brim of their caps on their crowns."

Young Lee continued:

From Kenneth Wiggins Porter, "The Oxford-Cap War at Harvard," *New England Quarterly,* 14 (March 1941), 77–83. Reprinted by permission.

These they were *permitted* to wear unmolested until the fourteenth of the same month, Saturday, when between the hours of twelve and two a tall negro (strange coincidence, a tall negro was ringleader in King st battle at the time of Stamp act and Tea tax Revolution) was seen parading in Tremont row with a large black-pasteboard square cap; designed as a burlesque upon our caps. he was met by law-student named Pickett, who very naturally knocked his cap off, the negro took to his heels, Pickett offered to fight any white man who would take his part, no one accepted the challenge. So far, so well. Silent contempt more judicious. Burlesques immediately became numerous and there were many rows. Boston people much excited.

The Boston *Morning Post*, May 16, 1842, reported this first skirmish in a fashion more likely to appeal to the local democracy, remarking temperately:

A portion of the Cambridge students have adopted the Oxford pattern for caps. The fashion of these caps being rather *outré*, their appearance in our streets excited some ridicule. On Saturday, a colored gentleman was seen walking in Tremont street with one made in the extreme of fashion—he was met by a student who knocked the cap from his head, whereupon the colored gentleman deliberately walked on bareheaded, while the student intimated that he was willing to meet any white man who was disposed to take up the quarrel; but as the persons about saw no occasion for fighting because the tastes of the colored man and student were alike in caps, the affair ended without further violence. In Washington street another student knocked a cap which looked something like his own from the head of a white boy, who turned upon the student and damaged him considerably. It is said that this latter circumstance has "raised the *dander* of the Boston boys" and that some of them threaten to knock off every "Oxford cap" they meet, and to drive every one from the theatre that may make its appearance there.

The next engagement in the Oxford-Cap War was the result of a decision by the "Boston boys" to "carry the war into Africa." War-Correspondent Francis Lee continues:

On the eighteenth, the West-Cambridge buss drove by in the morning with burlesquer upon the top, Henry Perkins and some other Freshmen, pelted him and H.P. knocked his cap off, the buss stopped and they had the usual amount of quarreling. During the day that *leetle* bird Rumor was occupied in stating that the buss would return in the eve, loaded with West-Cambridge bullies, but nothing confirmed its' statements; just after supper, the buss came along, the *fellows* Students were there and the burlesque appearing was saluted with a shower of missiles, and his cap knocked off but not down, the students pursued the buss, and, as it had a passenger just above there, they surrounded it when it stopped, a Freshman named Rowan went up on top and with one or two other fellows cleared the top of the buss of both man and driver and took possession of the cap. The man and driver jumped to the ground, the former immediately taking to his heels, he was pursued and whipped until picked up by a chaise passing by; it was found that he received nine shillings a day to wear that when passing through Cambridge. The cap was kept as a trophy.

To this account, the *Morning Post*, May 23, 1842, adds only that "in one case the students assailed an omnibus in which was a person with a burlesque cap on, and injured the vehicle to the amount of $80, which they 'forked over' to settle the business."

The next serious squabble was on the twenty-first Saturday. in Boston it took place in front of the Tremont, a large mob collected and threatened much disturbance, the Boston gentlemen sided with the students, there was not much real fighting so far as it went the students had rather the best of it, there were as many law-students there as undergraduates; Tucker parvus of the Tremont shut his doors upon everyone, after having turned every student in the house out into the street.

In an article captioned "Oxford Caps vs. Pasteboard Beavers," even the Democratic *Morning Post*, May 23, 1842, began to take a more severe view of the boisterous townsmen's conduct.

There were several rows in our streets on Saturday, between a portion of the Cambridge students and parties of Boston boys, oc-

casioned by the boys wearing burlesque imitations of the students'
caps. We have heard of several instances where the students were
grossly insulted, without the least provocation, and, on the other
hand, where the students were the aggressors. We are not surprised
that the students are annoyed by the ridicule attempted to be cast
upon them by the boys, and the fact that not one of them could
appear in our streets on Saturday without having a gang of rowdy
boys following and hooting after him, is disgraceful to Boston and
enough to provoke retaliation from the most forbearing. . . .
Philip Peak, truckman, was charged with having worn a certain
shaped cap for the purpose of exciting ridicule, and did thereby
cause a great number of persons to assemble together, said persons
uttering loud outcries and halloaing, and obstructing the streets.
Peak admitted that he wore the cap, or hat—with an oblong top
of pasteboard, two feet by one, with a tassle made of Manila rope—
in very rough imitation of the square-toed measle caps worn by the
collegians. Peak had attended a fire with his burlesque cap on, and
on his return walked around to the new City Hall, taking the middle of the street, and saying nothing to any body. A large concourse
of people had collected in and around the corners of Court street and
Court square—some to look at the original caps on the heads of the
collegians and some to look at the grotesque imitations. . . . Peak
. . . maintained that he had as perfect a right to wear a pasteboard
hat, as the collegians had to wear a square cloth cap, and he claimed
the right to wear it home. This of course was not allowed. . . .
About six o'clock a young man named Jacques was seized by the
police near the Tremont House, for striking a collegian.

The high tide in the Oxford-Cap War took the form of an invasion
in force of Harvard territory. Lee wrote:

About seven o'clock a mob composed of Port-Rowdies and Boston
truckmen, three hundred strong, (positively not exaggerated) came
out to Cambridge intending great deeds, "Harvard" was responded
to by about fifty students (many being absent, myself alas! one)
armed to the teeth with daggers pokers, pistols and clubs. The
Faculty rushed about, keeping the fellows within the yard, and
telling the mob that if they entered, they did so *at their peril*.
Quincy told the students if attacked to defend themselves in *any*
way, pistols implied [thereby winning, no doubt, a brief popular-

ity]. The mob having courageously broken *one pane* of glass, sneaked to Boston by Craig's bridge to evade the police.

The Boston *Morning Post*, May 23, 1842, was not so impressed by the students' militancy as Francis Lee and was able to discover rather more damage inflicted by the invaders.

> We regret . . . that a large number of rowdies, dressed in disguise and wearing pasteboard caps, went over to Cambridge on Saturday night for the purpose of having a battle with the students, but the latter were induced to remain in their rooms, by the urgent solicitations of the officers, and thus a conflict was prevented. The party from Boston, however, did not retire until they had broken several windows in the law school, and thrown stones at the other college buildings. A student by the name of Peabody, who happened to be returning to his lodgings before the party left, was assaulted and severely injured.

Shortly thereafter the war came to an end, without formal treaty. "Row expected the next three evenings, but we had none. 25th Burlesques died off, and war pretty much finished." No one appeared to prosecute "Jacquith," and the case against Peak was *nol. pros.* The War seems to have had its last flicker on Cambridge Bridge, probably on May 24. A "grease-and-ashes" man hailed two students and asked the price of caps. They offered to tell him with their fists; he promptly accepted the challenge by getting out of his wagon, whereupon one student, apparently doubting his manual expository power, reconsidered and advanced on the questioner with a cane. The man thereupon seized and brandished his cleaver, but when the second student produced a pistol, he leaped into his vehicle and drove off, "swearing most valorously"—thereby demonstrating that two Harvard students, a cane, and a pistol, were more than equal to a scavenger and a cleaver.

The students' side of the whole affair, with some additional information and theorizing, was summed up in a letter, May 23, 1842, to the *Post,* printed the next day:

> The first insult to the students is strongly believed to have originated at the office of the *Times;* who, in conjunction with several

clerks on Long wharf, dressed an "Ethiopean diabolus" in the "illegitimate Oxford cap," and sent him to walk the streets to provoke a fight. . . . A student met him on Washington street—went to a music store—procured a whip—followed him up on Tremont street—struck him across the cranium, and tore the cap from his head. A mob collected, and he offered to give any of them the same whip if they felt disposed to attack him.

Rowdies on Washington Street ordered students to doff their caps, according to the writer, who went on to give his version of the omnibus affair. Two students were attacked in Court Street but were assisted by law students. Students were locked out of the Tremont and thus left to the mercy of the mob. Some of them were that night attacked with clubs and stones.

The whole affair is interestingly revelatory of the unwholesome relations which then prevailed between Harvard and the commonalty of Boston and Cambridge—class-hatred and class-conflict on the lowest plane and in the simplest terms. Whenever the occupation of any of the embattled citizenry is mentioned, they turn out to be truckmen or something of the kind; it is unfortunate that they are usually referred to merely as "West-Cambridge bullies" or "Port-Rowdies." More significant is the ascription to the Boston *Daily Times* and "several clerks on Long wharf" of the responsibility for the initial clash. The *Times,* the first Boston penny paper, was a sensational sheet. "Police court reports constituted the major part of the local news." In the lack of local and contemporary scandal it published such material as the "awful disclosures" of the alleged escaped nun, Maria Monk. It is therefore quite understandable that it should have created news by sending out "burlesquers" to whip up a disturbance. But the Harvard student's charge against the clerks on Long Wharf, even though it may have been mistaken, indicates that clerkship was coming to be looked upon as a more or less permanent position, occupied by young men of a lower social and economic rank than that from which Harvard students of Boston residence were customarily drawn, instead of being as aforetime primarily the first rung of a ladder which the sons of prosperous merchants must ascend in order to attain to the position in mercantile circles occupied by their fathers; it further indicates that this incipient clerical proletariat was beginning to resent the young men some of whom would presently pass from Harvard through the counting-room *en route* to a partnership. There is, too, in the fact that two of the three students mentioned by name as active participants in the fray were Southerners, some confirmation for Thomas Wentworth Higginson's thesis that Southerners were disproportionately active in town-and-gown rows. They were particularly conspicuous at this time in the Law School, and the prominence of law students in the Oxford-Cap War has been noted. On the other hand, there is no question that students from staid New England were conspicuous in this and other college brawls. It is perhaps just as worthy of note that two of the three mentioned above did not receive Harvard degrees, and that one of these two was a New Englander of the New Englanders.

The *casus belli* apparently soon disappeared. Perhaps it would have speedily vanished even without opposition; but if, without the war that it inspired, the Oxford cap would have long persisted, generations of Harvard students are entitled to rise up and bless the Boston rowdies who all unwittingly fought in their cause.

This selection, by a former leader of the National Student League, analyzes the most important organized activity of the student movement of the thirties, the strike against war. Written from the viewpoint of the league, this essay does not give a balanced account of events, but it does capture the feeling and mood of activists in the thirties. Note the concern for fascism and the desire to counteract it.

18

Revolt on the Campus:
April 13, 1934–April 12, 1935

James Wechsler

Where was this insurgence to lead? We had become accustomed, by the end of 1933, to popular clamor against the revolt, certifying more plainly than anything else its penetration into new areas. For two years now the campus had witnessed a series of outbreaks, reverberations of which were often louder than the original sound. But most of these were momentary; hardly had they subsided than the peace of apathy and ignorance was restored. At first glance it did not seem that any great headway had been made; certainly, in terms of numbers or sustained activity, that was true. Although there had been a host of changes engendered in undergraduate attitudes—in their interests, their enthusiasms, their perspective—the trends were slow to assume organizational form.

A multitude of reasons could be cited for the lag. To an extent it was the fault of the rebels themselves; confident of their own position, supremely certain of their own analysis, they often lacked understanding of the web of student delusions, inertia and prejudice first to be undermined; they became impatient at lethargy and, instead of nursing it, denounced it; they could not fathom why others were not as swift as they to see. If this circumstance was partially responsible, it was far from the crux of the matter. The truth is that the American student was not, by education, by environment or by back-

From James Wechsler, *Revolt on the Campus,* pp. 166–181. © 1935, by James Wechsler; © renewed 1963, by Crown Publishers, Inc. Reprinted by permission.

ground, non-conformist. His training had developed just the reverse instinct. Whatever transient disturbances shook the world, he believed that they could not forever endure, and that he would once again be restored to a place of eminence in society. Although there was manifold data to indicate how precarious was his status, he preferred to regard it as a temporary phenomenon. A great illusion had been carefully nourished; why should it not survive? He had been taught to expect rewards from the world; he had seen his brothers before him carried along on the tide of boom-time dividends. To envisage for himself a similar life of comfort, of security, of advantage was a day-dream not easily shattered. Nor, as we have seen, did his education seek to rid him of the delusion. If the success formula might seem temporarily overturned, soon "inexorable forces"—the panacea of orthodox economics—would resurrect it. The vision was encouraged on every side—the same false hope and aspiration which animated the whole middle class. The student could not avoid its enticing conclusions. Like his father, he sought to embrace a mirage rather than face the readjustments entailed by the situation. Through two distressing years, his left-wing contemporaries had urged him to acknowledge that the vision was dead beyond recapture. Although he betrayed increasing concern over the issues of the day, although he might respond to a specific problem with fervor, his zeal was usually transient.

Why, in the face of all these difficulties and discouragements, did the insurgents not surrender? There was ever-increasing academic pressure, abetted from the outside, to stem the movement at its source, which augmented the obstacles of original preference. The student who was almost ready to involve himself in the revolt, after a long grapple with instinct and prejudice, was often restrained by the overt hand of his administrator. What kept the upsurge alive and gradually transformed it into a large-scale element? The answer is not to be found simply in the innate stubbornness of its constituents, although of brave persistence there was plenty. It can more readily be traced to the everyday facts of the world.

For by the dawn of 1934, had come the vindication of those predictions once derided as radical inventions or false-alarms. That is the primary clue to what was about to take place. Three years before,

a small group in Eastern colleges had joined together in the convic-
tion that this crisis was emphatically distinct from those which had
gone before. Pointing to the progressive severity of each depression,
they held that the existing one would be the most intense yet experienced. They were derided for their "pessimism"; economics professors
heatedly disputed their view, upholding the formulæ of automatic
"readjustment" and minimizing any singular aspects to the latest disorder. But by 1934 the "systematic laws" of capitalist economy had
still failed to assert themselves. At Chicago in 1932 the insurgents
had foreseen the reckless advance of the forces leading to war; the
two succeeding years had amply confirmed their judgment—to the
consternation of those who had vowed it could never happen again.
When, with Hitler's seizure of power, the dissenters had prophesied
the onrush of reaction throughout the crisis-ridden world, their fore-
bodings were ridiculed; but within twelve months repressive authority was being invoked on our own shores to stifle hunger-inspired
discontent.

This substantiation of their judgment was of wide import. It vastly
altered the relations of the student rebels with the other inhabitants
of the academic community. They could no longer be confounded
by orthodox professorial assurances; continued singing of revival was
far more incongruous than warning of doom. The average undergraduate, it must be emphasized, did not enjoy the revelation; he
clung valiantly to every hint that things would again right themselves. That faith endured for a disproportionate amount of time.
Perhaps no circumstance was more influential in its undoing than
the debacle of the New Deal. For Roosevelt's accession to office was,
for several months, a cause of jubilation on the campus as elsewhere;
he was to furnish the easy, unruffled way out of despair without any
basic realignment of the social order. The undergraduate was to regain his "privilege" status in a nation tempered by "social justice"
and "planned economy." While his place was solidified without "loss
of caste," the "New Era" was to be ushered in without strife or confusion. But the great transformation never occurred. Rooseveltism was
little more than the insurgents had declared it to be—a determined
but futile attempt to "patch up" an outworn structure without touch-

ing its foundations. When the Brain Trust went to Washington, a bright, eager coterie of young college graduates went with it; there were syndicated articles about the "young man in politics" and the emergence of idealism in government. The trek homeward was a sorrowful one; in unhappy procession, the talented Bachelors of Arts departed from Washington after a brief flirtation. Only a handful remained to "reason with big business."

Those were discomforting disclosures in the academic world. Out of them arose the prestige of the student insurgent. What he said commanded attention and, as often as not, respect. What he did was likely to be looked upon with more than cynicism or suspicion. What he thought ceased to be so alien an importation. It was not, of course, so simple a process. The rebels did not stand still and allow their predictions to be fulfilled. There were a hundred dramatic and animated phases of the revolt, some of which have been cited; there was the other side, less colorful to detail and less spectacular in conduct, but of equally great influence. I refer to the scores of discussion groups, conferences, symposia carried on by the National Student League and the League for Industrial Democracy throughout the country. The trend was manifesting itself in unobtrusive items; professors found their classrooms alive with at least a modicum of curiosity; often, to their uneasiness, they found that the stereotypes by which human disaster was customarily explained were no longer adequate. These were the background of such events as the strike of several thousand New York University students against the censorship of their press. And the background was of transcending importance, providing the prerequisites for broader activity.

In December of 1933 Henry A. Wallace, Secretary of Agriculture, was deploring the absence here of any "youth movement" comparable to those of other nations. His utterance was made at a conference of the "Student in Politics" in Washington, D. C.—a conclave at which the traditional entreaties to the student were made. He was being urged to join with all good Democrats and Republicans for the salvation of the Republic. But if Secretary Wallace had remained for the duration of the congress, he would have seen the startling beginnings of a youth movement—in terms vastly different from his own formulation. For that week the National Student League and the League for Industrial Democracy were holding their own conventions in Washington and many of their representatives sat in on the "Politics" assemblage. When they proposed certain resolutions for discussion, the controversial result was indicative of the leftward drift of the heretofore unorganized, detached throng of students whose emissaries had come to the conference. The possibility of a far broader, more concerted upsurge was visible.

For now, in the close of 1933, the point had arrived when a large number of American undergraduates were prepared to articulate their own dissatisfaction. The ferment which had begun nearly three years before was about to shift from passive to active form, from sympathetic interest to direct cooperation. The transformation would not occur overnight. But its inauguration was at least entirely conceivable. Its fulfillment was to depend on the clarity, vigor and adaptability of the left wing.

The most impressive, if perhaps incomplete, barometer for appraising the onrush of events in the fifteen months after the Washington congress, resides in two sets of figures. They do not signify the full and enduring importance of the period; they emphasize primarily how swift and far-reaching was the general upheaval in the ranks of American undergraduates.

In response to a call for a nationwide strike against the war preparations of the United States government, 25,000 students left their classrooms on April 13, 1934. That demonstration was unprecedented; nothing in the history of American undergraduate life was equivalent to it. Twelve months later, on April 12, 1935, there were 175,000 participants in similar demonstrations throughout the country. So startling and unique was the development that now, when it is still fresh in our minds, its dimensions are hardly appreciated. One leader of the national strike committee admitted that "we did not know our own strength." That impression was inescapable. Perhaps the outstanding aspect of the event was the fact that it had occurred. It was so sharp a departure from the "academic tradition," so tumultuous a contrast to the dead silence of inertia, that even the most detached could not fail to be shaken by it.

The scope of the walkout was literally nationwide.* There were at least 10,000 on strike in each of five major cities: Philadelphia, Boston, Chicago, Washington, D. C. and Los Angeles. New York City alone saw 30,000 students surge from the classrooms in dramatic unison. But the movement was not restricted to these centers. In small, out-of-the-way hamlets where an official emissary of the strike committee had never penetrated, there were spontaneous strikes. At little Phillips College in Oklahoma, 200 students—half the college—staged their own rally. In Oregon the entire student body of Reed College took part. More than 1000 students from three small institutions in Jackson, Tennessee—Union University, Lambuth and Lane colleges—streamed from their classrooms at 11 A.M. and marched through the streets. These were characteristic of the response in the minor, almost unknown colleges. While at large institutions like Chicago, Columbia and Minnesota there were thousands joining the strike, they were, it must be emphasized, not alone; overshadowing their importance was the sudden, unrivalled awareness which seized the schools in the backwoods, heretofore so assiduously sheltered from any such activity.

Those who responded to the summons were as divergent as the whole student population of the country. In 1934 the National Student League and the League for Industrial Democracy had sponsored and carried on the strike almost single-handed; one year later they were being immeasurably helped by such national groups as the National Council of Methodist Youth, the Middle Atlantic Division of the interseminary movement, two divisions of the National Student Federation, the American Youth Congress and others.† The

* In discussing the nature and meaning of the strike, I shall use as my general reference the walkout of 1935. The strike in 1934 was of vast importance in paving the way for the following year's response; it was, however, only a pale image of the succeeding effort. In 1935 more students struck in New York alone than throughout the nation on the previous occasion.

† These groups have, since that event, organized a permanent "Vigilance Committee" to insure the continuance of joint activity and to combat the concerted effort to outlaw the student anti-war movement as well as all insurgent movements. The presence of the American Youth Congress in that committee is notable; the Congress is the broadest, most heterogeneous youth group in this country today and serves as an excellent link between students and young people generally.

mixed opinion represented on this committee was even more vividly
evident among the students participating. We have seen how, in
earlier conferences and meetings, broad strata of undergraduates were
betraying increased interest in affairs beyond their own locality. But
those were merely preludes; they indicated a shift in pre-occupations,
a willingness to deal with controversial questions, a growing curiosity
—and often nothing more. To engage in them was to display one's
consciousness; it constituted no commitment beyond that. The strike,
I think it will be evident, was a profoundly different matter. And
yet, in the dominant proportion of schools, it was endorsed by campus groups of every allegiance. The chairman of the meeting at Columbia, for example, was a leading fraternity man. Nor was he an
exceptional figure; there were others everywhere with precisely the
same affiliations who gave freely of their energies and their enthusiasm. Five years before, they would have ridiculed such a project;
now they found themselves actively supporting it. No wonder that
a lone standard-bearer of preparedness at Mercer was almost in tears,
weeping that "everybody has gone communistic." He could not
fathom what was taking place—and so he accepted the most convenient label for it.

The conduct of the strike varied from place to place. In some
schools, "peace meetings" were held later in the day under administrative guidance; in others classes were cancelled and convocations
called; at a little Kansas college a prayer-meeting sufficed. But the
implications of the strike, whether it was such in actuality or not,
were felt almost everywhere: the solemnity, militance and determination associated with the term prevailed. It would be gross distortion to contend that every student, or even a large percentage, of
those who participated were radicals. They were not; many of them
were entirely unsympathetic to or ignorant of left-wing doctrine. To
believe that the 175,000 who joined hands from coast-to-coast were
declaring their hostility to the existing order is a grave delusion.
Many of them still believed in it and others did not think much
about it. Almost uniformly, however, they were manifesting their
opposition to one palpable procedure of that order—imperialistic war.
The radicals contended that imperialism was an essential, historical
outgrowth of capitalism, not a specific "policy" to be accepted or

rejected. The conservatives did not adhere to this view—or to the conclusions arising out of it. But whatever the disagreement on this point, there was accord on the problem in hand: resistance to imperialism as represented by the war budget of the Roosevelt government and the brewing conflict in Europe. In impressive unanimity students throughout the nation enunciated the Oxford pledge: "We pledge not to support the government of the United States in any war it may conduct." It was uttered in California and in New York and throughout the intervening territory. No one who heard it spoken could ignore the seriousness of the occasion and the deep-seated solidity which had been welded.

The strikers were drawn from every segment of the student community; that should be plainly understood. On the other hand, their action, in terms of traditional academic habit, was "radical." It was radical as a departure from the sanctified formulæ by which war was allegedly to be averted; it did not fly the dove of peace nor did it place faith in the divine benevolence of statesmen. The "strike" is a solemn weapon; directed against government policy it assumes even broader connotations. Those who endorsed the move, representing every political faith, did not do so because they were "out for trouble" or because they desired to "precipitate violence." They did so in acknowledgment of the immediacy of the issue and the incessant, overt pressure which the war danger demanded. No sinister hand forced the tactic upon innocent undergraduates; the American government, by adopting a program of arms expenditures unparalleled in peacetime, was responsible for the vehement form which this protest took. One conservative student, addressing a strike rally, stated this case admirably:

> I don't know whether it's radical to strike or not. I don't care. I do know that the government will listen to a strike a good deal sooner than it will heed a peace-picnic. And I'm not afraid of being called a communist or of working with communists. I'm a hell of a lot more afraid of the bankers and business men who make wars.

Even more noteworthy was the anti-fascist sentiment accompanying the protest. It was important because it signified an awareness of the roots of war and its present-day carriers. There was widespread recognition that the peril of conflict was inseparably linked with the existence of fascism abroad; and that, moreover, American involvement in such a war would be accentuated by the development of fascist tendencies in our own government. For fascism was nationalism epitomized; its leading exponents have not hesitated to say so, and if they had, the impending Italian invasion of Ethiopia would have adequately disproved their assertions. Mussolini believes that "imperialism is the eternal and immutable law of life" and cries "three cheers also for war in general." Hitler has echoed him, proclaiming that "an alliance whose aim does not include the intention of war is worthless nonsense" and that on his assumption of power "Germany struck out the word pacifism from its vocabulary." * These things were felt by the striking students; it was folly to oppose imperialist warfare without taking cognizance of its most ardent practitioners. And that was an understanding common to conservatives and radicals alike. Its most immediate meaning was the realization that the emergence of an American fascist régime would, in its first official legislation, illegalize any concerted protest against war. The omens of such measures were most acutely experienced by students at the hands of their administrators on April 12th; the details of this tendency will be recounted later, but its bearing cannot be omitted here. One of the prime convictions of the strike was this growing sense that fascism and war were inseparables, that they aggravated those international economic rivalries and local disorders which were the preliminaries to armed strife. Virtually every strike assemblage expressed this belief: fascism is the most extravagant, pronounced and pernicious phase of imperialism.

These were general assumptions underlying the event. Their specific relation to the campus was most concretely voiced by opposition to the Reserve Officers Training Corps. The hostility was based upon more than preparedness questions; there was, further, the intolerant, repressive credo of the R.O.T.C., and, of even more intimate concern, the vast funds which the corps required for its upkeep. At

* These quotations are from John Strachey's *Menace of Fascism*.

countless universities, there was organized on April 12th a determined campaign to end the rule of the military department—where such a campaign was not already in existence. It was an unhappy day for the generals.

The strikes were the expression of an idea, or of a set of ideas; yet their spectacular, colorful and dynamic qualities will not soon be forgotten. In 1934 undergraduates at Springfield planted white crosses on the campus on the eve of the walkout to commemorate the betrayal of 1917. At Vassar a throng of girls marched behind impressive placards declaring, not some illusion-tinged ode to peace, but "We Fight Imperialist War." Several weeks before the demonstration, students at the University of Washington hired a truck, draped it with appropriate jingoist placards and joined the Army Day parade sponsored by the American Legion. As the procession reached the center of Seattle, the students suddenly reversed their placards; on the other side were appeals to "Fight Against War." Legionnaires attacked the students, hurling them from the trucks; police arrived to arrest the victims of the attack. But the episode had served its purpose.

One year later 450 students jammed a room at the Carnegie Institute of Technology for a demonstration unequalled in the history of the institution. In the South, Negro students from Morgan College joined with whites at Johns Hopkins and Goucher, resisting the attempts of an R.O.T.C. band to disrupt their ranks. At little Dakota Wesleyan every church in the town and every campus organization joined together to prepare the strike; there were scores of townspeople at the actual meeting. That alignment between students and working-people in neighboring communities was repeated elsewhere; it testified to the solidification of those bonds essential to the movement. Thirty-five hundred students, assembled in the Columbia University Gymnasium, listened to a rendition of "Taps," and the chairman quietly declared that "these notes are in memory of those who died in the last war and in solemn determination that we shall not repeat their mistake." To an audience which overflowed the meeting-hall at Virginia, a speaker asserted: "If those who profit from

war insist upon bringing it on again, then we, with the mass of
American people, must take power into our own hands and force
peace upon the war-makers."

At Emory University in Georgia, where membership in the League
for Industrial Democracy is considered treason, 250 students braved
outside pressure to gather in a chapel peace meeting. And at New
Hampshire University 1000 of the 1300 undergraduates left their
classes at 11 o'clock to support the strike.

In every sector the move had gripped the imagination of American
students. The Cornell *Daily Sun* commented: "The Cornell undergraduate seems to have finally cast aside his usual cloak of apathy
toward world problems." The *Daily Princetonian* wrote: "The thinking and far-sighted youths of this country will no longer be restrained
but will shout their defiance of war so that all may hear it." Virginia's
student editor added: "Pro Patria Mori Is Bunk." According to the
Dartmouth Daily: "When war comes, an editorial like this achieves
nothing but an indefinite prison sentence for its writers. It is in time
of peace that we must build up anti-war sentiment to the point where
it will be able to fight cooperatively against the emotional hysteria
of war-time." The *Idaho Bengal*: "The cumulative effect of many
of these moves is bound to be great."

The strike was a militant gesture; the term itself was borrowed
from years of struggle against oppression by people of all creeds and
countries. But it was more than a momentary flare-up or one whose
effects would swiftly fade. Those demonstrations were a "dress re-
hearsal" for the immediate stand which students had vowed to take
should the government declare war. That point was reiterated on
every side. "Passive resistance" was not the prevailing tone; these
young men and women, as one speaker shouted to an earnest crowd
of thousands of students, "do not propose to be a lost generation—
and we are ready to fight for our lives."

On the same afternoon, a delegation of students visited the White
House to present a message from that nationwide assemblage. It was
addressed to Mr. Roosevelt and set forth the refusal of 175,000
American students to support the government of the United States
in any war it might conduct.

In the Spring of 1924 three conspicuous and celebrated feats agitated the American campus:

NEW HAVEN, CONN., March 9, 1924—A new record has been set for Old Eli. H. Howitzer and C. Souris took part in a marathon needle-work contest last week beginning at noon Tuesday and ending at 9.30 Friday.

IOWA CITY, IA., March 10, 1924—Two students of the University of Iowa, Dan Gilson and Judson Large, established an endurance record here when they played bridge for twenty-five hours consecutively.

MINNEAPOLIS, MINN., March 10, 1924—Swan Swenson of the University of Minnesota has for the past week been rolling a peanut around the campus, finishing last night at 10:30. He worked for 150 hours, making 90 circuits of the campus, a distance of 217 miles.

Eleven years afterward, a tabulation of the participants in the student strike against war disclosed the following totals, arranged by regions and with reports from certain sectors still incomplete:*

NEW ENGLAND		Radcliffe	300
Amherst	250	Simmons	700
Bennington	200	Smith	800
Brown	1,300	Tufts	300
Clark	100	Wesleyan	400
Colby	500	Yale	500
Conn. College for Women	400		
Dartmouth	500	MIDDLE ATLANTIC	
Emerson	250	American U.	500
Harvard	600	Barnard	400
M. I. T.	150	Brooklyn College (with	
Mass. State	43	Long Island U. and	
Mt. Holyoke	100	Seth Low)	6,000
New Hampshire	1,000	Bryn Mawr	500

* These figures are obtained from *The Student Outlook* which made the most exhaustive survey available of the strike total.

Buffalo	400	Tennessee	100
Carnegie Tech.	450	Texas U.	1,500
C. C. N. Y.	3,500	Texas Christian U.	1,600
Colgate	1,000	Tulane, Louisiana	500
Columbia	3,500	Virginia	1,000
Cornell	2,500	West Virginia	90
George Washington U.	1,200		

MIDDLE WEST

Goucher (with Johns Hopkins and Morgan)	2,000	Butler	200
Haverford	150	Central	500
Howard	600	Chicago	3,500
Hunter	2,200	De Pauw	1,000
Lafayette	1,000	Drake	300
New Jersey Coll. (with		Eden	100
Rutgers)	1,000	Hamline	500
New York University	2,000	Illinois	300
Penn. State	1,500	Iowa	250
U. of Penn.	3,000	Illinois Wesleyan	500
Pittsburgh	800	Lewis Institute	500
Princeton	1,000	Michigan State	50
St. Lawrence	400	Michigan	1,000
Swarthmore	500	Milwaukee State (with	
Syracuse	1,000	Wisconsin Extension)	2,500
Temple	2,500	Minnesota	3,000
Vassar	entire student body	Missouri	800
Wilson	500	Northwestern	1,200
		People's Junior College	750

SOUTH

		Washington U.	400
Berea	1,500	Wayne	500
Chattanooga	200	Wisconsin	2,000
College of the Ozarks	800	Wright Junior College	50
Emory	250		

OHIO

Florida State (with Rollins and Tampa)	1,000	Akron	250
Louisville	350	Antioch	350
Mercer	100	Denison	600
Morehouse	100	Fenn	200
Vanderbilt (with Peabody,		Marietta	175
Fisk and Scarritt)	250	Miami	500
North Carolina	1,000	Muskingum	500
Southwestern	200	Oberlin	1,200

Ohio State	400	Phillips	200
Ohio	1,200	Salina	300
Toledo	600	Wyoming U.	750
Western Reserve	2,000		
Wittenberg	700	**PACIFIC COAST**	
		California Tech.	400
ROCKY MOUNTAINS		U. of California	
Baker	38	(Berkeley)	4,000
Colorado U.	500	U. C. L. A.	1,000
Dakota Wesleyan	400	Linfield	200
Denver	800	Los Angeles J. C.	3,000
Friends University	300	Pacific College	600
Idaho U. (Southern and		Oregon U.	1,000
Moscow branches)	1,100	Pasadena Junior College	500
Kansas State	500	Reed	300
Kansas University	1,000	San Diego State	500
Montana	500	San Jose	500
Nebraska	500	San Mateo	800
North Dakota State Teach-		Stanford	1,500
ers College	400	Washington U.	500
North Dakota U.	No estimate	Whittier	500

The strike had grown seven-fold in one year. Dr. Stephen Duggan, writing in the *News Bulletin* of the Institute of International Education, predicted that by 1936 "the movement will be almost universally observed." How is this sweeping growth to be explained? Certainly the first year's demonstrations were part of the answer; they had attained a maximum of discipline and effectiveness despite the attempt of rowdies to disperse them. Even more important, they had broken an entrenched set of prejudices against precisely such action, paving the way for more decisive inroads. But this alone does not account for the increase. It was primarily due to the gathering of external forces, the ominous tempo of world events. Implicit in the student's response was the fear that the depression was to be "solved" by another international war and that he, as part of the "surplus population" was to be sacrificed for it. The signs of catastrophe were visible on every side. Growing out of this apprehension was his abandonment of traditional antipathies; he could not be dissuaded by appeals for "scholarliness"; the time had come when the organized might of mass opinion throughout the world would have to make itself heard. That had been, we have seen, the contention of the insurgents since 1932. By the spring of 1935, whether he liked the admission or not, the aware student had to grant their judgment. It was too late to contemplate the virtues of "restrained objectivity." It was hardly feasible to remain aloof from so intimate a peril. If the American undergraduate on April 12th was a changed, revitalized human being, that was because the world had changed from its post-war to its pre-war attire.

This essay, written by a professor who was a member of the faculty during the Berkeley uprising, is critical of the student radicals. It is also a careful analysis that explains what was unique in the Berkeley movement and what it had in common with student activism elsewhere.

19

"Student Power" in Berkeley

Nathan Glazer

Whatever students may be doing to change the world—and they are clearly doing a good deal—it could turn out that, in the end, it is rather easier to change the world than the university. This, it seems, is the inference to be drawn from four years of student rebellion at the University of California at Berkeley, where the present wave of student disorders—which has had such phenomenal impact in Italy, West Germany, and France—first began.

Four years after the Free Speech Movement exploded in autumn 1964, the world does look very different, and the FSM looks like a prophetic turning point; but the University of California looks very much the same, and it is this paradox that concerns me in this essay.

It may appear a case of distorted institutional loyalty to give Berkeley the primacy as the point of origin of the present wave of student civil disorder, and yet I think that what started at Berkeley in 1964 was rather different from the student violence of the years before—whether the student demonstrations of Japan in 1960, the endemic student violence of India, or the student rebellions of South Korea and Turkey that helped overthrow governments. There were five key differences:

1. The Berkeley student uprising occurred in an affluent country that, whatever the case with uneducated Negroes, treated the educated well. There was no problem of unemployment for the educated (as there was in India, South Korea, and other developing

From Nathan Glazer, "Student Power in Berkeley," *The Public Interest,* no. 13 (Fall 1968), 3–21. Reprinted by permission of National Affairs, Inc., © 1968.

nations). Thus the student uprisings could not be related to such issues as livelihood and status for the educated. It was new, then, in that it could find issues that were crucial to students despite their assurance of affluence.

2. It was new in that it was not directed against an oppressive national, local, or university regime—as "oppression" had been generally understood until that moment. In time, the student movement was so successful that the civil government of local communities (such as Oakland and Berkeley), and of the nation, and of the universities could be cast in an oppressive role, though they had generally not been seen in that light before. In contrast, much of the student disorder in developing countries was directed against military or dictatorial regimes; in Japan, the regime was democratic, but was nevertheless not considered so by many students and intellectuals. The new student movement that began in Berkeley was able to discover or create new issues pertaining to the basic constitution of a democratic government and the institutions within a democratic society.

3. It was new, too, in that it exploded at a time when there were relatively few great burning issues on the national agenda. One could still hope, in the autumn of 1964, that civil rights legislation and social legislation would rapidly enough satisfy the demands of American Negroes (white backlash seemed a more urgent problem then than black militancy), and Vietnam was not yet the overwhelming issue it was to become. But just as in Germany and France in 1968, student activists in Berkeley were able to create big issues on what most people felt was a relatively placid political scene.

4. It was new in its tactics. It found means of dramatizing its rebellion against an affluent and democratic society by forcing it to respond in ways that could be cast as repressive and authoritarian. The politics of "confrontation" was not original with the Berkeley students, but they nevertheless elaborated it in new and startling ways.

5. But perhaps the most striking novelty in the Berkeley student revolt was that the two ideologies which had played the largest role in sparking student uprisings around the world, Marxism (in demo-

cratic countries) and liberalism (in dictatorial and Marxist countries),
played a minor role in Berkeley. Marxists of various persuasions, and
liberals too, were of course involved, but neither the classic demand
for socialist revolution by the first, nor for civil liberties and democratic reform by the second could fully encompass the main thrust
of the Berkeley student revolt. Marxism and liberalism were rather
two wings of a movement whose center was poorly defined—though
"participatory democracy" thoroughly carried out in every institution
and social process was perhaps its clearest feature. It is revealing that,
when the Berkeley student rebels paused after their victory over the
administration, and cast about for representative figures who might
express their philosophy and help them to define their positive aims,
they chose Paul Goodman, who is not a Marxist, and invited him to
the campus. Goodman considers himself an anarchist, and the dominant theme in his voluminous writings is specific and detailed attention to the small social structures and institutions that immediately
affect people and their lives—predominantly the school, but also
housing, the neighborhood, local government, the work setting. In
radical contrast to the Marxists, who had banned as "utopianism" all
consideration of the details of how to reconstruct society, Goodman's
main achievement is to analyze and propose means of refashioning
those details. If Marxists traditionally wait for the revolution, and
in the meantime radicalize people by demonstrating that no change
but the largest can help them, Goodman does quite the opposite—
he hopes to show them that many small changes can help them.

Revolt Against Whom?

In summary, Berkeley to my mind is the first example of a student
rebellion that occurs in conditions where students are privileged,
their future is assured, where liberal, parliamentary democracy pre-
vails, and where the principal ideology of the student rebels is neither
Marxism nor liberalism but rather the effort to create a participatory
and somewhat communal democracy. It is the first student rebellion
to have considered what is still wrong in a liberal, democratic, and

permissive society, and by what tactics and strategy revolutionaries can bring larger and larger numbers to agree with them that a great deal is wrong.

It is, of course, not easy to escape from the past, particularly when so many problems of the present resemble those of the past. Thus Vietnam permitted and enabled Marxism again to become more prominent in the radical student movement—but let us recall that the Berkeley revolt precedes any large concern with the issue of Vietnam, and with the associated pressure of the draft, though these soon became the dominant issues of the movement. Moreover, the means of "revolutionizing the masses" inevitably are never entirely new. Thus it is known that when the police attack, one gains recruits and strength, and a good deal of attention must be devoted to the tactics that get the police to attack.

But what *is* new are the means of casting a liberal polity in the role of an oppressive one. Thus, the student activists place great emphasis on the constraints of organization and government (any organization and government), and as a corollary emphasize the importance of participatory democracy, which concretely tends to mean that any mob is right as against any administrator, legislature, or policeman. (Fortunately, up until now we have had left-wing rather than right-wing mobs, and they are milder.) In the thinking of the radical students, the IBM card that facilitates student registration can be cast in the same role as the police control cards of the tsarist state or the Soviet Union.

So the line that leads from Berkeley to Columbia, through the universities of Italy, West Germany, France, and England, marks something new. What is happening in Eastern Europe and Spain, in Brazil and Argentina, is easier to understand—it is the fight for freedom. But what then do the student uprisings of the affluent world represent? The answer isn't easy or clear. For from the beginning there was a central ambiguity in the student disorders here (as there are in those of other affluent countries). Were students protesting primarily against their *universities*—the institutions of higher education, with their special constitutions, rules, requirements, culture? Or were they protesting against their *societies,* with their unresolved problems and their "hypocrisies"?

The Primacy of Politics

It is not easy to disentangle the two sorts of issues, in practice, but they are clear in theory. On the one hand, we have issues that stem directly from the concrete institutional setting of higher education—relations among administrators, students, and teachers; roles in setting rules for the three groups; power to exercise discipline, and to define the actions that call for discipline; power to determine curriculum, criteria for admission and graduation, faculty appointments, and the like. On the other hand, we have the two great issues of American life in the late 1960's—the race issue and the Vietnam issue, and what they may be taken to reflect in society: racism, the dominance of the military, middle-class fears of Communism encouraged by the mass media, the power of corporations, etc.

From the beginning, in 1964, the university issues have played second fiddle to the political issues, even though this was often hard to see—for the actual battleground was generally the university and the representatives of "the establishment" under siege were the university officials. But the university, in effect, was standing in for the world and its problems—which made for dilemmas in knowing how to handle student rebellion, but which also meant that the central structures and institutions of the university were really not the chief target. According to the radical students, the university had to be reformed—but mainly in order to permit the political resistance or intervention of students in a corrupt society to become more effective. Thus, one reason why the impact of the student revolt on the colleges and universities has been moderate up to now was that issues of educational reform came up later and were secondary to the political issues.

In the thinking of the student radicals and their leaders, the primary problem was the society, not the university. How then does the university get involved so prominently in the act? The university gets involved because (1) the radical students demand that it offer a refuge and base for political action in the community; (2) they treat it as a surrogate for society in general—whether out of frustration, or because it was a nearer target, or in order to practice tactics and strategy for the larger offensive against the stronger institutions; and (3) they eventually hope actively to enlist it in their efforts at political education and mobilization. The university thus serves three possible functions for student radicals: as refuge and base, as surrogate for and representative of an oppressive society, and finally as potentially active ally in the attempt to transform society.

In the first case, the university simply—to use the language of the student radicals—"gets in their way." This was the origin of the Free Speech Movement: the students wanted the right to meet freely on campus, to raise funds, to recruit supporters, and to discuss the whole range of issues that concerned them, including the use of unlawful tactics in their political activities. This last was the sticking point in the first major Berkeley climax in December 1964, and it was left somewhat unresolved, with the faculty voting that only considerations of "time, place, and manner" should limit student political activity on campus, and the regents of the university insisting that considerations of legality should still limit the right to political activity on the campus. In the end, a kind of *modus vivendi* has emerged in which the radical students feel relatively unhampered in discussing the full range of present-day political issues and tactics, including of course a good deal that is unlawful, but in which the administration does not limit them unless major publicity is given to their actions—and even then it simply works out a compromise to demonstrate to the regents and to the governor that it can exercise some power over political activity on campus. Thus, when a "Vietnam Commencement" was proposed last spring to honor those who refused to be drafted, there was a good deal of negotiation between the organizers of the commencement and the university administration as to where and when it should be held and just what its content would be. But it was held.

The University as Surrogate

More significant has been the university's role as a surrogate or representative of society. Here, some of the chief issues have been whether the university should give special placement exams or report grades to draft authorities (when standing in class was a factor in drafting students), whether the university should permit representatives from such government agencies as the armed forces and the CIA and from Dow Chemical to recruit employees on campus, and the role of the university in classified and weapons research. Here the university is acting as part of or as agent for society—and the radical students have had the convenience of an agent of society being near at hand and also being more vulnerable to attack than some of the institutions it may be taken to represent. While in the first case—where the university serves as base and refuge—the radical students have insisted that the university make no judgment as to the legality or illegality of their actions and that it leave it to the civil arm alone to determine whether they have broken the law and should be limited in their political activity, in this second case the radical students insist that the university *must* make a judgment as to the morality of the activities it permits on the campus—and among those it must ban are any that serve the interests of the armed forces or the foreign policy of the government.

At Berkeley, the role of the university as a surrogate and representative of those forces in society that radical students oppose has been, for the latter part of the last academic year at least, in eclipse. The radical student movement has moved on from an attack on university practices in connection with Selective Service and military and government recruiting to a direct attack on Selective Service stations. The university has been superseded, first by the Selective Service headquarters in Oakland, and then by the police, with whom the radical students have clashed in Oakland in their efforts to surround and close the Selective Service station. Radical student antagonism to the Oakland police is now heightened by the alliance with the militant and armed Negroes of the Black Panther party, who have been harassed by the police. In addition, the city government of Berkeley and its police have been added to the list, since the police opposed, with tear gas, the efforts of radical students to close a major street ostensibly in order to hold a rally supporting the French students and workers. In addition, the radical students have been active in helping organize the Peace and Freedom party, which ran the writer Paul Jacobs for U.S. Senator, the former student leader Mario Savio for state legislator, and a variety of leaders of the Black Panther party for Congress and other posts. In all this, the university role as surrogate and representative of society has for the moment been eclipsed—the Selective Service authorities, the police, the local civil authorities, the state government, and the national government have for the time being at least taken its place.

But, after one gets the university to move out of the way, and after one prevents, through the manufacture of disorder, the representatives of government agencies from recruiting on campus and cuts the universities' ties with defense research (not that this has been fully accomplished, but the mechanisms for doing so have been well developed)—then what? The rules as to political behavior in a university are after all fairly incidental to its chief functions—unless matters come to the point where unpopular (that is, nonradical) opinion is intimidated. (While that has happened at Berkeley and elsewhere, it is owing less to the new rules, which are on the whole good, than to the attitude of the New Left to the expression of dissident opinion, which is bad. It also owes something to the ease with which people allow themselves to be intimidated.) Similarly, just who recruits on campus and how much classified research is permitted or exists is to my mind incidental to the central functions of the university. Classified research has in any case never loomed large. The huge laboratories that various universities direct for the Atomic Energy Commission have been cut off from the university, administratively and sometimes physically. It is hard to see that they have had a major impact on the university—which is perhaps one reason why it has been hard for the radical students at Berkeley to launch an attack on the university's relationship with Livermore and Los Alamos. These relationships could in any case be cut without any significant effect on either the university or the laboratories—just as relationships with IDA are now being cut by a number of universities.

The question remains: what about the heart of the university— the teaching of undergraduate and graduate students, the day-to-day research of faculty and graduate students? How are they affected by the student rebellion? The answer is that, up to now, there has been little effect. The structure of the university and its normal activities go on, suffering only minor impact from the events that have made student activism a major political issue in the state, the nation, and now in the world.

The "Free Universities"

We have suggested one reason for this—that the radical students have really not been primarily interested in educational reform. During Paul Goodman's visit, for example, the radical students were more interested in him as a radical social prophet than as a radical educational reformer. Yet there has been a section of the radical student movement that, together with some nonradical students and a few members of the faculty, has been interested in educational reform for a long time—this group began its activity even before FSM. FSM gave the reformers potentially much greater influence and a much larger audience. In the past, this group had run meetings which attracted little attendance and little interest. Meetings on educational reform after FSM attracted somewhat more student interest, though nowhere near the number that became involved in protest on the great political issues and in the confrontations with the university administration that the tactics chosen always seemed to lead to. And, revealingly enough, not one of these major confrontations with the administration since FSM has ever dealt with an educational issue. But if radical student interest in educational reform was not great, administration interest was. For it is natural and understandable for educational administrators to assume or hope that student unrest and disorder must reflect and must be curable by institutional reform. Acting Chancellor Martin Meyerson in 1965 and Chancellor Roger Heyns who succeeded him were eager to sponsor changes in the university. The question was, what changes?

The first expression in education of the student rebellion was the student-run free university. One was organized at Berkeley (it bears the unfortunate initials FUB), another at Stanford. At San Francisco State, owing to the greater strength of student radicals, or the greater acquiescence of administration and faculty, the free university seems to have been in effect organized within the college, under the control of students, but giving credit for work. There are three points to be made about the free university as a means of revolutionizing the university. First, it is not new. Radical and other ideological groups have always organized courses outside the university in order to push some specific outlook or to present material that they felt the university was slighting. Long before the free university, one could take courses off campus on "Revolutions of Our Time and Why They Failed," "Basic Principles of Marxism-Leninism," or the like. (Today's free university will generally have a course in guerilla warfare, picking up from Mao and Ché, and on the ideologists of Black Power.) There were other free, off-campus, noncredit courses that were and still are generally available around a university, often in the religious centers catering to students. Naturally, these courses would try to pitch themselves to student interests and could show a flexibility and rapidity in responding to current issues that the regular university departments could not. I imagine Kierkegaard was being taught in off-campus religious student centers before he got into the curriculum of many university philosophy departments; the off-campus pastors had a greater incentive to find something that might reach and excite students.

I mention this background only because it is my impression that the free universities are not so different from these previous efforts to supplement university education, though they are on a somewhat larger scale. But of course the ambition of the free universities is greater than this, as their name implies; it is to teach new areas of learning and experience, by new means, all of which would not be allowed in an "establishment" university. The problem is that almost anything that the law allows—and a bit more—is to be found in an establishment-run university, and you get credit for it besides. I would guess that the summer universities now being launched in the wake of the May days in France will have a greater impact— simply because their universities have been more conservative.

There is a second factor that limits the effectiveness of the free universities for revolutionary purposes. Just as the off-campus religious centers have to offer courses that are responsive to student interests and fashions, so too must the free university. Perhaps the organizers would like to give courses in urban guerilla warfare—and they do—but there is nothing they can do to make them more pop-

ular than courses in drug experience, meditation, sensitivity training, new forms of sexual and interpersonal relations, film-making, and
a variety of other present-day youth interests. The free university,
then, is limited in its effect, not only because it gives work in areas
that other extra-university groups have already covered, but precisely
because it is so responsive to its clientele and their shifting interests.

Finally, another reason for its limited effect is that the faculty,
many of them young and only recently (or still) student radicals
themselves, are by no means backward in adding to the curriculum
those new ideas that the radical students feel the university is suppressing. Frantz Fanon, Paul Goodman, Herbert Marcuse, and Ché
Guevara get into regular courses of the university as fast as they
get into the free university. This is perhaps one reason why drugs,
meditation, and sex, which admittedly are handled in a more academic way, if at all, in the establishment university, become a major
stock-in-trade of the free university. And this, in turn, helps to explain why the phrase "repressive tolerance" is now so popular on
the Berkeley scene—it is Marcuse's explanation of how the establishment draws the teeth of revolutionary ideas by spreading them
through university courses and the mass media.

Experiments at Berkeley

When the free university—the student-run university—gets within
the fold of the university, its effects are greater, but still not revolutionary. I have spoken of the student-run courses at San Francisco
State College, given for credit. The same development has occurred
at Berkeley, as part of a number of experiments in education that
flowed from the FSM. One of the results of the movement was the
establishment of a faculty Select Committee on Education at Berkeley
(the Muscatine Committee, as it became called after its chairman,
Professor of English Charles Muscatine), which issued a large and
substantial report.

The Select Committee reviewed the student rebellion at Berkeley,
recognized it had many causes and that many were beyond the
reach of the university, and then went on to urge reforms in educa-

tion at Berkeley. It proposed no new and large sweeping transformation of the university, though some of the faculty reacted as if it had. What it did propose was very many small changes, and one major institutional change, all designed to support experiments and innovations in education. In effect it proposed escape hatches for specific student and faculty interests, while the rest of the university was to go on its accustomed ways. Not clear as to how the curriculum of a huge university could be reorganized, it proposed a new institution—the Board of Educational Development—that would have the power to approve courses and courses of study outside the regular departments and would not require their approval or the approval of other faculty committees.

These courses could be initiated by students or by faculty. If initiated by students, they required a faculty sponsor, though his role could be minimal. The board has been established, has been in operation now for two years and has sponsored quite a number of interdisciplinary and nondisciplinary courses (twenty in the Spring 1968 quarter). There is as yet no new curriculum that has been proposed to it—though if one were, it could be approved. One of the most imaginative and unconventional of the courses it sponsored was one which sent some forty students to Washington in spring of 1968 to live with and observe the Poor People's Campaign. Students wrote papers and received credit, and were supervised by a faculty member. This course perhaps expresses best the kind of change the radical students would like to introduce, a course in which one becomes somewhat more expert in political activism and its understanding. However, even here the faculty sponsor imposed an academic discipline that was very likely felt as external and irrelevant by some of the activists who took the course.

There is also now a student-run Committee on Participant Education, which will develop courses that students show interest in. (These do not give university credit unless the student makes a special arrangement with a faculty member, but in view of the number of acquiescent faculty members, this is not hard.) These courses involve a few thousand students a year. The most popular this past year was a course on (or in) meditation. They can be best considered something of a cross between extra-curricular activities and course work. Once again, despite Board of Education courses and Committee on Participant Education courses, and the popularity of some of them, the university—that is, the departments and the research institutes, the faculty, the course work, the students—proceeds on its regular way, rather unaffected.

There have been other changes. Even before FSM, Professor Joseph Tussman of Philosophy and some faculty colleagues of various departments had been urging an experimental college, to conduct for some students the first two years of their college education, replacing the normally disparate collection of courses they take by a single unified curriculum, based on the treatment of four major periods of civilization. This program was approved experimentally, and about 120 students and five faculty members plus graduate assistants were provided with a former fraternity house and full freedom. The program has graduated one class, and has completed the first year of work with another. It is not easy to come up with an unambiguous verdict as to its success. One thing is clear however: having begun with five regular faculty members deeply involved and committed, it is now down to one, plus visitors brought specifically to teach in the experimental college. And rather than serving as a model for other experimental colleges, it seems questionable whether it can continue. This is no profound verdict on it—it merely confirms what everyone who has had some experience with experiments in higher education knows, that the departments and the disciplines define the greater part of college education, and it is very difficult to establish anything outside the regular departmental lines.

But having said this, one must also add that it is not at all clear that what would or could be established outside the regular departmental and disciplinary lines would be better than what exists within them. We should also add that the Tussman experiment, aside from the fact that its establishment was facilitated by the desire of the administration to encourage experiment as a result of FSM, has only loose connections with the student rebellion at Berkeley. It is not student initiated or student run, nor does the curriculum particularly reflect the new student interests. Although there is a great deal of faculty and student freedom in how to handle the curriculum, it still consists of fixed readings in fixed periods of civilization.

The Passing of General Education

The main thrust of student activism, in contrast, has been to further diminish the appeal of the notion of any fixed or required liberal arts curriculum. Here a good part of the faculty, with its specialist interests, agrees with the student radicals. One might say the educational ideal of both, at this point, if they have any, is better expressed by President Eliot of Harvard and his pure elective system than any available alternative.

While the Muscatine Committee Report, which moved somewhat in this direction, was approved by the faculty, with the unenthusiastic support of student radicals, another educational report, which tried to move in the direction of a more coherent curriculum that would reflect the ideal of a broadly accepted liberal arts education, was defeated by the faculty. At the time the Muscatine Committee was appointed, a second special committee (called the Herr Committee, after the historian Richard Herr who chaired it) was formed to review the undergraduate program in the College of Letters and Science, the largest unit on the Berkeley campus. The committee proposed that the undergraduate program should be more coherent. Instead of the common arrangement whereby each undergraduate was required to take some work in a number of fields which supposedly defined the well-educated man (science, social science, humanities, mathematics, languages, etc.) and was free to select what he would out of the wide range of courses offered in each field, the hope of the committee was that a more relevant undergraduate education could be structured, in part by developing special undergraduate courses attuned to the interests of students in other fields (science for literature students, and vice versa). Of course, this would mean either getting the faculty to agree to develop such courses and programs or recruiting new faculty. In effect, it meant breaking the pattern of organization that is so well suited to a faculty committed to disciplines and research and is organized in powerful departments. In such a situation—which characterizes Berkeley and most universities—the undergraduate curriculum is arranged by treaties between groups of departments in the various major areas, rather than by any agency reviewing undergraduate education from a nondepartmental perspective, and the introductory courses and the courses designed for those from other fields, the so-called "service" courses, generally get little attention. The Herr Committee proposals meant that a faculty gathered on the basis of research interests and capacities and disciplinary orientations would now have to devote more attention to undergraduate teaching and nondisciplinary concerns. In this case, the interests of the faculty coincided with the interests of politically activist (and other reform-minded) students, who wanted as little restriction and limitation as possible in getting through their four years in college. The Herr Committee report, as a result, did rather poorly, and its major proposals were voted down by the college faculty (only a small minority of whom in any case were interested enough to attend the meetings at which the report was discussed), in favor of a simpler student-formulated proposal.

The movement of the university toward greater fragmentation, greater specialization, strong independent departments, a weakening concern with general education, was either endorsed or at any rate not interfered with by these changes.

Toward Participation

Another major report came under consideration by the faculty, *The Culture of the University: Governance and Education*. This is the report of a faculty-student Commission set up in January 1967, after another major blow-up at Berkeley. This one was occasioned by radical students blocking military recruiters. When the administration called in the police, the predictable results occurred—the radical students gained a great deal of support, including that of liberal students and faculty, there was a student strike, and a faculty-student commission on governance was set up. The majority report of this commission is the first of the three I have discussed that expresses in some central way the ideas of the radical students.

The majority report, like the two reports before it, eschews any detailed discussion of the content of a desired education—who knows what that should be? But it does know what is wrong with the present education.

It argues:

> Some of the most thoughtful and serious students have come to repudiate many of the social goals and values they are asked to serve in the university and upon graduation. That repudiation is directed in part at the conditions of technological society which seem to threaten human dignity. The new world emerging seems to exact greater conformity, more routinized lives, more formalized relationships among individuals. . . .

Faced with the crises of race, urban violence and decay, environmental degradation, war,

> many students express intense dissatisfaction with the university, since it provides much of the knowledge and most of the trained personnel required by the technological and scientific society. . . . It is little wonder, then, that many students are no longer content to spend their college years preparing to "take their place" in such a society. Nor is it surprising that many students regard as irrelevant the miscellany of superficial, uncertain choices and professional training which often passes as the curriculum.
>
> Such discontent is deepened by the degree to which the university's atmosphere reproduces the characteristics of the society. The university is large, impersonal, and bureaucratic. The acquisition of specialized skills has often been substituted for education of persons, instead of supplementing it. . . .

The two crucial failures of the university, the majority report argues, are first, "its failure to develop a student body which respects the value of the intellect itself," and students therefore suffer from "passionless mind and mindless passion" (as well as mindlessness and passionlessness, on the part of the majority of the students, who are characterized by apathy and careerism), and second, its domination by "service." The "function of providing useful knowledge and expert consultants to assist society in its effort to satisfy human needs, has somehow gotten out of hand."

And the university is not well organized to deal with these problems: "Inertia and discouragement have combined to produce a situation in which fundamental educational problems are discussed only sporadically and then in so prosaic a fashion as to make education seem a dreary affair when compared with the drama of campus politics." The university *should* be an educational community, but it sees itself as if it were "any other pluralistic society populated by diverse interest groups and lacking a common commitment to anything more than the bargaining process itself."

This is roughly the majority report's analysis of the problems of Berkeley. In the light of all this, it is somewhat disappointing to discover that the major recommendations of the report, spelled out at elaborate length, are, first, an extensive decentralization of all the functions of the university to the departmental level, together with a great increase in the role of students in educational policy-making at every level, from the departmental up and down; and second, an elaborate system for exercising student discipline through various courts and panels and appellate bodies, whose aim is to ensure the fullest due process, but which strikes me as something only a lawyer could have written, and one suspects only lawyers can read or understand.

The majority report, despite the varied character of its writers and its strong commitment to a traditional view of higher education, has gained the support of the student radicals, because it does offer them a greater field of action. The report has been sharply criticized by a Commission minority of two faculty members. It has been presented to the faculty, where there is a good deal of dragging of feet at undertaking its detailed and extensive suggestions on decentralization, student participation, and new forms of handling student discipline.

The majority report reflects to my mind many illusions: that the university can and should remain fully separate from the state, criticizing it and training its self-proclaimed enemies but nevertheless gaining generous support from it; that service and practical knowledge are inferior to other kinds of education; that it is administrative arrangements that primarily prevent the kind of education that will involve radical students in their education rather than in transforming the world; that the modern university can or should be changed into a coherent educational community devoted to common ends (aside from its general ends of education, research, and service, which the majority finds inadequate); that the endless elaboration of due process and its required apparatus of courts, hearing officers, transcripts, appeals bodies, etc., will solve some basic problem of the university; that extensive decentralization and student participation can be introduced without adding to the burden of a faculty that even now tries to escape duties of all kinds, aside from research and graduate teaching. One has the feeling that the university that would emerge from these proposals would be a delight to student politicians, but to hardly anyone else.

One outcome of the report, supporting a trend that was already strongly evident, will be more student participation in academic matters at Berkeley. But what is not clear is the extent to which this will, or can, affect the general structure of university education. After all, we have had a good deal of experience with student participation, at colleges such as Antioch and Bennington, and in various graduate departments and professional schools on the Berkeley campus itself. I think student representation on a greater range of university, college, and departmental committees may introduce valuable points of view. But it does not transform education—it only demonstrates that the dilemmas of contemporary higher education are not simply of the making of conservative professors or administrators. And if students can be taught that by participation in faculty and administrative committees, well and good.

Left and Right, Black and White

The radical student rebellion has not yet affected the central functions and character of the university. It is still dominated by departments, and by a specialist-minded faculty. Research and publication are still the chief means by which faculty members gain status. Undergraduate teaching gets less attention than either graduate teaching or research and writing. Most students are interested primarily in jobs, careers, and credentials in colleges and universities, and no one has suggested how to change this, short of reversing the entire trend to mass higher education. The increasingly large support universities need comes from states, the federal government, parents, corporations, and alumni, on the assumption that they are a good thing for society, and help increase its wealth and solve its problems. Out of this massive support, the functions of the university that traditionalists and radicals alike would like to see increased—social criticism and the liberal arts—gain resources on a scale they have never known up to now. But one can see little prospect that the modern university can be transformed into the school of the revoltuion, though one sees a rather greater possibility that some universities will be destroyed in an effort to do so.

Interestingly enough, in a relatively brief period the rebellion of black students has had much greater impact on the universities than the years of disorder by white student radicals. The explanation is simple. As I have suggested, the student radicals don't quite know what they want to do with the university, and many of their demands (for student participation, for example), can be accommodated without major upset. Radicals are to be found on many faculties, as they always have been, and Marx and his successors are in the curriculum. All this does not make them happy, because the academic tone changes all, but they have found no means to affect this, and their major thrusts has been to such peripheral matters as to who recruits on campus and the university's formal relation with defense institutions.

On the other hand, the demands of the black students have been concrete, and have gone directly to curriculum and university organization. They want specific courses on American Negro history and culture, and African history and culture. They want programs to recruit more black students, tutor them, and support them. They want more Negro faculty. Whereas the impact of the white student radicals has been met by administrators as that of an external invading army, which they have tried to appease with educational changes which scarcely interested them, the attack of black students has been directly on educational issues, and can be met to some extent by changes in curriculum, and by student and faculty recruitment. Not that there are not critical dangers to the university developing in the black demands—there are. They are the implicit demand for quotas of students and faculties, the sometimes voiced demands for separate living quarters and separate and exclusive courses for black students, and involved in both is a potential attack on the ability of the university to maintain standards. But whereas the white radical students have fundamentally been interested in the university as a base for an attack on society, or as a surrogate for their attack on society, the black students, whatever their rhetoric, are fundamentally interested in changing it so it can do a better job of getting them *into* society. The university has to fight the first, but it can respond positively to the second. The problem here is the illusions of many black students as to just what is involved in getting into society. White radical students have convinced a good number of them that it is all or only a game unrelated to ability and effort.

There is a second reason why white radicals have not been able to change the university: their faculty allies on political issues have been split and on the whole, have been conservative on university issues. Even Herbert Marcuse has partially exempted the university, or at any rate the San Diego Campus of the University of California where he teaches, from the devastating critique to which he subjects the rest of society. Many a faculty member who has said "yes" to getting out of Vietnam or getting military recruiters off campus has said "no" to greater student participation in the shaping of the curriculum, or in the advancement and selection of faculty members.

But there is a third reason why the radical students have not reshaped the university: there is no image or vision, no outline or guide, no philosophy available, that tells us how to shape the university. The traditional liberal arts curriculum is dead. It can excite little loyalty from anyone, except for academic deans and the humanities faculty. Those parts of the university that prepare people for the more concrete and obviously meaningful tasks in the world remain relatively unaffected by student disorder—engineering, the sciences, the law and medical schools. Their students and faculty generally do not get involved, and do not see that the university needs reforming—or, if they do, they have rather positive and manageable proposals as to who and how to reform it. It is the social sciences and the humanities that supply the rebels, student and faculty, and of these it is the "softer" rather than the "harder" fields, sociology rather than economics, English literature and history rather than foreign languages. The crisis of the university is a crisis of those areas. How should students in these fields be educated, for what functions, what resources should be devoted to education in these areas, to what ends? It is the traditional liberal arts areas of the curriculum that are the sources of discontent and unhappiness—and here sociology, which provides by far the most student militants, is no exception, for it is not the technicians that sociology trains, but rather the social critics it forms, who become the rebels. Nor can the radicals be appeased, either by the university or the society. They insist that both must be overturned and transformed—to be replaced by what, remains vague, and to most people frightening.

A Scorched Earth Policy?

Perhaps the most serious current radical effort to define a program for radicals in the universities is the Radical Education Project of Ann Arbor, which publishes the Radicals in the Professions Newsletter. All the dilemmas of student radicals in higher education are there exposed. The newsletter reports on the little triumphs of academic radicals—such as how, through "a little planning and initiative," the American Society for Aesthetics was persuaded to take a stand on Vietnam.

But when it comes to what radicals can do to transform the university into a truly radical institution, matters get vaguer. One mathematics professor, writing on "Teaching Mathematics Radically," reports that he is still far from knowing how to do it—he has gotten as far as emphasizing the concepts behind the formulas, which one imagines is the kind of thing conservative mathematics teachers might well agree with. There is a report on having students grade themselves. There are proposals for research projects and community projects that are not very different from others for which one gets credit or gets paid. But one asks, are they truly capable of creating that totally different and transformed world that now excites the imagination of student radicals? And if they disappoint in achieving such an objective, as they must, will it not begin to appear more attractive to destroy the university rather than reform it?

It is rather ominous—for one concerned for the universities—to read a lengthy analysis in the Radicals in the Professions Newsletter of why universities and university faculties are really no places for radicals after all. It is also ominous, to me, that a growing proportion of students feels a fundamental alienation from the university administration and the faculty. In 1964, Robert Somers, a Berkeley sociologist, conducted a poll on the campus—which was conducted during the excitement of FSM—and 56 per cent of the students agreed that the campus administration can "usually be counted on to give sufficient consideration to the rights and needs of students in setting university policy." In 1968, after four years of moderate academic reform, with an administration far more responsive to student desires, the proportion agreeing with this formulation had dropped to 32 per cent. Only a slightly higher proportion in 1968 thinks that faculty can "usually be counted on," etc.—48 per cent. There is no question as to the increasing alienation of a very substantial part of the students. One finds the same phenomenon among Negro Americans—and in both cases I would argue strongly for greater participation, student and community. Not that I think it will solve the basic problems particularly faster, but it may convince those who now think of themselves as oppressed classes that the problems are not easy to solve.

In any case, there have been bombings and fires and window smashing on the Berkeley campus, which had not happened in the earlier years of intense student activism. Conceivably the student radicals may decide on a scorched-earth policy before they withdraw.

In the end, one must judge whether the student radicals fundamentally represent a better world that can come into being, or whether they are not committed to outdated and romantic visions that cannot be realized, that contradict fundamentally other desires and hopes they themselves possess and that contradict even more the desires of most other people. I am impressed by Zbigniew Brzezinski's analysis of the student revolution:

> Very frequently revolutions are the last spasms of the past, and thus are not really revolutions but counterrevolutions, operating in the name of revolutions. A revolution which really either is non-programmatic and has no content, or involves content which is based on the past but provides no guidance for the future, is essentially counterrevolutionary.

The student radicals come from the fields that have a restricted and ambiguous place in a contemporary society. They remind me more of the Luddite machine smashers than the Socialist trade unionists who achieved citizenship and power for workers. This is why the universities stand relatively unchanged—because despite their evident inadequacies the student radicals have as yet suggested nothing better to replace them with.

This essay deals with a unique problem in American universities, that of black-student activism in a white middle-class environment. Note the influence of the Berkeley uprising on Cornell, the objectives of the blacks, and the reasons for the authors' pessimism over change having a lasting effect on the university.

20

Confrontation at Cornell

William H. Friedland and Harry Edwards

Bandoliers across their shoulders, rifles and shotguns casually held ready, the black students of Cornell broke into American consciousness one morning last April [1969] like an advance patrol of that army of barbarians which is the special nightmare of the affluent and, for some, their dream of regeneration. In that moment, fear—which everyone on the campus, both black and white, had known for days—rippled out and touched everyone.

Cornell seems an unlikely, not to say preposterous setting for such an event. Tucked away in rural upstate New York, the college until recently was comfortably settled in an atmosphere of genteel WASP-ishness. There was also an Ivy League rah-rah spirit about the place which only partially obscured the substantial number of lower-class youths who came to Ithaca under State University auspices to study agriculture, education and home economics. True, there had been a riot in 1958 (memorialized in Richard Fariña's novel *Been Down So Long It Looks Like Up to Me*) over the right of students to have mixed parties without chaperons. But *political* activism came late to Cornell.

The trigger was pulled at Berkeley in 1964. After that, Cornell students began to organize themselves, somewhat feebly, into a group called Students For Education. SFE, before being washed away

From William H. Friedland and Harry Edwards, "Confrontation at Cornell," in Howard S. Becker, ed., *Campus Power Struggle* (London: 1970), pp. 79–99. Copyright © 1970 by TRANS-action, Inc., New Brunswick, N.J. Reprinted by permission.

by the Vietnam escalation of 1965, brought into being a good many study commissions and some small changes, among them the conversion of the campus bookstore into a bookstore rather than a purveyor of required texts, setting up an on-campus coffee house, and some very limited changes in the grading system.

But as the Vietnam war went on and was intensified, students at Cornell, like those elsewhere, stepped up their protests. One major confrontation took place during an ROTC review in the college's cavernous Barton Hall, which later figured so importantly in the events of the Spring. Throughout this period, most student activism revolved around the Students for a Democratic Society. Like SDS everywhere, the Cornell group was anti-organizational, anti-leadership, using consensus decision-making procedures, committed to spontaneity. Despite this (or because of it), SDS has been remarkably efficient in mobilizing on the part of the students and a few faculty members.

Until recently, the number of blacks at Cornell has been negligible. Indeed, into the early 1960's, those from outside the United States were far more numerous than American blacks. Furthermore, as at most American universities, the atmosphere at Cornell was almost unashamedly racist. Many fraternities, for example, constitutionally denied membership to non-Caucasians. But as the civil rights movement gathered force in the country, Cornell's liberals began to put pressure on the restrictive practices of the fraternities and tried to eliminate discrimination in off-campus housing. And Cornell students were among those who participated in the Freedom Summer of 1964, working on voter registration in Fayette County, Tennessee.

White involvement in civil rights activities fell off in 1965 however. The development of racial consciousness among blacks led to the belief that blacks had to make their own way and shed themselves of their white supporters if their movement was to be their own. Then, too, the escalation of the Vietnam war increasingly provided a focus for liberal and radical whites. At the same time, more significant changes were taking place at Cornell as the number of American black students began to increase. A Committee on Special Educational Projects (COSEP) was set up to locate and recruit black students and provide them with financial and other support. COSEP's success, while small, was such that by September 1968 there were 240 blacks at Cornell in a total of some 13,200.

But even before then, the presence of black students was causing considerable strain in the university. The separatist issue broke into the open when a black girl, living in the girls' dorms, experienced difficulties with her dormmates. The girl was referred to Cornell's clinic for psychiatric assistance and apparently found little sympathy there. Ordered to leave Cornell, she refused. This precipitated a crisis out of which came demands for separate housing so that blacks could be free of the pressures of living in a hostile environment. Reluctantly, the college made arrangements to establish several black co-ops.

Later, academic freedom seemed to many to be called into question when black students and others became convinced that a visiting professor was teaching racism. After complaining to every relevant agency of the university and being put off time after time, the blacks confronted the professor with the demand that he read a statement in class. When he insisted on reading it in advance and the blacks rejected this, he dismissed the class. The blacks thereupon sat in at the professor's department offices, holding the department chairman in his office.

On that same day occurred the assassination of Martin Luther King and the two events provided the university community with a rarely experienced shock. In addition, several fires were set and later, blacks used Cornell's memorial service to King as an opportunity to attack the university and America's whites.

If nothing else, these events during the year 1967–68 indicated that the blacks at Cornell had laid a strong base for their organization which soon everyone would know as the Afro-American Society.

In response to events of the 1968 spring term, the university moved to set up an Afro-American studies program. Throughout the summer and fall a committee made up of nine faculty and administration members and eight black students met to work out the program. But in the second week of December the black students revolted against what they saw as stalling tactics. They demanded total control of the program and refused to cooperate any further with the existing committee. The same week, six members of the

Afro-American Society forced three whites to leave their offices in a university building on Waite Avenue—a building that the administration had promised to the Afro-American studies program, and during the same affair a photographer for the *Cornell Daily Sun* was roughed up when he refused to turn over a film.

At the same time, however, covert negotiations between the black students and the administration continued over the demands for an autonomous black studies program, but little progress was made and the blacks saw this as another expression of Cornell's unwillingness to take their demands seriously. Consequently, one week before the Christmas recess, black students at Cornell staged a number of demonstrations. Groups of them marched around the quadrangles playing bongo drums, while another contingent entered the President's office with water pistols. They also pushed white students away from several tables in the student union and claimed them for themselves as "black tables." Another time, they carried hundreds of books from the library shelves to the checkout counters, and dumped them there as "irrelevant." They also went to the clinic and demanded treatment by a black physician. Despite their sometimes playful aspects, these demonstrations had an ugly and threatening undercurrent that left most whites tense. Nevertheless, the administration did move toward implementing a black studies program. Not all black demands were met, but a black was chosen to be acting director and compromises were worked out that made the program a degree-granting one. Another consequence was that the black students saw their demonstrations as part of a political program necessary to help them gain a meaningful education at Cornell.

Still, the faculty and administration response to the demonstrations had been hostile and the process of finding scapegoats upon whom retribution might be visited got underway. In January, six students were charged before the Student-Faculty Conduct Board. The decision with respect to these students was one of the important factors leading to the 1969 confrontation.

The disciplinary issues were complicated by what happened during a conference on apartheid sponsored by Cornell's Center for International Studies. The 25 speakers, of whom only three were black, were not greeted sympathetically by an audience composed for the most part of Afro-Americans, black Africans, and sds supporters. The latter moved rapidly from verbal hostility to more openly disruptive interventions. At a meeting on the second evening of the conference, the blacks turned out en masse to challenge Cornell President James Perkins on university investments in South Africa. As Perkins was speaking, one black student grabbed him by the collar and pulled him from the podium. Perkins, badly shaken, left the room. The campus reaction to this incident was hardly in favor of the blacks, despite the fact that there was an increasing sentiment that Cornell's endowments should be free of the taint of apartheid.

Meanwhile, preliminary to the trial of the six members of the Afro-American Society before the Student-Faculty Conduct Board, the aas was claiming that the demonstrations of December had been political acts for which the organization should be held responsible. Selection of a few members could only be regarded as victimization. Accordingly, the six refused to appear before the Conduct Board. Then followed a period in which the six students were verbally threatened with suspension if they failed to appear before the Board. When they didn't show up, letters were sent. In April, just before the events that brought Cornell into the headlines, an obscure clause was discovered that permitted the Conduct Board to take action without the black students being present. On April 18, the Conduct Board reprimanded three of the blacks, dismissed charges against two others, while the charge against the last student was dropped because of his departure from the university.

Throughout this period, campus groups had been enunciating principles to support their positions on the issues involved. For the Conduct Board (and implicitly for the faculty and much of the student body) the issue raised was: Is the university a single community? If it is a community, must all "citizens" adhere to its rules? The blacks not only challenged the idea of a community but put forward the principle that no man should be judged except by a jury of his peers. The blacks also challenged the legitimacy of the Board, contending it was not a voluntary product of the campus community but one imposed by the racist apparatus of American society. In partial justification of their statement, the Afro-Americans pointed out that there was no black representation on the Board. A second conflict of principle arose over the issue of how personal, in contrast to political, acts could be judged. Some university groups argued that individuals rather than organizations had to be held responsible for their acts; organizations could not be tried before the Conduct Board. The blacks asserted the reverse was true: their actions were political, therefore their responsibility was collective. The blacks also argued that the university was not only the aggrieved party but the judge and jury as well, and principles of Anglo-Saxon justice declared that this should not be done. The Afro-American Society suggested that "arbitration" as in industrial relations might be the appropriate model for a resolution of the problem.

In addition to the disciplinary issue, a number of other questions were deeply troubling to numbers of both students and faculty. During their seizure of the Waite Avenue building the blacks had insisted that their demands for an Afro-American studies program were "nonnegotiable." This was pure rhetoric, negotiations were going on through intermediaries, and most people knew it. Nevertheless, many faculty members interpreted the position of the blacks as needlessly intransigent. The black separatism issue had not gone down well with much of the university community either, especially those tables in the student union which had been claimed as black territory. Blacks moved around the campus in groups and were never found fraternizing with whites. This was upsetting to most faculty and students.

While attention centered on the blacks during the spring, a host of other issues affected large numbers of white students. SDS had made demands that the university provide housing not only for students but for the Ithaca community. Arguing that Cornell had thrown the burden of housing upon the community, SDS insisted that the university provide low-cost housing units for underprivileged groups in Ithaca. This issue generated considerable support in faculty and student circles: a network of housing organizations was created to bring pressures for a university commitment. A second issue burgeoned over the impending departure of several noted historians and humanities professors. Humanities has not been strong at Cornell; it is not an area to which the administration has paid any serious attention. So the issue was one that mobilized many Arts and Sciences students. Still other grievances were those of graduate assistants over financial support, and Cornell's South African investments. And, in mid-April, just before the confrontation, a popular sociology professor, one of the first winners of a teaching award, was refused tenure because of his weak publication record.

These issues, and others, created an atmosphere of tension that threatened to come to a crisis on Wednesday, March 12, when the university faculty was scheduled to meet. But when the day came, the faculty adopted a resolution supporting the integrity of the adjudicatory machinery of the Conduct Board and the situation continued to bubble with neither confrontation nor resolution.

At 3:00 A.M. on the morning of Friday, April 18, persons still unknown threw a burning cross on the porch of the black girls' co-operative. Responding to a call, the campus safety patrol reached the co-op where the fire was stamped out. What exactly the campus safety patrol did at the scene of the cross-burning is not clear, but apparently all seven officers covering the incident withdrew, ostensibly on other business, leaving no protection at the co-op. Much later, a guard was established, but by that time the blacks had evidently lost any confidence they may have had in campus protection. This was to be exacerbated as campus officials, while strongly deploring the incident, referred to it as a "thoughtless prank." To the blacks, the symbolism of the event was as powerful as if someone had burned a *Mogen David* in front of a Jewish fraternity. Had such a thing occurred, the blacks reasoned, all the powers of the university would have been brought to bear and the cries of outrage would have been mighty indeed. As it was, the somewhat cavalier attitudes of the university seemed still another reflection of institutional racism, less open perhaps than the occasional group of white boys who had shouted "nigger" at black girls, but racism it was, nevertheless.

As word of the cross-burning spread among the blacks, they assembled at the co-op to decide what action was necessary to protect their women. The defense of their own kind, this was to become a central symbol of the events that followed. As for their choice of target—the student union at Willard Straight Hall, this was in part dictated by the dramatic possibilities implicit in the fact that Parents' Weekend had begun and the opportunity to demonstrate before thousands of parents was tactically so tempting that rumors had been circulating that some group would seize some building somewhere regardless of the issue. How significant a role the rumors played in the deliberations of the blacks is not known, but the tactical impact of the seizure was clear. But it is clear that in deciding to take over the student union, the blacks were intent only on giving an emphatic warning to the campus to "get off our backs," they were not concerned with specific demands. Indeed, the original intent was to seize the building for one day only and then surrender it peaceably.

At 6:00 A.M. on Saturday, April 19, the blacks marched into Willard Straight Hall, calmly ordered service personnel preparing for the day's activities to remove themselves, expelled from guest rooms in the loft a number of visiting parents, and locked up the building.

News of the seizure soon spread throughout the campus; by 8:00 A.M. everyone knew the university was on the brink of another confrontation. For many of the students, particularly those at either end of the political spectrum, having an audience of parents probably served as a stimulus to action. The conservative students tend to be concentrated in a small number of houses that remain "lily-white" and in the fraternities. One of these, Delta Upsilon, is known as the "jock house," because of its unusual number of athletes. It is also one of the most WASPish houses and at present includes no Negro members. Around 9:00 in the morning, about 15 to 20 DU members attempted to break into Straight Hall, and some eight or nine succeeded in getting in before a group of SDS people prevented the rest from entering. While a good deal of pushing, shoving, and arguing was going on outside, inside there was a brief but violent battle between the blacks and the DU men. Three whites and one black were injured, no one seriously. The battle ended with the expulsion of the fraternity boys, but the blacks, even though badly shaken, announced that any other attack would be met by mounting escalation of force. SDS members, standing outside in sympathy with the blacks, rejected a proposal to seize another building and maintained a picket around the entire building to show their support.

The DU attack can be, and was, interpreted in various ways. But from the viewpoint of the blacks, it represented a university attempt to oust them from the building. The campus patrol was supposed to have been guarding the building to prevent entry. Therefore, the fact that the DU people had gotten in was all too easily understood by the blacks as administrative complicity, rather than what it probably was—a spontaneous, self-organized attempt by frat boys. For their part, the DU men insisted that they had entered the building to engage in discussion with black athletes inside and that there was no intent to recapture the building. (There is no evidence, however, that there were ever any black athletes involved in the seizure of the student union.) The DU men claimed that they went in empty-handed; the blacks insisted that they came in with clubs.

Following this incident, the campus gave itself up to an orgy of rumors. Throughout the day, it was circulated about that armed vigilante groups were preparing to mount an attack on Straight Hall. Inside the Hall, the blacks received continuous telephone messages about these vigilantes. By Saturday afternoon, according to the testimony of the blacks and the administrators in telephone contact with them, the occupiers were in a state of terrible tension. It was then that they decided to bring in guns to protect themselves. In the end, they were to have 13 rifles, and two shotguns.

Saturday night passed quietly, but the tension throughout the campus was approaching a critical point. By Sunday morning, Cornell administrators had decided that it would be necessary to end the occupation of the Straight at almost any cost.

That the occupation of the Straight was a precipitous act, probably triggered by the cross-burning, is attested to, first, by the lengthy time it took the blacks to formulate demands; and, second, the relatively flimsy nature of the demands. By Saturday afternoon, three had emerged from Willard Straight, of which one was subsequently withdrawn. The first demand called for a nullification of the three reprimands handed down by the Conduct Committee after the demonstrations of December; the second called for a full investigation and report of the Afro-American Society of the cross-burning incident. That the blacks would take such very serious steps for such tired and modest demands indicates their state of fear and tension. But this was never communicated to the campus, except to those in the administration, Dean Robert Miller especially, who were in direct contact with them. With the latter, the blacks entered into a six-point agreement to end the Straight occupation. It included a commitment to call a full faculty meeting and recommend that the reprimands be declared null and void.

However, the occupiers of Straight Hall were still determined to demonstrate to Cornell whites that they were no longer sitting ducks. So it was that despite pressure from administrators for a decorous exit, the blacks proceeded to make a dramatic exit, brandishing their weapons. It soon became convenient for the shocked white majority of the university to look upon this as a new escalation in student activism; while campus after campus had experienced confrontation, it was argued that this was the first time that students had taken up guns. It was within this context that Cornell arrived at a new level of internal tension on Monday, April 21.

The sight of armed students marching across their campus was too much for the overwhelming majority of the faculty. Unable to understand, or ignorant of, the black students' side of the story, their immediate reaction on Monday, April 21, was one of bitter hostility to any compromise or accommodation of black demands. Their antagonism focused on the six-point agreement reached between the administration and the blacks. Some forty members of the faculty, largely in the government and history departments, signed a statement declaring they would resign if the reprimands were nullified at the Monday faculty meeting.

Tension increased during the day as the opposition to nullification crystallized in the faculty. What the reaction of the blacks would be to a refusal to nullify was unclear, but there was an unspoken and widespread fear that Cornell might be headed toward some kind of shoot-out. In these circumstances, President Perkins called a convocation in Barton Hall just before the university faculty meeting. Some 10,000 students, faculty and staff assembled to hear an innocuous 20-minute statement by the President that left issues more undefined than before. There had been an expectation that presidential leadership was to be asserted.

Instead, in an atmosphere of diffuse fear and anger, in which the focused hostility of the government and history departments stood out, the faculty assembled at 4:00 P.M. in unprecedented numbers. The meeting began with a report by Dean of the Faculty, Robert

Miller, who introduced a formal motion calling for nullification of the reprimands. The Dean's assessment was that the danger to human life at Cornell was real and had to be avoided even at the cost of failing to sustain the authority of the adjudicatory machinery, the Conduct Board. This approach was rejected by the faculty. Instead, they voted a substitute motion that upheld the legitimacy of the adjudicatory machinery and took no action on the nullification of the reprimands. Continuing for over four hours of intricate parliamentary maneuvers, the faculty meeting showed that the majority was adamantly opposed to nullification, but there was also an obdurate, vocal minority supporting the blacks or concerned with the consequences of refusal to nullify. President Perkins had little political capital at this meeting despite his earlier proclamation of limited emergency, a statement that anyone carrying guns on university property would be suspended summarily, or that disruptive demonstrations would lead to immediate suspensions. Nevertheless, he was able to achieve minimal consensus with a resolution calling for the initiation of discussions between the Faculty Council and the Afro-American Society and calling for another full faculty meeting.

Dean Miller now tendered his resignation, stating that by the refusal to vote on his motion, the faculty was repudiating his estimate of the situation. He was promptly given a standing ovation, which neatly illustrated the faculty's dilemma. They respected him and wanted peace, but they felt they had to refuse to make concessions under what they saw as the threat of armed coercion. As the meeting ended at 8:15 and the faculty departed for long-delayed dinners, there was the sense that no solution had been found and that the campus was entering a new and more dangerous situation.

On Monday evening sds called a meeting attended by 2,500, but it ended inconclusively. sds was waiting for the blacks.

By Tuesday morning the campus was in chaos. Many classes did not meet, and in those that did the only topics were those raised by the confrontation. The university leadership, seeking desperately to remedy a deteriorating situation, consulted the deans of the colleges and proposed meetings of college faculties and the beginning of a broad-based discussion at all levels. The intent was to structure free-floating campus anxieties into organized meetings geared to a search for solutions. In the leadership vacuum created by the conflict between the administration's willingness to make concessions and an obdurate faculty, the administration sought only to keep a dialogue going. The fear of bloodshed was everywhere.

At noon, an ephemeral organization named "The Concerned Faculty," consisting largely of elements supporting the blacks, convened for several hours. Urged on by members of the Afro-American Society, "The Concerned Faculty" were unable to decide on anything more than gestures of solidarity. Twenty-six of those attending agreed to seize a building if necessary, while some 60-odd announced their willingness to strike.

Meanwhile, however, at meetings of the faculties of the various colleges, an apparent change in campus opinion began to be felt. The colleges of Arts and Sciences and Home Economics voted to recommend nullification of the Conduct Board's reprimands, and at its 7:00 P.M. meeting, the Faculty Council did the same, while calling for another meeting of the faculty for Wednesday noon. But several other faculties were still determined to maintain business as usual.

That same Tuesday, student opinion on campus began crystallizing around a call by SDS and the Inter-Fraternity Council for a teach-in at Barton Hall, the largest building on campus. By early evening, thousands of students had begun moving to the Hall. Like the faculty, they too seemed intent on avoiding violence between the blacks and other forces. Somewhere between 8,000 to 10,000 people gathered there and as the evening went on, a consensus emerged that it was vital for Cornell students to remain in the building and act as a pressure group on the Cornell faculty, which was scheduled to meet the next day, Wednesday, April 23. SDS speakers proposed that the students declare that they had seized the building, thereby defying President Perkins' new regulation prohibiting such actions. Only a handful objected, and later in the evening Perkins condoned the occupation of Barton Hall, though he persisted in defining it as a teach-in rather than as the seizure the students had declared it to be. This "legal" anomaly continued through the night. Thousands made preparations for the all-night meeting; a collection was taken and soon sandwiches and drinks were being passed out among the teeming mass of students.

As the evening of Tuesday, April 22 wore on, students organized according to their colleges to lobby faculty members for their vote on Wednesday. Around the edges of the Hall, there were dozens of meetings involving tens and hundreds of students. At 3:00 A.M. meetings were still continuing; they included not only groups from different colleges, but various ad hoc committees on the press, particularly the *Sun,* the university's student operated newspaper. One large group of biology students was attempting to deal with the problem of a professor who refused to cancel a quiz scheduled for the next day. The mood in Barton Hall was tensely hopeful; that such an incredible outpouring of students could take place showed that student sentiment had shifted to the blacks, although it was less clear whether the shift had occurred for substantive reasons or because of the fear of violence.

On Wednesday, April 23, the students were wakened by a banjo ensemble and the speech-making began again in the Hall. Elsewhere on the campus, hundreds of meetings were taking place as faculty members were visited by student lobbyists.

Soon after the faculty meeting was gavelled into session by Provost Dale Corson, it became evident that a clear shift had occurred among the members. Despite hardline speeches by government and history faculty members, a motion to nullify was replaced by a second motion which not only called for nullification but also for restructuring the university. The substitute was introduced by Professor Clinton Rossiter who had signed, only two days before, the statement threatening resignation if the reprimands were nullified. Biology professor William Keaton explained how a large delegation of his students from Barton Hall had asked him to change his vote, not because of the threat of violence, but because they wanted him to have faith in them. But the probable major reason for the shift was expressed by Nobel physicist, Hans Bethe, who said that since the moderates were moving toward the SDS left, it was necessary for the faculty to reverse itself to occupy the middle ground and isolate radicals. The resolution calling for nullification and restructuring the university carried by a voice vote probably on the order of three or four to one. The faculty now accepted a resolution by philosopher Max Black informing the students "We hear you. . . ."

A thousand faculty members then moved to Barton Hall where they received a standing ovation. The faculty action demonstrated to the students the latter's influence on the decision-making process; from this point, emphasis shifted to the second part of the Rossiter resolution on restructuring the university.

As the faculty arrived, Eric Evans, vice president of the Afro-American Society was talking. President Perkins came to the podium where, according to Evans, he put his arm around him, smiled in fatherly fashion, and said "Sit down, I want to talk." Evans refused to surrender the microphone. Nothing better demonstrated the students' new mood than the hilarious cheering that broke out when Evans informed them of this exchange. While Perkins fidgeted uncomfortably on the floor with the students and faculty, Evans continued a leisurely review of events leading up to the Willard Straight seizure. When he finished, Perkins spoke and was followed by a succession of others. Slowly the Barton Hall meeting achieved a catharsis from the tensions of the past five days. By 5:00 P.M. the teach-in had ended. Cornell now entered a new phase ostensibly dedicated to a restructuring of the university.

The period immediately following the Barton Hall catharsis was characterized by what can only be called organizational withdrawal symptoms. The most dramatic occurred within SDS which either could not or would not come to grips with its lack of organization and need for leadership. The faculty, too, lost the capacity to function coherently as a corporate body. The Afro-Americans managed to rename themselves the Black Liberation Front but otherwise they also retreated into themselves to try to decide how to relate to the college community under the new circumstances.

Administration officials and traditionally apathetic students also withdrew. The administration was in a state of shock; all that emerged from Day Hall, the administration building, were generalized statements reinforcing previous statements about guns and disruptive demonstrations. Beyond that, Day Hall demonstrated no capacity to provide any structure, guidance, or direction. As for the students, once catharsis had been achieved on Wednesday they lost the capacity to act.

In these circumstances, the tendency was to revert to the traditional, though weakened, institutional structure. Students and faculty turned to colleges and departments, that is, to more manageable social units. With this, the cooling-off process began. It was not that everyone's behavior was as in the past, but students once again came into direct face-to-face relations with teachers, to whom they had always exhibited deference. In a (crude) word, the "reniggerization" of the students had begun.

But the cooling-off took time. It was a week before student statements became more qualified and less concrete and hard-line. Faculty statements, too, became tougher as the teachers reverted to traditional issues of teaching vs. research, academic freedom, and the like.

What this means is that any action with respect to change in university structure, functioning, and priorities will be based on traditional university norms and values. Moreover, the summer will be used as a cooling-off period. Once again there will be the gradual accretion of "data," the rational consideration of infinitesimal details. This does not mean that the faculty will be unwilling to change at all; rather that change will be oriented toward maintaining basic structures. Cooptation of student dissidents will become the major mechanism for attempting to alleviate pressure, for it is evident that the major emphasis is now on alleviating pressure, not solving problems. More fundamental commitment to change in the governance of the university or the educational process remains small.

In the weeks following the adjournment of Barton Hall, the administration, the students, and the faculty have been inadvertently laying the foundation for the next confrontation by reversion to old structures.

But first, it is perhaps worth a short digression to examine why so few black students at Cornell have been able to create such enormous pressures (and we limit ourselves to Cornell here, although some of this analysis is appropriate to black-student experience at other universities).

There is, first of all, a reservoir of readily exploitable guilt in liberal academic circles, but much more depends upon the social situation of a relatively small number of blacks resident in an overwhelmingly white university. All students experience adaptation and living problems in residential universities. Thrown together for long periods of intensive community living and having to navigate a host of curricular and extracurricular problems and opportunities, most students have to find ways of making it all manageable.

As blacks increased at Cornell they experienced the usual problems that blacks undergo in a white environment. But the present generation of black collegians entered the university just as black-power ideology began to affect black intellectuals. This, and the antipathy they felt on the part of the whites, led black students into closer and more intensive relations with each other. The coalescence was further intensified by such incidents as that of whites yelling "nigger" at black girls. Each incident was stored away and became the subject of continual discussion. In these circumstances, black students began to act against their environment and their number was exactly right for the maximum cohesiveness needed to generate pressures. If larger numbers of blacks were present, this cohesiveness would be difficult, if not impossible.

But the main grounds on which we would predict further troubles for Cornell are the discrepancies between student hopes for change and the structural inabilities of universities to obtain significant change, especially in the educational process. This will create serious problems because the demand of students for restructuring the learning process remains unresolved. At the same time, the social conditions contributing to this demand also remain unresolved: poverty, discrimination, racism, the war in Vietnam, continue and are interpreted, probably correctly, as worsening. Most students are naive in that they think university reform will take place by itself, and many believe that something tangible will come out of Barton Hall. As students realize that little or nothing can emerge, they will find themselves increasingly frustrated.

The specific issue that will trigger the next action can come from a variety of sources: recruitment by employers (which most universities will not eliminate because a majority of students want it), pressures for open recruitment of blacks or other deprivileged groups, financial shortages as alumni react against campus actions, relations with the surrounding community, university investments, and so on. Thus, the institutional inabilities to change rapidly and drastically practically guarantee new confrontations in the next academic year at Cornell.

Selected Bibliography

Selected Bibliography

General Readings on Student Protest

Altbach, Philip G., ed. *Select Bibliography on Students, Politics, and Higher Education*. Cambridge, Mass., 1967. This is the most thorough and extensive bibliography on the subject.

Aron, Raymond. "Student Rebellion: Vision of the Future or Echo of the Past?" *Political Science Quarterly*, 84 (June 1969), 289–310.

Bell, Daniel, and Irving Kristol, eds. *Confrontation: The Student Rebellion and the Universities*. New York, 1969. An uneven yet helpful book.

Califano, Joseph A., Jr. *The Student Revolution: A Global Confrontation*. New York, 1970. The author, a former member of the Kennedy and Johnson administrations, visited various countries and talked with student leaders, university administrators and government officials. He provides a general yet useful analysis.

Cockburn, Alexander, and Robert Blackburn, eds. *Student Power*. Aylesbury, Great Britain, 1969. Written by various leftist British students.

Douglass, Bruce. *Reflections on Protest: Student Presence in Political Conflict*. Richmond, Virginia, 1967. This study contains an excellent article by Kenneth Boulding on the nature of protest movements.

Feuer, Lewis S. *The Conflict of Generations*. New York, 1969. Feuer has done a massive amount of research in providing the most thorough conservative critique of student protest.

Lipset, Seymour Martin, ed. *Student Politics*. New York, 1967. One of the better studies on student movements in underdeveloped countries.

Paloczi-Horvath, George. *Youth Up In Arms: A Political and Social Survey 1955–1970*. London. 1971. A broad and often impressionistic treatment, but current and stimulating.

Roszak, Theodore. *The Making of a Counter Culture: Reflections on the Technocratic Society and Its Youthful Opposition*. New York, 1969. The author presents a provocative analysis of the developing

youth culture in America and the nature of an adversary, the tech-
nocracy.
Stern, Fritz. "Reflections on the International Student Movement," *The
American Scholar*, 40 (Winter 1970–71), 123–137. Analyzes the
underlying historic causes of the movement and assesses it. The conclusion is negative.

I Medieval Student Life

Dodge, Bayard. *Muslim Education in Medieval Times*. Washington,
1962.
Gabriel, Astrik. *Garlandia: Studies in the History of the Medieval Uni-
versity*. Notre Dame, Indiana, 1969.
Kearney, Hugh. *Scholars and Gentlemen: Universities and Society in
Pre-Industrial Britain 1500–1700*. London, 1970.
Kibre, Pearl. *Scholarly Privileges in the Middle Ages*. Cambridge, 1962.
Laurie, S. S. *The Rise of Universities*. Edinburgh, 1886.
Rashdall, Hastings. *The Universities of Europe in the Middle Ages*.
Oxford, 1936. The basic source for any study of student life in the
middle ages.
Robb, James. "Student Life at St. Andrews before 1450," *Scottish His-
torical Review*, 9 (July 1912), 347–360.
Schachner, Nathan. *The Medieval University*. New York, 1962.

II Student Movements in Western Europe

Aron, Raymond. *The Elusive Revolution: Anatomy of a Student Revolt*.
New York, 1969.
Ashby, Eric, and Mary Anderson. *The Rise of the Student Estate in
Britain*. London, 1970.
Bair, Jake. "The Spanish Student Movement," *Studies on the Left*, 5
(Summer 1965), 3–20.
Besancon, Julien, comp. *Journal Mural Mai 1968: Sorbonne Odéon
Nanterre, etc*. Paris, 1968.
Bourges, Herve. *The French Student Revolt: The Leaders Speak*. New
York, 1968. The interview with Alain Geismar is excellent.
Ehrenreich, Barbara and John. *Long March, Short Spring: The Student
Uprising at Home and Abroad*. New York, 1969. Two American stu-

dent activists tour Europe and provide many perceptive insights of student rebellions in Western Europe. Their chapter on Italy is especially good.

Eyck, F. G. "Political Theories and Activities of the German Academic Youth Between 1815 and 1819," *Journal of Modern History*, 27 (March 1955), 27–38. The author describes how student activism can be used and deliberately misinterpreted by the government for political purposes.

Fields, Belden A. *Student Politics in France: A Study of the Union Nationale des Etudiants de France.* New York, 1970.

Habermas, Jürgen. *Toward a Rational Society: Student Protest, Science and Politics,* trans. by Jeremy J. Shapiro. Boston, 1970. Contains interpretive essays on student activism in the Federal Republic of Germany.

Halsey, A. H., and Stephen Marks. "British Student Politics," *Daedalus,* 97 (Winter 1968), 116–132.

Lutz, Rolland R., Sr. "Fathers and Sons in the Vienna Revolution of 1848," *Journal of Central European Affairs,* 22 (July 1962), 161–173.

Scholl, Inge. *Students Against Tyranny: The Resistance of the White Rose, Munich, 1942–1943.* Connecticut, 1970.

III   The Activist Tradition in Eastern Europe

Burg, David. "Observations on Soviet 'University Students,'" *Daedalus,* 89 (Summer 1960), 520–540.

Cornell, Richard. "Students and Politics in the Communist Countries of Eastern Europe," *Daedalus,* 97 (Winter 1968), 160–184.

Hans, Nicholas. *History of Russian Educational Policy, 1701–1917.* New York, 1964.

Kecskemeti, Paul. *The Unexpected Revolution: Social Forces in the Hungarian Uprising.* Palo Alto, California, 1961.

Kheraskov, Ivan. "Reminiscences of the Moscow Students Movement," *Russian Review,* 11 (October 1952), 223–232.

IV   Student Communities in Asia and Africa

Altbach, Philip G., ed. *Turmoil and Transition: Higher Education and Student Politics in India.* New York, 1968.

Cormack, Margaret. *She Who Rides a Peacock: Indian Students and Social Change.* New York, 1961.

Doolin, Dennis J., trans. and ed. *Communist China: The Politics of Student Opposition.* Stanford, 1964.

Fischer, Joseph. "The University Student in South and Southeast Asia," *Minerva,* 2 (Autumn 1963), 39–53.

Goldman, René. "The Rectification Campaign at Peking University May–June 1957," *The China Quarterly,* no. 12 (October–December 1962), 138–153.

Hanna, William John. "Students," in James S. Coleman and Carl G. Rosberg, Jr., eds., *Political Parties and Natural Integration in Tropical Africa.* Berkeley, 1964, pp. 413–443.

Hussein, Karrar. "Politics and Students," *Pakistan Quarterly,* 13 (1966), 141–144.

Kiang, Wen-han. *The Ideological Background at the Chinese Student Movement.* New York, 1948.

Lipset, Seymour M., ed. *Student Politics.* New York, 1967. An excellent group of essays dealing with emergent nations.

Lyman, Princeton M. "Students and Politics in Indonesia and Korea," *Pacific Affairs,* 38 (Fall–Winter 1965–1966), 282–293.

Ottaway, David B. "Algeria," in Donald Emmerson, ed., *Student Politics in Developing Nations.* New York, 1968, pp. 3–32.

Shimbori, Michiya. "Zengakuren: A Japanese Case Study of a Political Movement," *Sociology of Education,* 37 (1964), 229–253.

V Latin America's Student Power

Albornoz, Orlando. "Student Opposition in Latin America," *Government and Opposition,* 2 (October 1966–January 1967), 105–118.

Bonilla, Frank, and Myron Glazer. *Student Politics in Chile.* New York, 1970.

Havighurst, Robert. "Latin American and North American Higher Education," *Comparative Education Review,* 4 (1961), 174–182.

Rotblatt, Miguel. "The Latin American Student Movement," *New University Thought,* 1 (Summer 1961), 29–36.

Scott, Robert. "Student Political Activism in Latin America," *Daedalus,* 97 (Winter 1968), 70–97.

Spencer, David, ed. *Student Politics in Latin America.* Philadelphia, 1965.

Suchlicki, Jaime. *University Students and Revolution in Cuba, 1920–1968.* Coral Gables, Florida, 1969.

Walker, Kenneth N. "A Comparison of University Reform Movements in Argentina and Columbia," in Lipset, ed., *Student Politics,* pp. 293–317.

Walter, Richard. *Students and Politics in Argentina.* New York, 1968.

VI   Student Rebellion in the United States

Axelrod, Joseph, *et al. Search for Relevance: The Campus in Crisis.* San Francisco, 1969.

Barlow, William, and Peter Shapiro. *An End to Silence: The San Francisco State Student Movement.* New York, 1971.

Cox, Archibald, *et al. Crisis at Columbia.* New York, 1968, especially pp. 3–18.

Draper, Hal. *Berkeley: The New Student Revolt.* New York, 1965.

Draper, Hal. "The Student Movement of the Thirties: A Political History," in Rita James Simon, ed., *As We Saw the Thirties: Essays on Social and Political Movements of a Decade.* Urbana, Illinois, 1967, pp. 151–189. This is a rambling, reminiscent account by a former student activist.

Erlich, John and Susan, eds. *Student Power, Participation and Revolution.* New York, 1970. Essays on the movement of the 1960s.

Foster, Julian, and Durward Long, eds. *Protest! Student Activism in America.* New York, 1970. Analyses of the events of the 1960s.

Goodman, Paul. "The New Reformation," *New York Times Magazine* (September 14, 1969), 32–33, 142–155.

Handlin, Mary and Oscar. *The American College and American Culture: Socialization as a Function of Higher Education.* New York, 1970.

Heirich, Max. *The Spiral of Conflict:* Berkeley, 1964. New York, 1971.

Jencks, Christopher, and David Reisman. *The Academic Revolution.* New York, 1968. Maintains that the confrontation between old and young is the central feature of college life.

Kahn, Roger. *The Battle for Morningside Heights, Why Students Rebel.* New York, 1970.

Keniston, Kenneth. *Young Radicals: Notes on Committed Youth.* New York, 1968.

Lipset, Seymour M. "Student Opposition in the United States," *Government and Opposition,* 1 (May 1966), 351–374.

Lipset, Seymour M., and Sheldon Wolin, *The Berkeley Student Revolt.* New York, 1965.

Michener, James A. *Kent State: What Happened and Why.* New York, 1971. This book also contains a conservative analysis of the student unrest of the 1960s.

Miles, Michael W. *The Radical Probe: The Logic of the Student Rebellion.* New York, 1971.

Otten, Michael. *University Authority and the Student: The Berkeley Experience.* Berkeley, Calif., 1970. An historical and sociological treatment, 1869–1970.

Strout, Cushing, and David I. Grossvogel, eds., *Divided We Stand: Reflections on the Crisis at Cornell.* New York, 1970.

Weaver, Gary R., and James H., eds. *The University and Revolution.* Englewood Cliffs, New Jersey, 1969.

Wechsler, James. *Revolt on the Campus.* New York, 1935.

Alexander DeConde, Professor of History at the University of California, Santa Barbara, was graduated from San Francisco State College and received his M.A. and Ph.D. degrees from Stanford University. Previous to his present position, he taught at Stanford University, Whittier College, Duke University, and the University of Michigan. The 1949 co-winner of the annual American History Award of the Pacific Branch of the American Historical Association, Professor DeConde has also received awards from the Social Science Research Council and the American Philosophical Society as well as a Fulbright and two Guggenheim Fellowships. His books for Scribners include *A History of American Foreign Policy*, *The Quasi-War*, and *Half-Bitter, Half-Sweet*.

Da